international
SCHOOLS &
international
EDUCATION

international
SCHOOLS &
international
EDUCATION

improving teaching, management & quality

Edited by
MARY HAYDEN & JEFF THOMPSON

**KOGAN
PAGE**

First published in 2000

Apart from any fair dealing for the purposes of research or private study, or criticism or
review, as permitted under the Copyright, Designs and Patents Act 1988, this publication
may only be reproduced, stored or transmitted, in any form or by any means, with the
prior permission in writing of the publishers, or in the case of reprographic reproduction
in accordance with the terms and licences issued by the CLA. Enquiries concerning
reproduction outside these terms should be sent to the publishers at the undermentioned
addresses:

Kogan Page Limited   Stylus Publishing Inc.
120 Pentonville Road   22883 Quicksilver Drive
London   Sterling
N1 9JN   VA 20166-2012
UK   USA

© Mary Hayden, Jeff Thompson and the named authors, 2000

The right of Mary Hayden, Jeff Thompson and the named authors to be identified as the
authors of this work has been asserted by them in accordance with the Copyright,
Designs and Patents Act 1988.

British Library Cataloguing in Publication Data

A CIP record for this book is available from the British Library.

ISBN 0 7494 3368 X

Typeset by Saxon Graphics Ltd, Derby
Printed and bound in Great Britain by Clays Ltd, St Ives plc

Contents

Notes on contributors

Samia Al Farra

Samia Al Farra started her career as a science teacher in Kuwait and has held senior management positions ever since. She is currently the Principal of Amman Baccalaureate School, Jordan, the first school in the region to implement the International Baccalaureate Primary Years and Middle Years Programmes. She is a member of the International Baccalaureate Academic Affairs Board and the Jordan National Council of Education, and in 1995 received the ECIS Award for Promotion of International Education. Samia Al Farra was an International Baccalaureate Heads Representative Committee member for six years and, in Jordan, Education and Higher Education Sector Committee Member for Preparing the Economic and Social Development Plan for the period 1998–2002. She initiated the establishment of the Middle East International Baccalaureate Association (MEIBA) in 1995 and was its President until 1999. She is now undertaking Doctoral research on international education at the University of Bath.

Keith Allen

Keith Allen is Academic Vice-Principal at St Clare's, Oxford. His involvement in international education started in British comprehensive schools and led to his appointment to teach Biology at the United World College of South-East Asia in Singapore. Subsequently, he has frequently found himself involved in the development of new IB schools. This includes working as Area Manager for Curriculum Development at the first City Technology College in the UK, managing the development of a bilingual school in Argentina and acting as Chief Executive Officer for the New International School of Thailand.

Joseph Blaney

Dr Joseph J Blaney retired in 1998 after 11 years as Director of the United Nations International School (UNIS) in New York City. He was also Director General of the International School of Geneva between 1981 and 1983. Dr Blaney served as Superintendent of Schools and

Executive Deputy Commissioner of Education for New York State. He is a former member of the Boards of the International Baccalaureate North America and the International Schools Association and a present member of the Board of the American Forum on Global Education in New York City. He has been instrumental in establishing several new international schools, chaired accreditation teams and conducted management seminars for international school Heads and Boards.

Gail Bradley

Gail Bradley began her teaching career in Wales, where she gained experience teaching at a variety of levels, from nursery to adult education and with various subjects, including Welsh as a second language. In conjunction with teaching for a local authority, she has worked for the Workers Educational Association and the British Council. In 1989, she obtained her first overseas teaching post in a multinational school in Abu Dhabi. Between 1994 and 1999 she enjoyed the opportunity of teaching at Dover Court Preparatory School, Singapore – an inclusive, international school. In addition to mainstream teaching, she was the Early Years of Schooling Coordinator, closely involved with the organization of inclusive practices, and she also spent some time on the Senior Management Team as the Head of the Infant section. She has returned to the Middle East and is currently teaching at Qatar Academy in Doha. She was recently awarded an MA in Education by the University of Bath, and is continuing her studies at Doctoral level at the University of Bath.

James Cambridge

James Cambridge has been a biology educator in Britain, North Yemen, Lesotho and South Africa in both national and international schools. He is currently a Research Officer with the Centre for the study of Education in an International Context (CEIC) at the University of Bath, and his research interests focus on schools in an international context and, in particular, on the organizational and national cultures associated with them.

Michael Fertig

Michael Fertig is a lecturer in the Department of Education at the University of Bath, and a member of the Centre for the study of

Education in an International Context (CEIC). He has held teaching and senior management positions in secondary schools in England for over 20 years, is an OFSTED-trained school inspector, and is an examiner in History for the International Baccalaureate. Michael Fertig is currently involved in teaching on the modular Masters-level courses offered to teachers and educational administrators worldwide, primarily in the area of educational management. This has involved him teaching at Summer School and at a range of overseas Study Centres, as well as presenting a range of INSET programmes. His research interests lie in the areas of school effectiveness and school improvement, with particular reference both to international schools and to the developing world.

Brian Garton

Brian Garton is the Director of the Anglo-American School of Sofia in Bulgaria. He was previously the Head of international schools in Moshi (Tanzania), Lusaka (Zambia) and Baguio (the Philippines). He was also the Head of an all-Nepalese boarding school in Kathmandu, for which services he was awarded the Prabhal Gorkha Dakshin Bahu by HM King Birendra. From 1986 to 1988 he was a member of the Management Committee of the Headmasters' Standing Conference of the International Baccalaureate Organisation. His wife has taught in six different international schools, and both of their sons graduated with IB Diplomas from an international school.

Mary Hayden

Dr Mary Hayden is a senior lecturer in the Department of Education at the University of Bath, and is Head of the International and Comparative Education Research Group, as well as being a member of the Centre for the study of Education in an International Context (CEIC). She has particular responsibility for directing the campus-based Summer School and overseas Study Centre dimensions of the modular Masters programme in Education offered to teachers and administrators based around the world. Mary Hayden's involvement in international education began when she took up a post in 1982 with the International Baccalaureate Organisation: her recent and current research interests are based in the field of international schools and international education, an area in which she has published widely.

John Lowe

Dr John Lowe is a lecturer in the Department of Education at the University of Bath, prior to which he worked for many years in Kenya and the Solomon Islands as a science teacher and in various aspects of curriculum and examinations development. More recently he has worked as a consultant in Poland, Eritrea, Somalia and Lesotho on a range of educational development projects. John Lowe is a member of the Centre for the study of Education in an International Context (CEIC), with research interests in the role of education in national development, particularly in response to globalization trends. Among his most recent work is a study, still in its early stages, of the role of internationally available qualifications in relation to the globalization of labour markets.

John Mackenzie

John Mackenzie has held senior management positions at The Grange School, Chile, where he is currently Head, and formerly at Santiago College, Chile. He has been involved with the International Baccalaureate since 1983, when he joined the Philosophy and Theory of Knowledge Subject Committee, and was Chief Assessor for Theory of Knowledge from 1995 to 1999. Having studied Sociology and Politics, his present academic interests are in Philosophy of Mind, Philosophy of Language, Ethics, Theory of Knowledge and Educational Theory.

Anne McKillop-Ostrom

Anne McKillop-Ostrom began her teaching career in India, and later taught in a variety of schools in Canada, Scotland, Kenya and Vietnam. Anne completed her MA with the University of Bath, where she focused her dissertation on addressing transition issues in international schools. As an offshoot of her theoretical and practical research, she has conducted many workshops and published a variety of materials on transition, transition teams and internationally mobile children. Anne is the parent of two internationally mobile children and has recently relocated to Helsinki, Finland, where she continues her research at Doctoral level through the University of Bath.

Niall Nelson

Dr Niall Nelson is Headmaster of Jakarta International School in Indonesia. He has held headships and teaching positions in Tanzania, Libya, Italy, Russia, the United Kingdom and the United States of America. He has also taught graduate-level courses for the Principals Training Center (PTC) and the College of New Jersey. An Irish national, Niall Nelson holds a Bachelors degree from the University of Sussex and Masters and Doctoral degrees from Harvard University. He is a member of the International Baccalaureate Heads Representative Committee and a former member of the IBO Council of Foundation. Niall Nelson serves on the ECIS and EARCOS (East Asian Regional Council of Overseas Schools) governing boards, and is Board President of the recently established Academy for International School Heads.

William Powell

William Powell has served as an international school educator for the past 25 years. He has Masters degrees in education from Manhattanville College and the College of New Jersey, and has taught in the United States, Saudi Arabia, Indonesia, Tanzania and Malaysia. From 1991 to 1999 he served as the Chief Executive Officer of the International School of Tanganyika in Dar es Salaam, Tanzania, and is currently the Headmaster of the International School of Kuala Lumpur in Malaysia. Bill Powell has served as the Chairperson of the Association of International Schools in Africa (AISA) and as a co-opted member of the International Baccalaureate Heads Representative Committee. He is a frequent workshop presenter at educational conferences, and is also a teacher for the Principals Training Center (PTC), and serves on the Board of Directors of the Academy for International School Heads. He is also a regular contributor of articles to educational journals and magazines.

Carol Thearle

Carol Thearle started her career in international education in 1979 in El Salvador. Subsequently she taught at Vienna International School, the United World College of South-East Asia in Singapore, the International School of Paris, and St Dominic's International School, Portugal; she is currently Head of the Secondary School at the Bavarian International School, Munich. In 1997 Carol Thearle was awarded an MA in

Education (Educational Management) through the Centre for the study of Education in an International Context (CEIC) at the University of Bath, her dissertation being focused on a number of issues relating to women in senior positions in international schools.

Jeff Thompson

Professor Jeff Thompson, CBE, is Director of the Centre for the study of Education in an International Context (CEIC) and Professor of Education at the University of Bath. He is also Director for International Education with the International Baccalaureate Organisation. Jeff Thompson first became active in international education in the 1960s when working with Alec Peterson at the University of Oxford Department of Educational Studies, and has continued his involvement since that time in a number of different capacities. He was Chair of the IB Examining Board and member of the IB Curriculum Board, Executive Committee and Council of Foundation; his current roles with the IBO also include being Director of the IB Research Unit based at the University of Bath. His major research interests are linked to the fields of assessment and curriculum, in both national and international contexts.

George Walker

Professor George Walker, OBE, is Director General of the International Baccalaureate Organisation and Visiting Professor in the University of Bath, through the Centre for the study of Education in an International Context (CEIC). George Walker's earlier career was in science education, and included a spell as an educational consultant for Imperial Chemical Industries (ICI); he subsequently took a central role in the development of comprehensive education in England. He was Deputy Head and Head in a number of schools in Britain before taking on the role of Director General of the International School of Geneva, a position he left to join the IBO in 1999. George has also participated in a number of ECIS accreditation teams and, in his capacity as Visiting Professor, teaches and supervises Masters and Doctoral students at the University of Bath.

Peter Zsebik

Peter Zsebik has Bachelors degrees from McGill University and the University of Western Ontario, as well as a Masters degree from the

College of New Jersey. His career as an international educator has encompassed the teaching of music, ESL, physical education and IB Theory of Knowledge in international schools around the world, including the American International School, Kuwait, the Overseas Family School, Singapore, the Canadian International School, Singapore, the Thai-Chinese International School and, most recently, Vienna International School. He is currently undertaking research into issues relating to the concept of an international curriculum as part of his studies towards a Doctorate with the University of Bath.

Preface

Since the publication in 1998 of our first edited collection of contributions from experienced practitioners in international schools, *International Education: Principles and Practice*, a great deal of interest has been expressed in what was written. Clearly it was the case that this volume filled a gap in what, as we pointed out, was a relatively thinly researched field at that time. One pleasing feature of the response to *International Education: Principles and Practice* has been the strength of the interest shown in the work both from practitioners in the field, whether classroom teachers or educational administrators, and from those who are researching and developing the more theoretical aspects of the area: indeed, that book was intended by its subtitle to achieve such a twin target.

In producing this second collection, and prevailing upon colleagues to contribute to it, we have attempted to generate a similar mix of those involved directly in research and enquiry in the field, together with those who deploy leadership and teaching roles in the context of the practice of international education. Our thrust this time focuses not so much on issues arising from a consideration of what fundamentally constitutes international education, but rather on the set of concerns that would need to be addressed in building quality into the process of international education in both international and national schools.

In inviting authors to contribute to this volume, a range of perspectives has been sought from those who are researching in the context of the Centre for the study of Education in an International Context (CEIC) of the University of Bath, and from those who are involved in the promotion of international education from their positions of leadership within schools and worldwide organizations such as the International Baccalaureate Organisation (IBO) or the European Council of International Schools (ECIS). The result is a range of quite different conceptual and practical perspectives, which we anticipate will be of interest to those working within different spheres of international education.

The way in which the book has been organized relates directly to the large areas of influence which systematic research has shown to be central to the development of international education, in whatever institutional context. In Part A we include a range of perspectives on those curricular topics that may not always have received the level of consideration that an international education would seem to require. Thus, while John Lowe addresses issues concerned particularly with assessment, his arguments range much more widely than those relating merely to summative assessment for accreditation and qualification purposes, encompassing also consideration of the formative dimensions of assessment and their impact upon quality in the educational process. Gail Bradley's chapter highlights the area of inclusive education in the international school, which has, arguably, tended to be rather neglected in this context. While focusing on the experiences of one pioneering school, she also draws on a range of issues that may well have relevance within the wider international school arena. Catering for students with special educational needs within school is almost certainly as much concerned with the non-traditional disciplines as it is with the more subject-based curriculum, and John Mackenzie's consideration of what has been described as the 'interstitial' curriculum (that which arguably holds together the 'subject' components of the curriculum) identifies the part played in bringing coherence to the international curriculum by the Theory of Knowledge element of the International Baccalaureate Diploma programme. In the following chapter, by Samia Al Farra, are found a number of pertinent issues relating to international education in the Moslem world and how teachers can be supported in promoting this form of education. Peter Zsebik's chapter, similarly, takes a cross-curricular theme in considering the politics of international education, in so far as this relates to both explicit and implicit value systems, to choices of what to include in the curriculum, how it is taught and how the organization is managed: all factors which contribute – intentionally or otherwise – to the development of the students attending the school in question.

In Part B, issues are addressed which relate to that crucial dimension of any school: the people – as individuals or collectively – without whom the school would not exist. Anne McKillop-Ostrom identifies aspects relating to student mobility and the so-called 'global nomads' or 'third culture kids', a phenomenon which is fortunately now being given increasing attention in terms of how schools can best support students who experience a relatively transient lifestyle as they accompany their parents around the world. Chapters 8, 9 and 10 in this part of the volume focus on three aspects of the role of teachers within international schools. Brian Garton's chapter picks up on the theme of transition in the recruitment of teachers for international schools, including orientation. Issues more broadly concerned with professional development for teachers are discussed by Bill Powell, who goes on to make a number of practical suggestions relating to the encouragement of reflective practice within the international school context. A further dimension relating to teachers is just who actually deploys the role of classroom teachers and administrators; Carol Thearle asks a question about the balance between men and women in these positions, and challenges us to consider how a more even balance at senior management levels might be achieved within the international context. The last chapter in this part considers the local community as a dimension of human resources, with Keith Allen arguing strongly for the importance of two-way links between international schools and the communities within which they are located.

Issues related to school management and organization are explored in Part C. Michael Fertig's contribution reflects on the topical and well-researched (in some national contexts, at least) fields of school effectiveness and school improvement and discusses the implications such thinking may have for the management of international schools. This is followed by two views of institutional planning. Within the context of international schools and their transient teaching and administrator population, the notion of long-term/strategic planning throws out particular challenges and, according to both authors, is of particular importance. Joe Blaney draws on his wide-ranging experience of educational leadership in both North America and Europe in making a strong case for the importance of strategic planning as a whole-school activity. Niall Nelson takes up this theme in considering a range of views on strategic planning and, in particular, highlights the role of the Board, before describing some practical action taken at Jakarta International School. The organizational culture of such schools is explored by Jim Cambridge, who raises another topical issue, that of globalization, and proposes that awareness of Hampden-Turner and Trompenaars' 'seven cultures of capitalism' will lead to better understanding of the tensions inherent within the diverse culture of an international school.

The volume is completed with George Walker's chapter, which focuses on international education in the context not only of international schools but also of national schools. It is based on a paper given to the biennial meeting of the Heads' Standing Conference of International Baccalaureate Schools, held in Accra in March 2000, and was presented in his capacity as Director General of the IBO. The chapter begins by challenging the perception that international education was created for the internationally mobile student. In going on to pick up issues of globalization raised by Jim Cambridge, George makes the case that international education is not something that should be the preserve of international schools alone but should also be viewed as an aspiration for national schools worldwide.

In reflecting upon the different chapters that make up this volume, we are impressed by the quality of what has been written by our contributors, and grateful for the patience and goodwill which has been demonstrated by them all throughout the process of drafting, editing and redrafting which has, we are sure, cut across many evenings, weekends and holidays since we first approached them to be a part of this publication. It can be argued that most good pieces of writing lead to as many new questions being asked as they do to questions being answered, and it is certainly the case that the various chapters in this volume have proposed solutions and raised challenges in equal measure. Thanks and appreciation must be extended to our authors for the stimulating nature of their writing, which, we hope, will make a positive contribution to the developing field of international schools and international education, and to those who have assisted that process by patient technical editing and publishers' guidance. We are grateful to them all.

Mary Hayden
Jeff Thompson

Chapter 1

Quality in diversity

Mary Hayden and Jeff Thompson

Diversity in international schools

The first edition of the *International Schools Journal* of the new millennium begins with an editorial by Edna Murphy (Murphy, 2000), who highlights some of the questions which have been raised not infrequently in recent years within the context of international schools. In raising again the questions 'What is an international school?' and 'What is an international education?', Murphy comes to the conclusion that:

> Maybe it is time... to stop trying to organize the unorganizable by dint of words alone... We might want to accept, finally, that we do not, in this community, speak with one voice; that we are educators with different experiences and backgrounds working in many different kinds of schools for different reasons, and whose common enterprise reflects a rich variety of approaches; and that we may or may not eventually arrive at a point where we conform to a single vision.

Almost by definition, such an argument will not meet with complete agreement amongst the wide community of international educators – such agreement might, indeed, serve to disprove the very point she makes. There will be few, however, who would take issue with the underlying premise that the community of those involved in the world of international schools is a diverse one. A striking feature which most of us would associate with our own mental picture of international schools or international education is a lack of homogeneity. Such an absence of homogeneity – or a presence of diversity – can itself be viewed from a number of differing perspectives. It may be considered, for instance, from the point of view of the wide variety of schools that claim to be international schools. Murphy (2000) reminds us that quite what is meant by the term 'international school' remains a moot point, since 'No one has so far come up with a definition of "international school" that does not exclude some schools which consider themselves international, and does include others which may not' as well as highlighting the absence of a shared perception of the meaning of the term 'international education'. Indeed, our own contribution to the same journal highlighted our perception that the two terms are not well defined and do not share the one-to-one relationship which seems sometimes to be assumed. Such a lack of shared agreement notwithstanding, it seems likely that there are currently at least one thousand such institutions (Hayden and Thompson, 1995a) which include amongst their number those with differing philosophies, whether these be essentially utilitarian, pragmatic or ideologically focused (Hayden and Thompson, 2000).

Clearly then, diversity in this context can be seen to manifest itself at what might be described as the global level, the 'macro' diversity which means that it is almost certainly true to say that, even taking into account groupings of international schools that share the same underlying philosophy, there are no two international schools that share precisely the same characteristics. Although diversity of this type has its drawbacks – no doubt the very nature of the differences to be found between such schools is at the root of the difficulties experienced in arriving at a definition of the 'international school' label that suits all – it also has its attractions, and many of those teachers and administrators who have chosen to spend their professional lives in the transient world of international schools undoubtedly find a career spent in a number of different cultural contexts stimulating, challenging and personally and professionally fulfilling.

Diversity in international education

To revert to the consideration of international education, however – and we would wish to argue that it is the promotion of international education and an associated set of values, rather than the counting or definition of international schools, that is important – such 'macro diversity' does not appear to have an obvious role to play in the promotion of such a set of values or, as it has been described elsewhere (Hayden and Thompson, 1995b), an 'international attitude'. The development of such an attitude is more likely to be promoted in the context of another, familiar, manifestation of diversity, that which is found at what might be described as the local level, the 'micro' diversity that characterizes so many individual international schools in terms of the large numbers of different nationalities, different cultural backgrounds, different languages spoken and different religious beliefs to be found amongst the student, and perhaps teaching, body. The extent of such diversity will clearly vary, according to the school's basic *raison d'être*, whether catering for a largely expatriate, transient population or for a more stable population of students drawn largely from the local community or indeed, as in the case of the United World Colleges, catering for a student population deliberately selected in order to capitalize on cultural diversity and to make that diversity a major feature of the student experience. Our own research (Hayden and Thompson, 1996) suggests that many students in international schools value interaction with those of other cultures as one of the fundamental characteristics of international education which promotes the development of an 'international attitude', a feature which, as Walker (2000) points out, is put to good effect as 'many of these schools claim to do more than just encourage the "rubbing of shoulders". The deliberate, planned interaction of students from different cultural backgrounds is widely regarded as a cornerstone of international education.'

Clearly this type of diversity within a school can make a positive contribution to its efforts to promote international education. Even if, to coin Walker's phrase, no attempt is made actively to build on the 'rubbing of shoulders', the relationships formed across cultural and linguistic divides may well lead to the modification and development of attitudes amongst the student population. It could, however, be argued to be – as could the diversity amongst schools already noted – at a relatively superficial (though not unimportant) level. To draw an analogy with the concept of validity, it could be described as 'face diversity' – that which is 'obvious' to the passer-by or transient visitor – as compared with a more fundamental notion of what might be described as 'construct' diversity. Diversity at the 'face' level will be most obvious in those schools with students, teachers and administrators from a wide range of cultural, national and linguistic backgrounds. Amongst those schools with populations which are less diverse (monocultural schools within national systems, or essentially monocultural schools which are 'displaced' from their own national context) such diversity will be less in evidence to the observer. This does not necessarily mean, however, that diversity at deeper levels cannot be built into the students' experience as a means of promoting international education, whatever the nature of the school in question. In discussing the development of a model for international education, Thompson (1998) argued for the importance of Board members, administrators and teachers arranging 'a learning environment that will provide opportunity, encouragement and support to those who are participating in it, and through which international education has the possibility of being experienced', going on to argue that the principal ingredients of such an environment could be represented in what have been termed the three dimensions of international education: a balanced formal curriculum, opportunities for celebrating cultural diversity and a range of appropriate administrative styles. These three dimensions could, it is argued, act as the three major strands in which diversity is manifest, with the three major 'constructs' being curriculum diversity, diversity of cultural experience and administrative/organizational diversity. These three constructs will be considered in more detail as follows.

Diversity through the curriculum

Opportunities for building in diversity to the curriculum will vary according to the nature of the school, its underlying philosophy of education and the nature of the student/teacher population. A school that wishes to promote international education, but within a context where it is constrained by commitment to the formal curriculum of a national system, will clearly have less opportunity than one in which no particular external curriculum is adhered to or, if it is, where that external curriculum is one that attempts to build in diversity as a means of promoting international education. Choice of formal curriculum, therefore, where that is possible, will clearly affect the possibility of diversity. Taking the definition of curriculum, however, in its broadest sense to include not only the 'subject' dimensions of the student's school experience, but also every other dimension – the informal as well as the formal – it is clear, as Thompson (1998) pointed out, that opportunities for 'interstitial learning' can be built in within and around whatever formal curriculum is espoused. Diversity can thus not only be built in terms of, for instance, the opportunity to study some subjects in greater depth than others, or some subjects in different ways from others by incorporating different styles of teaching to cater for different preferences in styles of learning; diversity can also be built in by encouraging students to be members of groups in different social and cultural contexts – perhaps by encouraging links between older and younger students, or links between students and other members of the community – in addition to the normal context of student and teacher relationships.

Diversity of cultural experience

Again, it is clearly the case that diversity in terms of interaction with, and knowledge of, different cultural contexts has the potential to be built in more easily to some school contexts than to others. For some, a rich resource is available in every lesson and in every student interaction in extracurricular activities. For others, operating within an essentially monocultural context, such opportunities may need to be more actively engineered but, in most cases, will nevertheless be feasible in organizational terms. There would be very few schools in the English national system, for instance, that would not be able to build into the curriculum (whether formal or informal) input from, and links with, those of other cultural backgrounds from the dominant culture of the school.

Diversity through organization and management of the institution

The organizational basis for any school is clearly crucial in determining everything else that arises within that school; management styles, decision-making processes, and school mission statements being among the explicit features into which diversity can be built. The more 'hidden' dimensions such as relationships between colleagues, or gender and cultural balance in senior positions, are also features where awareness of the importance of diversity can contribute to a richer experience for the student in terms of encouraging the development of an international outlook.

Concepts of quality for international education

We have been arguing thus far that diversity is not only an inherent feature of international schools, but is also a crucial aspect of the process of international education which must be purposefully built into the dimensions of the student's experience, where it may not necessarily be present as a natural part of that experience in any given context. However, it is clearly important to go on to ask the question 'If diversity, in all these kinds of manifestation, is at the core of international education, how can we, as international educators, ensure not only that appropriate forms of diversity are included in the programmes offered to students but also that the quality of provision is the highest attainable?'

The notion of quality is not a new one, either in its relation to the wide range of goods and services we receive as a part of our daily lives, or in relation to the many aspects of the various processes of education going on in different contexts around the world. The literature is full of debate and discussion about how best to define, implement, measure, assure and control quality in respect of those processes. Such approaches, however, rely on an assumption that quality has a universality, a stability and an objectivity that some would find difficult to accept. On the contrary, quality, it has been argued, is subjective, value-based and dynamic and the concept of quality for proponents of such an argument is problematic not primarily because of the technical issues of its measurement (such as an obsession in national debates about the so-called 'league-tables' of school performance) but much more fundamentally because of the 'philosophical issue of value and dispute' (Dahlberg, Moss and Pence, 1999). Although these authors are arguing in relation to studies in early childhood education, the points they are making in respect of the concept of 'quality' have much wider application and are certainly worthy of consideration in an international education context. They argue that 'quality' is not a neutral term but is socially constructed, arising from a '... "discourse of quality", which is itself the product of several related forces, including Enlightenment thinking and a particular rationality found in the world of business. Above all, the concept of quality makes sense within a philosophical framework, a way of understanding the world, what Habermas (1983) refers to as the "Project of Modernity"' (Moss, 1999). As Moss goes on to make clear, this philosophical perspective, which values certainty, linearity, objectivity and universality, has had a hold on the world for over three hundred years. In such circumstances it is very difficult to reconceptualize the notion of quality to accommodate diversity, subjectivity and multiple values – all characteristics which have been identified with dimensions of international education. In order to work with such complexity, Dalhberg *et al* (1999) have proposed a Project of Postmodernity, in which making sense of, or evaluating, educational institutions requires a different discourse which they refer to as 'meaning making'. The authors explain that whereas 'the discourse of quality attempts to judge the conformity of practice to predetermined criteria, the discourse of meaning making, in contrast, is first and foremost about constructing and deepening understanding of the institution and its projects, especially pedagogic work – to make meaning of what is going on' (Moss, 1999).

Such arguments notwithstanding, it would have to be recognized that the concept of quality, in a more traditionalist form, already exists implicitly within the international education community, though not necessarily based on a totally shared perception of what precisely it might mean. When students from international schools are striving to perform sufficiently well in end-of-school examinations in order to be accepted into the university of their choice, when they participate in team games with students of other institutions, when they are encouraged to participate in experiences such as the Model United Nations or debating societies which encourage the development of skills which are not formally assessed but which are nevertheless valued by those promoting the concept of international education, when features such as these are part of the student's experience, it is clear that concepts of quality exist within the institutions promoting international education. Whether understandings of such concepts are shared amongst those institutions is another issue, and it will almost certainly be the case that a variety of different understandings will come to light when the question of quality is discussed amongst any group of international educators. In editing this book, we have set out to address the question of what quality might mean in the context of international education by focusing on the three major areas already identified above, and within these three areas a range of issues relating to quality have been addressed by our contributing authors, all as they relate to international schools.

Issues relating to quality in assessment, in the interstitial curriculum, in national schools, in the politics of international education and in the extent to which international schools are inclusive are all raised in the first section with, in each case, arguments being made in relation to how quality can be determined with respect to the dimension in question. Quality in the context of issues relating to the 'human resource' dimension of international education, students (student mobility), teachers (recruitment, professional development, women in senior management roles) and the local community is discussed in the next section, with the last section focusing on school management: school effectiveness/school improvement and its implications for quality in international schools, long-term planning/strategic planning as a means of building in quality to the organizational elements of school, and some suggestions arising from the recent research relating to globalization which may help to support the development of quality in the international school context. Consideration of the links between the global context of international schools and the national context of many other schools also acts as the basis for discussions relating to how quality may be enhanced not only in one particular context.

Towards international standards setting

The task of generating a quality framework for international education rests on the extent to which an appropriate *system* of standards can be established in relation to criteria for judgement. In turn, this also raises important questions relating to *authority,* and the associated issue of the nature of the constituency which properly generates, protects and maintains that authority. The ultimate credibility and status of international education, and of the institutions through which it is promoted, are intimately bound up with the standards which are consistently demonstrated by them. In some respects the growth in the number and styles of international schools has mirrored the growth in the multinational commercial sectors, and in searching for a definition of standards for the international education context it may be appropriate to consider whether there is anything to be learnt from the notions of globalization in the commercial world.

From one perspective the growth of international standards is seen as part of the development of a worldwide advanced industrialized society, which requires a set of technical rules and conventions to enable it to function properly. Under such an arrangement a dominant player in the market, such as a global software producer, may occupy a key position in the determination of standards, as a result of which the standard is one that will be imposed. A quite different perspective rejects the notion that standard setting is merely a technical matter. In social policy fields the plurality of stakeholders with a wide range of differing interests results in approaches to standards, in quite specific circumstances, relating directly to the nature of the individual interests. The consequence is that any kind of international standards which emerge from such a *milieu*, and which do so after juxtaposed processes of cooperation and conflict have been evident, must be taken back and evaluated in terms of each of the competing interests, which may, in turn, give rise to further challenge and adjustment to the standards proposed. The situation with respect to international schools is certainly more likely to be identified with the latter perspective than with the former, given the case that has been made here for the diversity of the constituency.

Alongside the question of approaches to standard setting lies the issue of interpretation of the form of globalization that will be most appropriate in the context of a debate about quality in the network of international schools. Although there is already an extensive literature in existence on the subject of globalization, and it is one that is hotly contested within both academic and commercial spheres, there are three broad forms that may be identified (Room, 2000) as follows:

> *Market globalisation* involves the removal of barriers to the free movement of capital and labour, goods and services, so that entrepreneurs can develop their activities outside the constraints of national markets. *Political globalisation* involves the construction of new supranational systems of governance with a regional or even global mandate, in part to manage this global market. *Social globalisation* involves the convergence of social and cultural values, transcending the previously segregated national social debates. None of these forms of globalisation is neutral or even-handed in its effects, and even the language or discourse in which the dominant actors welcome its benefits or decry its costs is worth critical scrutiny.

In some parts of the world international schools have already become what may be described as market actors, and the stage on which they operate is becoming increasingly global. Escalating costs, together with a strong profit-motive (in admittedly only a relatively small number of cases) drives such schools to the market-driven end of Michael Matthews' categorization of schools (Matthews, 1988). In all international schools the task of management, through individual Heads or Chief Executives and School Boards, has seen a shift in the balance of skills away from academic leadership towards entrepreneurial imperatives to satisfy recruitment needs, with possible implications for academic standards.

Political globalization has been no less evident on the world stage so far as education is concerned for a considerable period of time, and common frameworks for discussing policy, sharing experience in the management of education systems, establishing value for money (by a regional or national system), organizing exchange programmes and the forging of links between national systems have been promoted at supranational levels by a range of organizations, such as OECD. Across international schools political globalization is already evident in both explicit and implicit forms. The creation of the International Schools Association (ISA) in 1951, based in Geneva, was one of the earliest attempts to incorporate supranationality, which if not exactly intended to establish governance certainly accepted a mandate to inform and develop on a global scale. More recently the European Council of International Schools (ECIS) has occupied a central role in the generation and implementation of criteria for the accreditation and professional development of its member schools. The International Baccalaureate Organisation (IBO) is a burgeoning political global player, with a full complement of programmes covering the K-12 range, its experience in evaluating the suitability of institutions for participation in its curricula and examinations, and its support for the work of teachers in international schools through its extensive range of workshop activities and school-based curricular developments. All of these organizations have sought to establish standards in the respective areas in which they operate globally, whether that be accreditation, professional development or curriculum, and there are many more examples of such organizations operating within the educational sphere throughout the world. However, having created the sets of conventions, rules and practices that constitute such societies, potential new members or participants are often required to subscribe to the established order and unless a mechanism for dynamic change is built into such organizations, what passes for the maintenance and upholding of standards can sometimes become a rigidifying influence in the concretizing of criteria which no longer have validity in a changing educational scenario.

The convergence of social and cultural values involved in social globalization offers, perhaps, the most appropriate way forward for international schools in relation to the range of characteristics for such organizations as discussed above. Under such circumstances the development of a charter, enshrining institutional obligations, and individual rights and responsibilities, would be a task for the group of international schools constituting the network, or for an association of those (schools, universities, and other international organizations) that share a common goal in the promotion of international education in national or international schools worldwide (Hayden and Thompson, 2000). Central to such an approach to globalization is the interests of all the stakeholders in the enterprise, and although international schools are, in general, autonomous institutions, they are also dependent on their interaction with a number of other key players in the field. It was for that reason that we have suggested elsewhere that the way forward with respect to the setting of international standards can only be through processes of collaboration, partnership and cooperation, between all the stakeholders. An Alliance for International Education (Hayden and Thompson, 2000), seen as an inclusive society, will have the mission not only of seeking to establish the meaning of 'quality' in international education, but of translating that understanding into the improvement of practice, for the benefit of students everywhere.

References

Dahlberg, G, Moss, P and Pence, A (1999) *Beyond Quality in Early Childhood Education and Care: Postmodern perspectives*, Falmer Press, London

Habermas, J (1983) Modernity: an incomplete project, in *The Anti-Aesthetic: Essays on postmodern culture*, ed H Foster, Port Townsend, Washington

Hayden, M C and Thompson, J J (1995a) International schools and international education: a relationship reviewed, *Oxford Review of Education*, **21** (3), pp 327–34

Hayden, M C and Thompson, J J (1995b) Perceptions of international education: a preliminary study, *International Review of Education*, **41** (5), pp 389–404

Hayden, M C and Thompson, J J (1996) Potential difference: the driving force for international education, *International Schools Journal*, **XVI** (1), pp 46–57

Hayden, M C and Thompson, J J (2000) International education: flying flags or raising standards?, *International Schools Journal*, **XIX** (2), pp 48–56

Matthews, M (1988) *The Ethos of International Schools*, MSc thesis, University of Oxford

Moss, P (1999) *Difference, Dissensus and Debate: Some possibilities of learning from Reggio,* conference paper, Reggio-Emilia, June

Murphy E (2000) Questions for the new millennium, *International Schools Journal*, **XIX** (2), pp 5–10

Room, G (2000) Globalisation, social policy and international standard-setting: the case of higher education credentials, *International Journal of Social Welfare*, **9**, pp 103–19

Thompson, J J (1998) *Towards a Model for International Education*, in *International Education: Principles and practice*, eds M C Hayden and J J Thompson, Kogan Page, London

Walker, G R (2000) One-way streets of our culture, *International Schools Journal*, **XIX** (2), pp 11–19

Part A

THROUGH THE CURRICULUM

Chapter 2

Assessment and educational quality: implications for international schools

John Lowe

Within many national education systems the past 20 years or so have seen an unprecedented growth of interest in the use of examinations and other assessment tools as means of enhancing the quality of education. This chapter will consider some of the approaches to achieving this end that have been tried or suggested, as well as some of their limitations, and will offer reflections on their application to the context of international schools. A distinction must first be made between the terms assessment and examinations, as they are to be used here. Assessment is taken to include any means of obtaining information about the achievement of learners, from day-to-day observations and questions in the classroom through to annual national, or international, formal examinations. Examinations are just one form of assessment, characterized by a degree of formality and a separation from the daily processes of teaching and learning. The most common form of examination is the written question paper, but various forms of oral and practical examinations are also in use.

Assessment as quality control

The simplest link between assessment and educational quality is in the use of assessment outcomes to monitor performance of the system at one level or another – international, national, regional, school, department or even the individual teacher or learner. To use the terminology of industrial management, this is a 'quality control' approach in which assessment is used to determine whether or not pre-specified 'product' parameters of quality have been met. Used in this way, assessment results are an indicator of what is perhaps the simplest interpretation of quality in an education system, namely its effectiveness in meeting predetermined targets (Hawes and Stephens, 1990).

There appear to be two approaches to this use of assessment data for monitoring purposes. The first relies on norm-referenced standardized testing. In this approach an assessment instrument is first 'calibrated' by being used with a reference population. The performance of this population is then used as the standard against which to judge that of other groups or individuals subsequently taking the test. (The need for 'fair' comparisons means that all aspects of the assessment must be standardized and this almost inevitably leads to the use of formal tests.) This is, in essence, the model for the Scholastic Assessment Tests (SATs) of the USA (Nitko, 1996). One of the advantages claimed for this approach is that it allows a monitoring of changes in educational outcome standards over time. Indeed, declining average SAT scores in the USA over time have been interpreted as being indicative of deteriorating educational quality (Madaus and Raczek, 1996). It should be noted, however, that such an approach is sensitive to the selection of an appropriate reference population in the initial 'norming' process. A comparison of performance between two groups may tell us more about differences in other characteristics of the groups than about the quality of their educational experiences. For example, the initial calibration of SATs was carried out in 1941, when a much smaller proportion of young people went on to college than do so today. The initial group used for calibration purposes represented the academic elite of its time (and probably, also, the socio-economic elite). It is rather invidious, if not meaningless, to make comparisons of the achievement of the vastly broader range of college-bound students of today with that elite. Outcomes may genuinely indicate a performance inferior to that of the earlier normative group, but the interpretation of this difference as an indicator of declining quality in the system does not necessarily follow. This is one reason why it was decided to recalibrate (or 'recentre') the SAT scores from 1995, using performance from a more recent population sample (College Board, 1998).

An alternative approach to devising assessment for monitoring is one based on criterion-referencing. In this approach, performance standards are embodied in a series of achievement statements rather than in the performance of a reference population. This is essentially the approach adopted in the English National Curriculum, with its 'Attainment Targets' (Gipps and Stobart, 1990) comprising a hierarchy of performance levels. In principle at least, the achievement level of any learner can be determined through an assessment which directly addresses the description of performance indicative of that level. Such an approach should preclude the need for standardized tests and allow the use of a wide range of assessment modes and tools, since the standard of achievement of an individual or a group is defined with reference to a set of fixed criteria, not to a particular assessment tool. In reality the situation is more complex, for at least two reasons. The first is the difficulty of writing statements that define achievement levels unequivocally for all who use them. The second is that the performance of an individual is dependent on a range of context factors that includes the form of assessment, thereby weakening our ability to define achievement independent of the means by which it was assessed. The latter problem can be addressed by defining achievement levels either in terms of best performance demonstrated in any assessment situation, or as an aggregate performance from a range of assessment opportunities. The former problem can be approached in two ways. One is to increase the level of detail in the criteria statements, with the danger that they become unmanageably complex for even the simplest of tasks. An alternative approach which has been adopted with regard to the English National Curriculum is to supplement broad statements of achievement with exemplar material illustrative of different performance levels, opportunities for teachers to discuss meanings and reach a consensus, and various processes of assessment outcomes moderation.

The criterion-referenced approach has immediate appeal in that it gives us information about actual learning outcomes of the system being monitored. Unlike a norm-referenced model it tells us what learners know or can do. It should be noted, however, that this information is not in itself a measure of quality. Judgements of educational quality will ultimately involve a comparison, a norm-referencing of some sort which often focuses on a historical comparison with an earlier population of learners, as in the United States example mentioned earlier. Such comparisons are commonly made both by national systems and by individual schools in order to monitor trends in quality over time. Schools may also make a comparison between their own assessment outcomes and those of other schools within the system. Increasingly, too, national systems are seeking to make comparisons of their achievements with those of other systems. The international comparisons carried out by the International Association for the Evaluation of Educational

Achievement (IEA) have been important in both driving and responding to this tendency, although it could be argued that both are part of broader patterns of increasing global awareness and competition (Kellaghan, 1996).

The warning given earlier about the need for caution in making comparisons is repeated here and is perhaps particularly significant for international schools seeking to use assessment data to monitor their performance. If comparisons are to be meaningful, they must be based on comparable data and must be made between similar populations. The comparable data may be that produced by taking the same external examinations as the 'target' schools with which comparison is to be made, or by working with the same set of defined performance criteria, such as the 'level statements' of the English National Curriculum. If working with the latter, the scattered nature of international schools may lead to difficulties in participating fully in the consensus-generating and moderation procedures that encourage uniformity of interpretation of the performance criteria. There may be further problems in seeking an appropriate population with which to compare performance. Schools taking nationally based examinations may use corresponding national norms for comparisons, but it should be noted that these norms them-selves derive from a very diverse population. It is increasingly common for schools in England, for example, to compare their performance not with the national results but with the performance of schools having a student intake from a similar socio-economic background. The nature of the student body in an international school may make such a socio-economic location difficult, but a comparison which does not take student background into consideration is of little value in making judge-ments about the quality of the educational experience provided.

The need to allow for differences in student characteristics when judging schools has led to the development of a more sophisticated monitoring model in which the 'value added' rather than crude output data is used to make judgements of quality. Models for value-added measures are becoming increasingly sophisticated, but the basic principle in all cases is that of using the achievement gain since entry to the school as a measure of quality, rather than the single measure of final performance. This, of course, demands the use of two comparable achievement measures, one at entry and one at exit. It appears at first sight to be a 'fairer' measure of the quality of the education that a school offers, but in practice it is bedevilled with at least as many difficulties as the simpler model, some of them very similar. At the basic level, some means of judging the amount of value added is still required and this, once again, requires a comparison with a norm taken from somewhere –

a value-added rather than a final-outcome norm. Furthermore, the use of value-added measures to judge the quality of the education provided by a school assumes that all, or the majority, of this added value can in fact be attributed solely to the school rather than to external factors such as home background. An assumption of this kind is naïve in the extreme. We are again left with the problem of choosing a suitable population with which to compare the degree of value that has been added.

For international schools, value-added approaches retain many of the problems of the cruder model when it comes to judging quality, and may also bring with them the added expense of having to buy into another external examination. For those schools with a fairly high turnover of students – as is the case in many international schools – there are the added difficulties of establishing the baseline measure for all students, and of deciding how much of any added value can be attributed to that school rather than to the other schools that many students may have previously attended.

Monitoring for quality improvement

If our aim is not only to report on current educational standards but also to attempt to improve them, the limitations of a simple monitoring approach are quite clear. Such an approach makes a summative use of assessment: it provides educational achievement measures at the end of a block of teaching and learning which may be several years in length, particularly if we are relying on external examinations as the monitoring device. If any deficiencies in quality are detected, it is too late to attend to them for the cohort of students that has been assessed. The students may be encouraged to repeat part or all of the educational process, but very often even this highly inefficient option is not available and the system has to accept that it has turned out 'failures'. Quite apart from efficiency arguments, it is difficult to justify such an approach when dealing with children rather than with industrial products.

Two responses to this limitation can be observed. One of these attempts to extend the impact of summative assessment further back into the educational process than the moment at which it is adminis-tered. This impact is commonly referred to as an assessment 'backwash' effect, with the extent of the backwash being directly dependent on the 'stakes' of the assessment concerned: the significance of the outcomes of the assessment for those who are preparing for it. By raising the stakes of an examination its impact can be intensified and extended further back into the teaching and learning process. If this is accompanied by the setting of achievement targets that are higher than those currently being reached, an improvement in standards is the anticipated outcome. This combination of monitoring, target setting and the use of assessment backwash is a central component of many models in the field of School Improvement.

The means by which an examination becomes 'high stakes' and for whom it actually has this status may vary. In many cases it is the students for whom an examination has important consequences, when examination results are used to select for scarce and desirable opportunities in education or employment. This commonly leads to the phenomenon of 'credentialism', which has important consequences for educational quality (Collins, 1979; Dore, 1997). Such a form of selection-led credentialism is of great significance, but is rather different from the management-led raising of stakes which is of concern here and so will be dealt with in a later section.

Within models of educational systems management, it is often the teachers or the schools for which examination stakes are deliberately raised as a means of forcing improvements in outcomes, as measured by examination results. The most blatant form of this was the 'Payment by Results' approach that was a feature of the English state system in the nineteenth century and is now being considered for reintroduction, in a marginally more sophisticated form, by linking teachers' salaries to the examination performance of their students. Other models rely on a pseudo-market mechanism that is supposed to operate by making a school's examination results publicly known so that parents will use this information when choosing schools for their children: schools with better examination results will have a market edge over those with poor results which will, as a consequence, attempt to improve their examination performance to stay 'in business'. The evidence from state education systems suggests that this mechanism is, at best, imperfect in its operation if only because parental choice of school is often restricted in practice and is commonly not based solely – or even at all – on a school's examination results (Lauder and Hughes, 1999). The applicability of these findings to private schools in general, and to international schools in particular, can only be guessed at and is likely to depend enormously on the nature and context of each school. My own research suggests that perceptions of the quality of education provided by such schools can be an important factor in attracting clientele and that examination results may play a significant part for some parents in judging this quality, but the situation is far from being as simple as this. The specific examinations on offer, the language(s) of instruction, facilities and extracurricular opportunities, perceptions of quality of the local state system, the social class of the existing clientele, and a host of practical considerations all play their part (Lowe, 2000).

A second response to the limitations of assessment for monitoring is to increase the frequency of the monitoring so that remedial action, if needed, can be embarked upon at an earlier stage. Such an approach has been adopted, for example, in England, where national external tests are either compulsory or optionally available in all of years 3 to 9 (ages approximately 7 to 14 years). National performance data from these tests is made available for schools to judge their own results (QCA, 2000). Taken to its logical conclusion this leads to a process of continuous quality monitoring. For practical reasons, however, if for no other, we are then taken into a very different model of the role of assessment in relation to quality. The key practical reason is that continuous monitoring cannot realistically rely on external assessment but must hand over control of the process to the teacher – and even to the learner. When coupled with a feedback mechanism that deals with 'faults' as they are detected, this development leads us to what is essentially the monitoring of process rather than product and into formative rather than summative assessment.

Formative assessment and quality improvement

Gipps and Stobart (1990) distinguish 'managerial' and 'professional' purposes of assessment: assessment to help manage an education system, and assessment to help the teacher in the process of educating, respectively. The uses of assessment considered so far fall very clearly into the former category. They treat assessment as a managerial tool, the purpose of which is to monitor or 'drive' an education system or sub-system. The model within which such approaches commonly work is that of the teaching and learning process itself being an unopened 'black box' into which there are inputs which somehow influence outputs – commonly measured by examination results. The mechanisms within the black box by which inputs are transformed into outputs remain largely unexplored (Gipps and Stobart, 1990). The past 20 years or so have seen managerial approaches to assessment become increasingly dominant across national systems and agencies working with such systems (Lockheed, 1996). There is evidence now, however, of the re-emergence of interest in the importance of assessment for the 'professional' purposes of supporting the teaching and learning processes; in other words, formative assessment. Two key proponents of this trend have, rather significantly, published one account of their research findings under the title *Inside the Black Box* (Black and Wiliam, 1998).

Formative assessment must, almost by definition, be under the control of teachers and learners, but Black and Wiliam refer to evidence of concern in several countries over the poor quality of assessment practice in the classroom. Thus, two decades or more of unprecedented growth of interest in assessment amongst policy makers, managers and academics may have had little impact on the assessment practices of teachers themselves. Perhaps this is not surprising when one considers that such growth has been predominantly in assessment for managerial purposes, which is almost certain to be in external hands, and it is in these hands rather than amongst teachers that expertise has developed. A side effect of the 'managerial approach' to raising educational standards, however, is that teachers come under increasing pressure to use or copy external tests in order to monitor their progress towards meeting the externally set targets embodied in these tests and may, in doing so, become deskilled in setting and using their own assessment tasks for other purposes.

What makes this report of the poor quality of classroom assessment practices more disturbing is the analysis that follows of research evidence relating to the impact of formative assessment. Black and Wiliam conclude from this analysis that the strengthening of formative assessment practices is in fact one of the most effective ways of raising attainment and that it 'helps the (so-called) low attainers more than the rest, and so reduces the spread of attainment whilst also raising it overall' (Black and Wiliam, 1998). They go on to identify key elements in effective formative assessment methods: targeted feedback, self-assessment by students, and interaction and dialogue between student and teacher. This work has been extended by the Assessment Reform Group (1999), which summarizes the characteristics of assessment to promote learning as follows:

- it is embedded in a view of teaching and learning of which it is an essential part;
- it involves sharing learning goals with students;
- it aims to help students to know and to recognize the standards they are aiming for;
- it involves students in self-assessment;
- it provides feedback which leads to students recognizing their next steps and how to take them;
- it is underpinned by confidence that every student can improve; and
- it involves both teachers and students reviewing and reflecting on assessment data.

Together these two documents present a model for the role of assessment in raising educational standards that is radically different from the currently dominant managerial model, in that the teachers and learners in this model take centre stage as active and skilled participants. The implications of the two models for systems and schools, in terms of resources and professional development, are very different, with the formative assessment model focusing on the development of in-school assessment capacity rather than external testing agencies and materials, and on new classroom practices rather than management structures: 'policy ought to start with a recognition that the prime locus for raising standards is the classroom... Attempts to raise standards by reform of the inputs and outputs to and from the black box of the classroom can be helpful, but they cannot be adequate on their own' (Black and Wiliam, 1998).

Black and Wiliam's suggestions for strategies to improve classroom assessment practices have interesting implications for international schools. They begin with the warning that there is no 'quick fix' for improving formative assessment. There are no existing rules or detailed models that can be followed in any classroom context. The answers to practical questions have still to be worked out and are likely to be different in different contexts. They advise a school-based approach to the development of formative assessment techniques but argue that this will work best amongst a collaborative group of local schools which will promote exchange and dissemination of new ideas and good practice, while still requiring external training inputs. For schools working within the same system and in proximity to each other such an approach is feasible. It is not at all clear, however, how it might work with international schools which may be operating on quite different bases, with different curricula, and which may even be in competition with each other.

One further difference between these two strategies for using assessment to enhance quality is that good formative assessment will make use of a much wider range of assessment techniques than is possible in managerial and external monitoring models. The latter are more likely to rely predominantly on formal testing, for reasons of reliability and comparability that are inherent to their purpose. It should be noted, however, that formal external assessments are unlikely to disappear from educational systems. Even if the development of formative, classroom assessment is seen as the most effective way to improve quality, it is likely that the measure of the 'standard' of many education systems will remain performance in formal, external, summative examinations. More significant than this, however, is the fact that such examination performance is now one of the key devices used for the allocation of life chances in many societies. The impact of this role on educational quality has received considerable attention and is the focus of the next section.

Credentialism and the quality of education

In many societies, the allocation of life chances in employment or in further or higher education is now largely determined, in the first instance, on the basis of performance in public examinations. This credentialism leads to key examinations becoming very high-stakes affairs that can have a devastating backwash effect on teaching and learning. When educational credentials become the gateway to occupational opportunity their acquisition tends to become the chief purpose of education. The closer in time an examination is and the higher its stakes, the more teaching and learning become focused on preparation for that examination, to the exclusion of all else. If an aspect of the curriculum is not to be examined, learners will not learn it and teachers will not teach it – the practice of 'teaching to the test' (Somerset, 1996), an approach commonly perceived as having negative consequences for educational quality. In his study of the impact of credentialism in the USA, Collins suggests that for American students 'the reasons for going to school are extraneous to whatever goes on in the classroom' (1979). In his 'diploma disease' hypothesis, Dore laments credentialism as leading to 'ritualistic examination-oriented learning' but argues that its most damaging effect extends beyond this to the production, in turn, of 'ritualistic, performance-evaluation-oriented workers' (1997).

These critics of the effects of credentialism are not judging educational quality in terms of examination results. Indeed, one consequence of credentialism is that educational outcomes improve, in the sense that more students gain higher levels of qualifications. This is a response to the 'positional competition' engendered by the use of these qualifications for occupational access, but one of its main effects is 'qualification inflation': the decrease in exchange value on the labour market of any given qualification as more people possess it (Hirsch, 1977). Success in the occupational selection competition is dependent on relative advantage, not some notion of absolute value of educational credentials, so there is a constant drive towards obtaining ever-higher levels of credentials. One interpretation of the rapid expansion in many countries of the numbers of schools offering 'international' qualifications is that they are a response by local elites to a stiffening of the local positional competition on the one hand and a globalization of that competition on the other. As more people gain local educational qualifications, those who can afford to do so seek a new competitive edge by taking qualifications that they hope will give them a local advantage. At the same time, it is hoped that these international qualifications will give access to a labour market that is becoming increasingly globalized – for the most advantageous occupations, at least (Ilon, 1997). The value of international credentials (a term which includes national credentials recognized outside their country of origin) may be in their being perceived as certifying a higher quality of education, or they may simply provide prospective employers or university admissions officers with an extra screening device, or, yet again, their value may derive from other sources, such as their certification of competence in English (Lowe, 2000).

There are those who, while recognizing the potential or actual negative impact of examination backwash on educational quality, argue that this backwash can in fact be harnessed to positive effect. Their argument is that the negative impact of backwash arises from examinations of poor quality – examinations that primarily test recall of facts and emphasize rote learning, for example – and, if the quality of the examinations is improved by making them valid tests of valuable educational objectives, any backwash on teaching and learning will be a good thing. This is the rationale behind the influential 'Measurement-Driven Instruction' (MDI) movement in the United States (Popham, 1987; Gipps, 1994). Some interesting work on this examinations-led approach to quality enhancement has also been undertaken in Africa, where, in many countries, key selection examinations between primary and secondary school or between junior and senior secondary school are enormously high-stakes and have correspondingly powerful backwash effects (Kellaghan and Greaney, 1992). What seems to emerge from studies of these effects is that while poor examinations do damage educational quality and good examinations may help to enhance quality, their impact is mediated by a whole range of factors beyond the examinations themselves. Key amongst these are the capacities of schools and teachers to respond to the demands of higher-quality examinations. Ultimately, teachers cannot be forced by examinations to do what they do not know how to do, and any examination-led attempt at quality enhancement must be accompanied by professional development support for teachers.

Quality in broader educational terms

There remain some fundamental issues about the capacity for examinations to improve educational quality. There is an element of circularity in

using examinations to drive educational quality improvement if one
then uses performance in those same examinations as the measure of
enhanced quality. One is left in need of an independent measure of
educational quality and cannot be sure whether examination
performance is really anything more than just that: performance in an
examination. If education has a significance beyond examinations then
one must look for a measure of quality in a broader set of educational
purposes. At best, examinations are a proxy measure of the real goals of
education, which relate to preparation for various aspects of life viewed
in the longer term. We assume that success in the proxy promises success
in the 'real thing'. In practice, evidence that this is so is limited, often
negative, and is, in any case, contaminated by our deliberate decision to
use examination success to limit access to many life chances in which
success might be demonstrated. It is very difficult to test the validity of
an examination in predicting, for example, success in the next stage of
education if one uses that examination to select who may go on to
demonstrate success in that next stage.

A further problem arises with high-stakes assessment, which is that its
high-stakes nature tends to limit the forms of assessment that can be
used. If assessment outcomes are used for the allocation of opportunity,
then the assessment must retain public confidence and be seen as 'fair' to
all. This almost inevitably leads to the use of formal written examinations, at least as the major component of the assessment, and very often
produces pressure for particular forms of those examinations such as
those based on 'objective' multiple-choice items. One consequence is
that only a limited range of educational aims can be assessed. These are,
first of all, likely to be largely in the cognitive domain and, within that
domain, likely to be limited to the simpler skills. Proponents of MDI
(such as Popham, cited in Gipps, 1994) argue that these are the 'basic
skills' and therefore central to a good education, but this does not alter
the fact that they represent a limited range of desirable educational
outcomes. Such proponents are guilty of promoting what Rowntree
(1987) refers to as McNamara's Fallacy: the tendency to give importance
to that which is easily measurable rather than trying to find a way of
measuring that which is really important.

Finally, those who counter the negative backwash critique of examinations by arguing that the backwash is acceptable as long as it is from
good examinations are, I believe, missing the point. It is not the form or
content of the examinations that is at the heart of the critique, but the
attitudes towards learning that are developed as a result of the uses to
which examinations are put – selection for limited opportunity – which
ultimately provide the rationale for these examinations. With the current

concern for developing propensities to lifelong learning to meet the demands of an uncertain and rapidly changing future, attitudes towards learning must become a central component of our concept of educational quality. Is there something in the nature of examinations that is fundamentally opposed to educational aims of developing reflective lifelong learning? The latter concept is about participation in and control of one's own life and learning. Examinations – at least, in the way they are most commonly used – are a way of meeting someone else's expectations, on their terms, not our own. If examinations *per se*, or the uses we make of them, contribute to the development of ritualistic or negative attitudes to learning, then they are undermining rather than supporting attempts to improve educational quality.

References

Assessment Reform Group (1999) *Assessment for Learning: Beyond the black box*, University of Cambridge School of Education, Cambridge

Black, P and Wiliam, D (1998) *Inside the Black Box: Raising standards through classroom assessment*, Kings College School of Education, University of London, London

College Board (1998) The effects of SAT scale recentering on percentiles, *Research Summary 5*, New York, Office of Research and Development, The College Board, October
(also available at The College Board Web site: www.collegeboard.org)

Collins, R (1979) *The Credential Society: An historical sociology of education and stratification*, Academic Press, New York

Dore, R (1997) *The Diploma Disease: Education, qualification and development*, 2nd edn, Institute of Education, London

Gipps, C (1994) *Beyond Testing: Towards a theory of educational assessment*, Falmer Press, London

Gipps, C and Stobart, G (1990) *Assessment: A teachers' guide to the issues*, Hodder and Stoughton, London

Hawes, H and Stephens, D (1990) *Questions of Quality: Primary education and development*, Longman, Harlow

Hirsch, F (1977) *Social Limits to Growth*, Routledge and Kegan Paul, London

Ilon, L (1997) Educational repercussions of a global system of production, in *International Handbook of Education and Development: Preparing schools, students and nations for the twenty-first century*, eds W K Cummings and N F McGinn, Pergamon, Oxford

Kellaghan, T (1996) IEA studies and educational policy, *Assessment in Education: Principles, policy and practice*, **3** (2), pp 143–60

Kellaghan, T and Greaney, V (1992) *Using Examinations to Improve Education: A study in fourteen African countries*, World Bank Technical Paper no. 165, The World Bank, Washington, DC

Lauder, H and Hughes, D (1999) *Trading in Futures: Why markets in education don't work*, Open University Press, Buckingham

Lockheed, M E (1996) Assessment and management: World Bank support for educational testing, in *Assessment in Transition: Learning, monitoring and selection in international perspective*, eds A Little and A Wolf, Pergamon, Oxford

Lowe, J (2000) International examinations: the new credentialism and reproduction of advantage in a globalising world, *Assessment in Education: Principles, policy and practice*, **7** (3), pp 363–77

Madaus, G F and Raczek, A E (1996) A turning point for assessment: reform movements in the United States, in *Assessment in Transition: Learning, monitoring and selection in international perspective*, ed A Little and A Wolf, Pergamon, Oxford

Nitko, A J (1996) *Educational Assessment of Students*, 2nd edn, Merrill, Englewood Cliffs, NJ

Popham, J (1987) The merits of measurement-driven instruction, *Phi Delta Kappa*, May, pp 679–82

QCA (2000) Optional tests at Key Stage 3, *OnQ*, (8), March, p 4, London, Qualifications and Curriculum Authority (also available at the QCA Web site: www.qca.org)

Rowntree, D (1987) *Assessing Students: How shall we know them?*, Kogan Page, London

Somerset, A (1996) Examinations and educational quality, in *Assessment in Transition: Learning, monitoring and selection in international perspective*, eds A Little and A Wolf, Pergamon, Oxford

Chapter 3

Inclusive education in international schools: a case study from Singapore

Gail Bradley

Introduction

> People want a curriculum for the 21st century that goes far beyond traditional
> academic domains – a curriculum that both reflects and supports the inclusive
> education in concept.
>
> (Udvari-Solner and Thousand, 1995)

A new dawn begins. The twenty-first century arrives, bringing with it renewed hope and success for the future. Many people aspire to peace throughout the world, an end to poverty, further progress in technology, improvements in health care and worldwide eradication of various diseases; in the field of education, aspirations are focused on equal opportunity and education for all. Inherent in such aspirations is the fact that the whole of mankind is becoming more interdependent as each day progresses.

Throughout the world, the web of international schools seems to acknowledge the enriching experience of cultural and linguistic diversity among its students: indeed, many of these schools actively provide for such diversity. One of the characteristics of international schools is the fact that the wide diversity of culture and languages can be utilized to enrich the curriculum. However, such provision rarely seems to extend to diversity of ability. There is little mention about utilizing the variety of human *achievement*. For whatever reason, whether due to economics, lack of expertise or negative attitudes towards people with special needs in the host country, students with special educational needs appear to be the 'forgotten children' in this web, a point highlighted by Hollington (1994). Furthermore, inclusive education, regarded as a worldwide phenomenon by sources including Ainscow (1999) and Florian and Rouse (1996), seems largely to have escaped the attention of international schools, although, given the increased global movement of population over the past 50 years, many would at some time have had the challenge and opportunity of providing for such students. An inclusive system may, I would argue, be regarded as a necessary requirement for all international schools if they are to be considered as institutions that cater for all the children of the world.

For families with children who fit the 'norm', confronting the whole issue of global mobility and the difficulties that often accompany it can be a daunting task. For parents of a child with special educational needs, however, problems are manifold. As has been made evident in one unique international school, Dover Court Preparatory School (DCPS) in Singapore, such problems could include physical disabilities, specific learning difficulties, and mild, moderate or severe learning difficulties. Those with special needs could include the hearing impaired, children with Down's syndrome or autism, students with speech and language disorders, students with epilepsy, gifted or talented students, those with cerebral palsy and those with difficulties related to a variety of syndromes. As Waldron (1991) explains, making appropriate educational provision for such children is not an easy task in a national system, and the problem in international schools is magnified, as there may be little available in the form of appropriate education for the children of those who for reasons of employment have to live abroad. Such a situation suggests that we should be asking why, if international education is being promoted in international schools, it is not designed to cater for the needs of students of *all* abilities.

It is becoming increasingly necessary for international schools to open their doors to children from a wider range of abilities; in most cases the need is there, and such a policy would lead to the schools providing a broad and balanced, quality curriculum for all students, since 'If all our young people and adults who are learners in our education system are to enjoy an appropriate curriculum in settings which do not reduce their status as full members of the mainstream community, then everyone has to be seen to be of equal worth, not only in principle but also in practice' (Booth *et al*, 1995). One distinguishing feature that separates Dover Court from the majority of other fee-paying international schools is the fact that it opens its doors to all and, in so doing, it can lay claim to have pioneered inclusive education in an international setting. The notion of inclusive education in an international context is complex and implementation could be regarded as problematic. From reviewing the literature on inclusion in national systems, and from my own experience of teaching in a unique inclusive international school (DCPS) where 12 per cent of the population were students with special needs, it transpires that certain factors can be identified as either inhibiting or facilitating the whole process. With this in mind, I embarked upon research to discover such barriers and facilitating factors within that school, with a view to identifying possible strategies for successful implementation. Foremost in my thoughts was the possibility that international school teachers may well learn from such institutions as Dover Court and in turn develop a 'code of practice' for use in international schools more widely. Such an outcome would be a major contribution to the dimension of quality in international education.

What is inclusive education?

> it means that students with special needs are entitled to have their special needs met in regular education... it stands for an educational system that encompasses a wide diversity of students and that differentiates education in response to this diversity.
>
> (Meijer *et al*, 1997)

Inclusive education is a diverse and complex field which has been introduced in some contexts as an alternative to segregated special education. Many experts see inclusive education as an evolving process, rather than as a fixed end point, which aims to offer a system that is not only more humane but also more effective and productive for *all* students: a notion supported by many educationalists, including McLaughlin (1996), Mittler (1995), Florian and Rouse (1996), Stainback, Stainback and Jackson (1992), and Udvari-Solner and Thousand (1995). The main argument made for inclusion is that segregation is ethically wrong and educationally inefficient. Ainscow (1995) considers that there is a vital link between school effectiveness and inclusive education, in that they should both improve the school. Inclusive education involves consideration of social values, classroom practice, school policies and innovative ideas of human rights, as elaborated upon by Clark, Dyson and Millward (1995). It has become part of an entire school reform movement throughout the world, with Australia, Canada, Italy, New Zealand, Scandinavia, the UK and USA all making attempts to move towards implementation. Admittedly, inclusive education may not be the highest priority for many national systems, especially in less developed countries where children with special needs are often ignored. However, it would be wrong to believe that no action is taking place. Families throughout the world are striving for, and insisting upon, community-based education and many schools are opening their doors and attempting to provide an inclusive programme (Mittler, 1995). Belonging, it is argued, is a basic human right and not one that should need to be 'earned': inclusion, as the opposite of segregation and isolation, could foster this basic human right. Further thoughts on such issues can be found in, *inter alia*, Ainscow (1995), Allen (1999), Mayor (1994), McLaughlin (1996) and Udvari-Solner and Thousand (1995).

Inclusive education and international schools

An inclusive school caters for students of a wide range of abilities, and is a school where nobody is turned away simply because of their lack of capability. The diversity of the learning group is valued and accepted, as is the case in Dover Court. All students experience an appropriate education, share in all school events and are regarded as equal members of the school community. Valuing the diversity of its students, there is the minimum of separation between them. In short, everybody is catered for under the same umbrella. The driving force for inclusive education has indeed gained much support over recent years. It is argued that inclusive education could become the training ground for an inclusive society that respects the dignity and differences of all human beings, as high-lighted by UNESCO (1994) when it adopted the 'Salamanca Statement on Principles, Policy and Practice in Special Needs Education and a Framework for Action'. In support, Ainscow (1999) and Mittler (1995) state that the move to include all disabled children in education is now an essential part of the United Nations' 'Education for All' programme. Federico Mayor (1994) suggests that 'All concerned must now rise to the challenge and work to ensure that Education for All effectively means FOR ALL, particularly those who are most vulnerable and most in need.' UNESCO calls upon all governments to adopt principles of inclusive education, and upon the international community to endorse an approach of inclusive education. If such considerations are taken alongside Bartlett's (1998) suggestions in the context of the International Baccalaureate Primary Years Programme that 'Skills, habits of mind and attitudes, a common knowledge base... are developed by many years of contact with important ideas', then there are significant implications for those who teach in international schools. Many of our international school students may eventually hold positions of leadership throughout the world and could well be able to influence governments and public opinion on such issues. Maybe it is time for us as international educators to ask the question 'How much longer can most of our institutions continue to ignore a particular group of students?' Some international schools claim to be inclusive, but, in many cases, views of inclusive education have been restricted to specific dimensions such as dyslexia or a mild learning disability; examples of truly comprehensive, inclusive education are very hard to find. Some schools do offer support, but it is mostly in the area of English as a Second Language (ESL) (Haldimann, 1998). In others, appropriate facilities are not available and specialist staff are not employed. Even schools linked to a national system that endorses inclusion often seem to follow a different philosophy when they are established in other parts of the world. As educationalists we have an opportunity to change the segregated approach to education in the context of international schools, which results in a climate of separateness and isolation and tends to foster stigma. The question for the future in this context, I would argue, is not 'Is inclusion the right thing to do?', but rather 'How can inclusion best be implemented?'.

It would be understandable if many readers perceived obstacles in the path of developing inclusive education in the international context. Recent research (Bradley, 1998) showed that providing for an inclusive education in such a context is not an easy task, and that certain factors do indeed inhibit the development and implementation of inclusive education. On the other hand, evidence was also found of elements that facilitate inclusion in this setting. The benefits of inclusive education in the international school may be seen as outweighing the difficulties, and recommendations from this piece of small-scale research could aid those international schools which are considering opening their doors to all and in turn improving the quality of the curriculum. Jenkins (1998) raises the issue of the nature of the curriculum in the international school of the twenty-first century. Udvari-Solner and Thousand (1995) would not hesitate to proclaim that it should be one that incorporates the philosophy of inclusive education. Mittler (1995) insists that 'The key to inclusive education lies in planned access to a broad and balanced curriculum, designed from the outset (and not as an afterthought) as a curriculum for all.' Inclusive education in an international context may be regarded by some as being simply a dream, but the successes of tomorrow often begin as the dreams of today. The reality of making this dream come true must lie in improving the quality of the curriculum.

The curriculum

> Managers of excellent schools will be very aware of the range and impact of all curriculum experiences on students, and will attempt to harness their power in the interests of improving the quality of every child's education.
>
> (Beare *et al*, 1992)

In the Salamanca report (UNESCO, 1994) there is a call for a curriculum that is flexible and adaptive and differentiated to students' needs and interests, with support for students with special needs in assisting them to experience the same curriculum as experienced by others. Evaluation should be incorporated into the process in order to identify difficulties, as well as to provide assistance to overcome them. In addition, there should be a continuum of support and technology that is appropriate and affordable to enhance success in the curriculum. Jenkins (1998) believes that the curriculum for the future should originate quite differently from the traditional curriculum. Although he agrees that an emphasis on vocational skills and knowledge is important, it should not, he argues, be at the expense of other dimensions, and a balanced curriculum should start with 'values, attitudes and a commitment to service'. Furthermore, Jenkins maintains that it is the responsibility of those of us who are international teachers to foster the qualities of 'cooperation, compromise, understanding and respect'.

Many educationalists, including Morrison and Ridley (1988) and Kelly (1987), would agree that the curriculum is something that students not only experience at school but also take away with them. Promoting the intellectual, physical, social and emotional development of students, the curriculum includes the school ethos, can be hidden or planned, and contains elements of the pastoral and academic. According to Soper (1989), 'The more a curriculum can be seen as a whole which has something to do with life and living, the more valuable it will be.' Wider than the formal timetabled offerings, it includes formal and informal activities, events, celebrations, extracurricular activities, clubs and societies.

Hayden and Thompson's research suggests (1996) that we owe it to *all* our international students to include those with widely diverse levels of ability. Reflecting on this research, it seems that confidence, enrichment, responsible attitudes and the understanding of others are generally promoted in international education, whether through the hidden or planned curriculum. I believe that all our students deserve an opportunity to experience these dimensions of international education, regardless of ability, and that, as in Dover Court, curriculum opportunities should be provided for *all* students to interact with children and adults of varying personalities, backgrounds, abilities, interests and ages.

An important question to ask, therefore, is how is the affective domain being catered for in the international school? What better way to embrace and improve the quality of the affective domain and develop emotional intelligence, to meet the mainstream students' need for tolerance and empathy, commitment, care and respect (all attitudes advocated by the International Baccalaureate Primary Years Programme, IBPYP), than to include special needs students in the school intake? Although the curriculum of the future cannot be predicted, it is certain that in this shrinking world people are becoming increasingly globally interdependent and are having first-hand experience of a growing variety of cultures. The development of global values, which will act as foundations for all systems, is therefore vital. The values that appear to play a major part in inclusive education are also an important dimension of international education in the sense of fostering ideals such as human rights and global citizenship. Aims associated with moral and social sensitivity are essential for all, bringing us back to the main premise of this chapter: a curriculum is needed which fosters inclusive education. To be a world citizen we have to feel a responsibility towards *all* humankind. If we are to provide a quality education for our international students, we have to incorporate such notions into the curriculum.

For international schools these arguments are underpinned by the fact that for globally mobile parents of special-needs children, there is rarely a school available which is able and willing to provide an appropriate curriculum. Special-needs schools experience curricular limitations, including the fact that there are fewer specialist teachers, and these are usually teachers trained for working with specific learning difficulties. A limited knowledge of specialist subject areas restricts the curriculum as students are usually taught by generalists; skills are often confined to a particular area of school such as the senior school (Southgate, 1995) and there are few opportunities for children to achieve their potential by being challenged by mainstream peers. The potential of such students may be high in some areas of the curriculum: some children with special needs in cognitive areas may outshine their mainstream peers in Physical Education or Art, for example. In Dover Court, everybody wanted Chris, a special-needs student, to be on their sports team because of his physical skills. In my present school, which admits children with specific learning difficulties (referred to as ACCESS children), a specialist Art teacher declared, 'If it were not for the ACCESS children, my classes would be two-dimensional.'

There is further support for the notion of linking emotions and feeling to areas of the curriculum from Kelly (1987), who sees the affective and cognitive domains as being interwoven. Such a view is endorsed by Goleman (1996), who sees 'emotional intelligence' developing character and states that 'character development is a foundation of democratic societies', as well as arguing that emotional intelligence 'goes hand in hand with education for character, for moral development, and for citizenship'. If such notions are to be sustained, there is a vital need to make curriculum provision for the development of the affective domain, which is essential to human development and learning. Stone McCown agrees, and suggests that 'Being emotionally literate is as important for learning as instruction in math and reading' (Stone McCown, 1996). Basing a curriculum purely on the cognitive domain may well lead to traumatic consequences; Villa *et al* (1995) point out that, at the time of the Holocaust, Germany was the most highly academically educated society that had ever existed.

Inclusive education and quality in the curriculum

If as international educators we are aiming for excellence, achieving quality and setting high standards, then a number of issues pertaining to inclusive education in the international school require consideration. What, for instance, does quality in the curriculum mean in this context? Is quality merely about obtaining good examination results and qualifications? Such indicators provide one way of determining quality, but as they do not allow for all forms of diversity, many children are excluded if these indicators are employed for such purposes. Should quality instead be about the extent to which all students are welcomed into the school? Or does achieving quality in the international school apply only to mainstream students? A different type of question is 'Can mainstream students experience a quality education if special needs children are excluded?'. Many educationalists would give a negative answer to this question. For example, Kelly (1987) believes that we should be offering a balance of experiences, and not just a balance of subjects, to all our students; such experiences, it could be argued in the international school context, should include interaction with students of diverse abilities as well as with those from diverse cultural and linguistic backgrounds. 'How does a child become more open-minded? What kind of curriculum makes a person reflective?' asks Bartlett (1998), before going on to suggest that 'it is necessary to examine rather more closely the structure of the curriculum model' in the international school. Furthermore, Stainback and Stainback in Lombardi (1994) believe that the inclusive situation allows all students to benefit from diversity, and

Strully *et al* (1992) argue that 'The rejection of any group has a direct impact on the quality of *all* learners.'

Benefits for international schools

What then are the reasons for excluding special-needs children in the international school context? In fairness, it needs to be pointed out that there are many difficulties in implementing inclusive education (Bradley, 1998). It is time-consuming and requires a high level of human resources. It has to be carefully monitored and well planned in order to cater for the needs, and not just the rights, of the special-needs child. In my experience, inclusive education does not work for practical and economic reasons if over 15 per cent of the population are special-needs children: in this situation it may not be economically viable. Given that many international schools are profit-making institutions, such economic considerations may have serious implications. In some countries, international schools might face opposition from parents if they were to implement an inclusive system, and not only on economic grounds. Most importantly, the introduction of an inclusive approach requires input and support from those who are committed to its ideology and values.

There are, however, many benefits to accrue from an international school being inclusive. Apart from that of being able to cater for market needs, other advantages are numerous, including the fact that all children are catered for on a continuum of skills and abilities. Significant consistent achievement for all students has also been demonstrated in a number of contexts. An inclusive approach facilitates and encourages staff teamwork, caters for individuals' rights, works towards eradicating stigmas, provides opportunities for special-needs children to function in the real world and to demonstrate their strengths, and raises awareness of mainstream achievement in special-needs teachers. It develops relationships and creativity that would not be possible in segregated situations.

It is not only special needs children who benefit from an inclusive approach to education. For mainstream students there are also other benefits. On the practical side, mainstream students can use the facilities of therapists whose services are provided primarily for those with special needs. Inclusion can strengthen the school and enhance provision for all children. Students from inclusive schools speak warmly of increased opportunities and of learning through diversity, challenging traditional views that special-needs children in mainstream classes lower the overall standards (CSIE, undated). Familiarity and associated tolerance reduces fear and rejection and as a result inclusive schools better prepare mainstream children for living in an inclusive society. The system provides a range of learning opportunities, develops emotional intelligence and fosters qualities of tolerance, empathy, respect, generosity, self-confidence, compassion, caring and responsibility – all necessary ingredients for the adult of the twenty-first century. Encouraging mainstream students to face challenges, and not to run away from them, leads to learning outcomes for such students which cannot be generated from a book.

Linking benefits to all areas of the curriculum, Wendy Cassey and colleagues in London followed the progress for two years of 36 children with Down's syndrome; half in mainstream, the other half in special schools. At the end of the two-year period, the children placed in mainstream education performed better on all outcome measures. As the children were carefully matched for ability at the initial stage, the gain cannot be explained by differences in ability (CSIE, undated). Various other positive results of research relating to special needs and mainstream children are cited by the Centre for Studies on Inclusive Education (CSIE, undated), by Van der Cook *et al* (1991), and by Villa and Thousand (1995).

My own small-scale study suggested that certain factors can affect the development of inclusive education in an international situation in either a negative or a positive way, depending on how they are managed. Although it was beyond the scope of the study to generalize to international schools more widely than the one in which it was conducted, and although each school is different, lessons can often be learnt by considering what has happened in a particular context: in this case, an inclusive system already in place in one international school. For these purposes, a set of brief guidelines for schools wishing to implement an inclusive system was produced (Bradley, 1998).

Conclusion

Gardner (in Udvari-Solner, 1996), looking at intelligence from a broad perspective, examines alternative ways of assessing children. His theory exposes peculiarities in learning styles and argues for the need to differentiate the curriculum, thus recognizing diversity as the 'norm'. If such an approach is considered when the policy for student intake in international schools is being formulated, then quality in the curriculum would be fostered and improved in a number of respects. In catering for market needs and thus offering a broader curriculum for special-needs children, we would in addition be improving the school and educating all children more effectively, as argued by Ainscow (1995), Florian and Rouse (1996) and Murphy (in Florian and Rouse, 1996). In addition, we would be catering for the development of the emotional needs of mainstream children with a 'hands-on programme'.

As regards quality, Strully *et al* (1992) suggest and elaborate upon three ways of measuring quality in inclusive schools:

1. determining if students are welcomed into the school;
2. observing peer interaction and assessing the nature of that interaction; and
3. evaluating what is being taught in the classroom.

When we witness four-year-old children helping less able children to stand up, to climb steps, or to mime actions to a song, all unprompted by an adult, it is clear that there is a magic in this system that works. As we enter a new century, there is an opportunity to make segregation a thing of the past. A positive action programme for the implementation of inclusive education could regenerate our very slow-to-change attitude towards education for all, and embrace those special people who have for the most part been forgotten or ignored by international educators. In the words of an international educator on whose belief system Dover Court Primary School is based: 'The world of international schools should all be working towards it. They all have at least a small number of special needs students. Inclusiveness includes gender, it includes ability, it includes culture' (Roach, 1997). Basically, it includes ALL, as echoed by Ainscow (1999), who summarizes the point succinctly by saying:

> All for the children,
> For all the children.

References

Ainscow, M (1995) in *Towards Inclusive Schools?*, eds C Clark, A Dyson and A Millward, David Fulton, London

Ainscow, M (1999) *Understanding the Development of Inclusive Schools*, Falmer Press, London

Allen, J (1999) *Actively Seeking Inclusion*, Falmer Press, London

Bartlett, K (1998) International curricula: more or less important at the primary level?, in *International Education: Principles and practice*, eds M C Hayden and J J Thompson, Kogan Page, London

Beare, H, Caldwell, B J and Millikan, R H (1992) *Creating an Excellent School*, Routledge, London

Booth, T, Swann, W, Masterton, M and Potts, P (eds) (1995) *Policies for Diversity in Education*, Routledge, London

Bradley, G (1998) *Inclusive Education in the International School: A study to discover the facilitating factors and barriers with respect to the implementation of inclusive education in a particular international school*, MA Dissertation, University of Bath

Centre for Studies on Inclusive Education (CSIE) (undated) *Notes for Students*, CSIE, Bristol

Clark, C, Dyson, A and Millward A (eds) (1995) *Towards Inclusive Schools?*, David Fulton, London

Florian, L and Rouse, M (eds) (1996) *School Reform and Special Educational Needs: Anglo-American perspectives*, Institute of Education University of Cambridge, Cambridge

Goleman, D (1996) *Emotional Intelligence*, Bloomsbury Publishing, London

Haldimann, M (1998) Special learning needs in international schools: the optimal match concept, in *International Education: Principles and practice*, eds M C Hayden and J J Thompson, Kogan Page, London

Hayden, M C and Thompson, J J (1996) Potential difference: the driving force for international education, *International Schools Journal*, **XVI** (1), pp 46–57

Hollington, A (1994) A very special international education, *International Schools Journal*, **27**, pp 27–33

Jenkins, C (1998) Global issues: a necessary component of a balanced curriculum for the twenty-first century, in *International Education: Principles and practice*, eds M C Hayden and J J Thompson, Kogan Page, London

Kelly, A V (1987) *Knowledge and Curriculum Planning*, Harper and Row, London

Lombardi, T P (1994) *Responsible Inclusion of Students with Disabilities*, Phi Delta Kappa Educational Foundation, Bloomington, IN

Mayor, F (1994) *The Salamanca Statement and Framework for Action on Special Needs Education*, UNESCO, Paris

McLaughlin, M J (1996) in *School Reform and Special Educational Needs: Anglo-American perspective*, eds. L Florian and M Rouse, Institute of Education, University of Cambridge, Cambridge

Meijer Cor, J W, Pijl Sip Jan and Hegarty, S (eds) (1997) *Inclusive Education: A Global Agenda*, Routledge, London

Mittler, P (1995) Special needs education: an international perspective, *British Journal of Special Education*, **22** (3), pp 105–08

Morrison, K and Ridley, K (1988) *Curriculum Planning and the Primary School*, Paul Chapman, London

Roach, M (1997) Conversation on inclusive education at Dover Court School, Singapore

Soper, S (1989) *Primary First*, Oxford University Press, Oxford

Southgate, T (1995) Finding a new place: changes in role at Ormerod Special School, in *Policies for Diversity in Education*, eds T Booth, W Swann, M Masterton and P Potts, Routledge, London

Stainback, S, Stainback, W and Jackson, J (1992) in *Curriculum Considerations in Inclusive Classrooms: Facilitating learning for all students*, eds S Stainback and W Stainback, Paul Brooks, Baltimore, MD

Stone McCown, K (1996) in *Emotional Intelligence*, ed D Goleman, Bloomsbury Publishing, London

Strully, J, Buswell, B, New, L, Strully, C and Schaftner, B (1992) in *Curriculum Considerations in Inclusive Classrooms: Facilitating learning for all students*, eds S Stainback and W Stainback, Paul Brooks, Baltimore, MD

Udvari-Solner, A (1996) Theoretical influences on the establishment of inclusive practices, *Cambridge Journal of Education*, **26** (1), pp 101–19

Udvari-Solner, A and Thousand, J (1995) Effective organizational, instructional and curricular practices in inclusive schools and classrooms, in *Towards Inclusive Schools?*, eds C Clark, A Dyson and A Millward, David Fulton, London

United Nations Educational, Scientific and Cultural Organization (1994) *The Salamanca Statement and Framework on Special Needs Education* (World Conference on Special Needs Education: Access and Quality), UNESCO/Ministry of Education and Science, Salamanca

Van der Cook, T, York, J, Sharpe, M, Knight, J, Salisbury, C, Le Roy, B and Kozleski, E (1991) The million dollar question, *Impact*, **4** (3), pp 1–20, Institute on Community Integration, University of Minnesota

Villa, R and Thousand, J (eds) (1995) *Creating an Inclusive School*, ASCD, Alexandria, VA

Villa, R, Van der Klift, E, Udis, J, Thousand, J, Nevin, A, Kunc, N and Chapple, J (1995) in *Creating an Inclusive School*, eds R Villa and J Thousand, ASCD, Alexandria, VA

Waldron, M (1991) International schools: perspective of a parent with a handicapped child, in *World Yearbook of Education 1991: International schools and international education*, eds P Jonietz and D Harris, Kogan Page, London

Chapter 4

Curricular interstices and the Theory of Knowledge

John Mackenzie

I say that habit's but long practice, friend,
And this becomes men's nature in the end

(Evenus)

Virtue, then, is a state of character concerned with choice...

(Aristotle)

In the closing chapter of the companion volume to this collection (Hayden and Thompson, 1998) Thompson, in his suggested metaphor for 'internationalism', coins the phrase 'interstitial curriculum' to refer to the mortar that holds the curricular 'bricks' together. The interstitial curriculum represents that learning which takes place either between subjects, because it arises from subjects that cross boundaries, or because it derives from structures such as pastoral care, discipline codes, assemblies, and so on. This learning is experiential in nature, he tells us, and can be very useful in fostering an international attitude. In his words, 'it will constitute the institutional "cement" for internationalism'.

Bricks and mortar is not an easy metaphor to accept for someone brought up on a regular diet of Pink Floyd, but all educators will know what Thompson is pointing to, and would no doubt agree that it constitutes an important, even central, part of a school's ethos. Some of what is being referred to comes about as a matter of design, and to that extent can be made explicit, and some results from management or teaching styles (which might be more or less conscious) as well as from the unintended consequences of our designs or actions.

The problem with notions that pack so much in, however, is that they easily become unmanageable, so I would like to focus on a particular element of curricular design: the Theory of Knowledge (TOK) programme in which all candidates undertaking the International Baccalaureate Diploma programme (IBDP) must have participated as part of their course of studies. In doing so, I will look at the interstitial objectives the programme seeks to achieve, including, of course, those related to its international outlook. While I am deliberately narrowing the focus, much of what will be said could equally apply to many other elements of conscious interstitial design within the IB programmes, whether they are other elements at the centre of the familiar Diploma hexagon (Thompson, 1988) such as the Creativity, Action, Service (CAS) component, and the Extended Essay, or the Areas of Interaction of the IBO's Middle Years Programme (MYP) (IBO, 1998a), or the guiding questions and values of the Primary Years Programme (PYP) (IBO, 1998b). What these all have in common is that they aim to create attitudes or dispositions, which on the one hand are life skills or 'know how', and on the other (and equally importantly) are habits which result in what Aristotle above calls 'states of character'. The unconscious and unreflective nature of habits has made them a rather unpopular term in education, with the exception of the rather dull sounding, though important, *study habits*. But many of our important life-skills are of this automatic, ingrained sort of knowledge, which comes, as Thompson suggests, from experiential learning.

I will start by looking at experiential learning, and at what we mean by things that are *caught* rather than *taught*, and then at what TOK offers in this respect to the objectives of international education.

Varieties of knowing, varieties of learning

One of the first things that many students of the IB Theory of Knowledge course will be taken through at the beginning of their studies is the variety of meanings we can find in the ways in which we use the word *know*. Students are shown the difference between the sense of *to know* which Russell termed *knowing by acquaintance*, that is, in his words, 'the knowledge that a dog lover has of his dog' and *knowing by description*, or 'propositional' knowledge, which is the sort of knowledge to which most of our teaching is related (Russell, 1912). The former is a type of knowledge which cannot be transmitted to others by means of language (or, if it can, only very imperfectly) and depends on personal experience or acquaintance. The latter involves the public knowledge that we typically share with others.

A similar, though not identical, distinction is made by Ryle in distinguishing between *knowing how* to do something (such as knowing how to play the guitar, or swim, or knit) and *knowing that* something is the case (Ryle, 1949). The common element between these two distinctions is that the latter form involves language, whereas the former requires a personal experience, which cannot be transmitted fully by language. In knowing *how*, of course, personal acquaintance is not enough, because skills require practice before one is in the position to say one *knows* how to do something. But skills cannot simply be transmitted through language, so personal practice is a must.

A related notion comes up much earlier in Oakeshott's analysis of skills, and his distinction between *technical* and *practical* knowledge. Hirst (1993) summarizes it as follows:

> There is, on the one hand, what he calls technical knowledge, a knowledge of rules, techniques and principles, that can be formulated comprehensively in propositions, which can be learned, remembered and put into practice. On the other hand, there is practical knowledge which exists only in use, which is not reflective and cannot be formulated properly in rules. Its normal expression is in a practice of some sort, in a customary or traditional way of doing things. These two kinds of knowledge Oakeshott considers distinguishable but inseparable, both being involved in any concrete activity. Together they make any skill or activity what it is... Practical knowledge is not simply some blind unstructured executive competence that applies rules and principles. Practical knowledge consists of organized abilities to discern, judge and perform that are so rooted in understanding, beliefs, values and attitudes that any abstracted propositional statements of those elements or of rules and principles of practice must be inadequate and partial expressions of what is involved. Practical knowledge is acquired by living within the organized social world to which we belong, structured as it is by institutions and traditions of a great variety. In education, as in any other area of activity, we come to understand the activity, its problems and their answers from engagement in the activity itself. Then gradually, by a variety of means, we can improve and extend our knowledge of how to pursue it, analysis of the activity and reflections on its rules and principles having their part to play in that process.

Learning and expertise

In *Mind over Machine*, Hubert and Stuart Dreyfus distinguish a series of five steps to learning that go from 'novice' to 'expert', and outline a view of learning and expert knowledge that goes heavily against our common understanding, particularly the philosophical tradition in which the more conscious we are of what we are doing, the greater its epistemic value. In this view of things, conscious awareness leads us to ever-greater heights of knowing, and of greater practical wisdom (Dreyfus and Dreyfus, 1988). Our capacity to stand back from our actions, as it were, and to examine them in a detached manner, would be the hallmark of human rationality in this Cartesian tradition which can be traced back to Socrates (Dreyfus and Dreyfus, 1991).

Dreyfus and Dreyfus argue that it can easily be shown that expert human action operates at what can only be viewed as an intuitive level with a very low level of conscious awareness of why, and how, one is doing what one is doing. Anyone who has watched sports stars painfully try to explain how they made the 'decisions' they made, has seen this truth illustrated to an extreme. And we also know that if we needed to think about the next dance step, or ponder the exact pressure to apply to the brakes as we exit from a major motorway, the results could be disastrous. High levels of consciousness are necessary for learning at early stages, where one learns procedures in a relatively explicit algorithmic fashion, but become less and less necessary, and even a hindrance, at a higher level of expertise. The *detached* approach, which is typical of certain forms of problem solving, only arises when we are faced with what we perceive to be a problem: when things do not work as expected, or when we are seeking explanations. But both of these situations are the exception rather than the norm where human action is concerned. In our ordinary going about things, we can take our expertise for granted and never be aware that it is there.

This view of Dreyfus and Dreyfus, with its origin in the writings of Heidegger, has strong echoes in the discoveries of Anthony Damasio. Damasio argues that intelligent behaviour depends on the emotional development and learning which underpins our thought processes, and by studying patients with damaged brains, where the area controlling emotions has been damaged, he illustrates his argument with persons who have brilliant IQs and yet are totally incompetent when it come to coping with even minor difficulties in daily life (Damasio, 1996). In educational circles this notion of 'emotional intelligence' has become a major theme since the publication of Daniel Goleman's book on the subject (Goleman, 1995).

All these distinctions of types of knowledge will have their correlative distinction of ways of learning, but not as a one-to-one relationship. It must be recognized that some of these ways are more propositional and language-based than others, and some are more experiential. Even within subjects where propositional learning is high, experiential learning is involved to a greater or lesser extent. Learning laboratory skills is a mix, for example, but there is far more experiential learning involved in becoming proficient than there is a following of rules. Students who are very good at laboratory work will avoid typical pitfalls without having to think about what they are doing.

The Theory of Knowledge programme

The Subject Guide for the Theory of Knowledge states at the outset that 'The Theory of Knowledge (TOK) programme is central to the educational philosophy of the International Baccalaureate' (IBO, 1987). This course had been termed a 'key element' in the previous guide, and has always been thought to have this key or central role since its inception (Peterson, 1987 and the IB Diploma Guide, 1987). Its current aims are to:

- develop an understanding of why critically examining knowledge claims is important;
- develop a critical capacity to evaluate beliefs and knowledge claims;
- make interdisciplinary connections;
- become aware of the interpretative nature of knowledge, including personal and ideological biases;
- consider that knowledge may place responsibilities on the knower;
- understand the strengths and limitations of individual and cultural perspectives; and
- develop a concern for rigour in formulating knowledge claims, and intellectual honesty.

These aims are interstitial, as indeed is the course, in the sense in which Thompson uses the term; it is not surprising, therefore, that the course has often been seen as the 'cement' or 'glue' that binds together the different curricular areas of the IB Diploma's hexagon. Its objectives are clearly not tied to any one of the six IB subject groups, but rather have always been viewed as the sort of meta-learning that can give meaning to knowledge acquired in the subjects which students must study.

One of the IB Diploma's chief architects (Peterson, 1987) grounds the rationale for a course such as this with the following quote from Bruner:

> Teaching specific topics or skills without making clear their context in the broad fundamental structure of a field of knowledge is uneconomical in several deep senses.... [one of which is that] knowledge that one has acquired without sufficient understanding to tie it together is likely to be forgotten. An unconnected set of facts has a pitiably short half-life in memory. Organizing

facts in terms of principles and ideas from which they may be inferred, is the only way of reducing the quick rate of loss of human memory.

The Theory of Knowledge course would achieve this, Peterson argued, by helping the student to:

> think about the questions which underlie the nature of knowledge as presented in the school disciplines and his daily life, about such questions as the grounds for accepting as valid a proposition in logic, in mathematics, in physics, in sociology, or in history; as the importance and limitations of quantification in different academic disciplines; as the basis and interrelation of moral, aesthetic, and religious beliefs; and so, using Jean Capelle's image, to bring back from the garden of his studies his own bouquet, his own deepened understanding and enjoyment of his own experience, rather than a collection of individual flowers unrelated to each other and selected by an outside arbiter on the basis of the boundaries of the 'disciplines'.

What is referred to here as 'Capelle's image', an idea borrowed from Montaigne, is quite a forceful statement of the constructivist notion of 'meaningful learning', even if not necessarily an intended one, but perhaps more interestingly it highlights the extent to which even in its design, TOK was conceived of as *experiential* learning. It is precisely its experiential nature that can allow TOK to develop that very personal outlook referred to as one's 'own bouquet'.

The aims quoted above all refer to developing something in students, whether this be an awareness of aspects of knowing, or a particular attitude (intellectual and/or ethical), or more likely a combination of both which we may separate analytically, but which in fact will be present simultaneously in a student's later actions.

Teachers in a TOK classroom have a terrible time trying to *teach* TOK in the more traditional sense of the term, precisely because it is more an experience to be undergone than some particular *thing* to be learnt, at least in the propositional sense of learning. The learning occurs as a result of undergoing the experience; it is, in the sense that Thompson and others have used these terms, *caught* rather than *taught*. And the proof of this is in the course's subject matter. There is none, in the usual sense of the term; merely a list of questions that people have found worth asking, and particularly worth asking if one wishes to affect the intellectual maturity of students in important ways (as outlined in the aims). In TOK there is an assumption that the regular practising of guided reflection on these questions, and an exploration of what are termed the 'ways of knowing', and the 'areas of knowledge', and of how these relate, will result in the achievement of the aims mentioned above. It is not primarily what teachers say that determines the success of a TOK class, though this can be very helpful, but what they get their students to do. This is what allows certain skills, ideas and values to be *caught*.

The theory of knowledge and internationalism

But let me now turn to the issue of 'TOK and internationalism', which has a long history within discussions of the IBDP curriculum. The purpose of doing this is to show how the nature of this course contributes to a major *interstitial* objective of the IB – its internationalism. As stated above, this is only one of the ways in which the IBO seeks to achieve this objective. Other requirements of the Diploma, including its subjects, contribute to this objective, as do other IBO programmes.

TOK has often been criticized within the IBO for representing what to some is an element of ideological bias typical of Western thought. This at times does not go beyond stating that it must be so because of its origins, but then I suppose this could also be argued of the generic fallacy implicit in the argument – a perfect example of catch-22! If this were the sole complaint, however, one might choose to ignore it, but the stronger indictment is to argue that TOK actually undermines one of the central interstitial aims of the IBDP – its *internationalism*. This is not an argument that will go away easily, and I certainly do not expect to lay it to rest, but I would like to offer a personal appreciation of what is sometimes a very muddled discussion.

The first way in which we can try to clarify what is being argued is to say that the word 'internationalism' can stand for many things, and is often used in many differing ways when levelled as criticism. It is one thing to talk about issues such as representation on governing bodies or management structures, or about the choice of examiners, or about which languages are offered as 'official' IB languages. It is another to argue that certain forms of knowledge are of differing value to different communities (are weighted differently, perhaps) and that a curriculum that is truly international should recognize this fact. And it is yet another to argue that a truly international curriculum should somehow embrace all valuing and cultural discourses as equal, and integrate them into a coherent whole. If internationalism is somehow viewed as accepting all things at once, where any attempt to be critical from a particular perspective is viewed as hegemonic pretensions, then we are faced with an insurmountable obstacle.

An enormous problem behind some of this arguing at cross-purposes is the assumption that what humans beings do in *knowing* the world is to describe it objectively. In this view, words are symbols for natural things that we can perceive, and therefore there are clearly correct and incorrect uses of words, whose meaning is given by the objective things to which they refer. Internationalism, in this account, is a word that, like all others, captures some essential feature that we must ensure is captured by our usage. We do not, however, have a privileged access to, or window on, the world. There is no way in which we can know whether our interpretations of the world, which is all we have, are true representations, except in the sense that we can agree on standards from which we assess our interpretations, and can therefore have a powerful notion of what constitutes a truth.

At the same time, words such as internationalism mean what we choose them to mean, not in the arbitrary fashion claimed by Humpty Dumpty, but in an evolving collective usage. Internationalism does not, in fact, point to any particular *thing*. It is a word, with which we assess particular practices, and find them appropriate or wanting. It is a term that serves to judge, not to describe. This sort of word implies a standard by which we make the judgement, and this is where I think the Theory of Knowledge ties in so well with the mission of the International Baccalaureate as it has been variously stated over time. The IBO has always sought to educate students so that they will see themselves in the broader context, and be prepared for life in an increasingly interconnected world.

All of us hail from one culture or another, and at times from quite widely differing ones. Each of these cultures, in turn, can be seen as an interpretation of the world, and a set of institutionalized practices, so that all of us are part of what is now often termed a discourse or narrative, with a greater or lesser overlap between them. There are two ways in which one can be a part of a narrative, however: blindly, or self-consciously. If students are able to see themselves as part of a discourse or narrative, and to understand that what they consider obvious and natural (their 'common sense') is the result of belonging to this tradition, and sharing some of the, perhaps unquestioned, assumptions that go with this belonging, then I, for one, would be happy that education was serving the interests of internationalism.

These are clearly the ambitions of the TOK course, whatever cultural tradition it may have grown out of; in this sense, at least, it is therefore well aligned with the IBDP's major interstitial objective. No other major educational curriculum has this aim so clearly embedded in it, and the quality of the IBDP's overall curricular design depends to a great extent on this feature.

To return, finally, to Aristotle and Evenus, we could say that what the IB programme is aiming to achieve, in its 'interstices', are natures or states of character that share certain habits. One works on the habits of rigorous critical thinking, openness, sensitivity and commitment, making explicit what one can. But this can only take us so far. Students must be brought up in a 'way of doing things', as Oakeshott says, and this practice will in itself become habitual. Much of this practical knowledge can be reflected upon in ways in which the practice itself becomes improved and consciously valued, and in so doing we help them to become not only habits of the mind, but also habits of the heart!

References

Aristotle in *The Nicomachean Ethics of Aristotle*, (1990) Sir David Ross (tr), Oxford University Press, Oxford

Damasio, A R (1996) *Descartes' Error: Emotion, reason and the human brain*, Avon, New York

Dreyfus, H and Dreyfus, S (1991) From Socrates to Expert Systems: The limits and dangers of calculative rationality, http://socrates.berkeley.edu/~hdreyfus [Spanish version in *Estudios Publicos* (1992), **46**, pp 25–41]

Dreyfus, H and Dreyfus, S (1988), *Mind Over Machine: The power of human intuition and expertise in the era of the computer*, The Free Press, New York

Evenus in *The Nicomachean Ethics of Aristotle*, (1990) Sir David Ross (tr), Oxford University Press, Oxford

Goleman, D (1995) *Emotional Intelligence: Why it can matter more than IQ*, Bantam Books, Toronto

Hayden, M C and Thompson, J J (eds) (1998) *International Education: Principles and practice*, Kogan Page, London

Hirst, P H (1993) Educational theory, in *Educational Research: Current issues*, ed M Hammersley, Chapman Press, London

International Baccalaureate Organisation (1987) *General Guide: Fifth edition*, IBO, Geneva

International Baccalaureate Organisation (1998a) *Guide to the Middle Years Programme*, IBO, Geneva

International Baccalaureate Organisation (1998b) *Guide to the Primary Years Programme*, IBO, Geneva

Peterson, A D C (1987) *Schools Across Frontiers*, Open Court, La Salle, Illinois

Russell, B (1912) *The Problems of Philosophy*, Oxford University Press, Oxford

Ryle, G (1949) *The Concept of Mind*, Hutchinson, London

Thompson, J J (1988) Validity and reliability issues in International Baccalaureate examinations, in *Admission to Higher Education: Issues and practice*, eds M C Hayden, P N Richards and J J Thompson, (1995), International Association for Educational Assessment, Dublin

Thompson, J J (1998) Towards a model for international education, in *International Education: Principles and Practice*, eds M C Hayden and J J Thompson, Kogan Page, London

Chapter 5

Images of international education in national and international schools: a view from Jordan

Samia Al Farra

Introduction

No country in the world can live in isolation. Interdependence has become the norm, enhanced by advancements in technology and the emergence of the Internet and satellites. In a matter of seconds, someone in Jordan can know what is happening in the USA, China, South Africa or Japan. Gone are the days when people of a certain country would stay there for life. People are moving, interacting and understanding each other more; cultures are crossing borders; languages are inter-mixed; first-hand experience and primary sources are more easily at hand.

Since the early years of the twentieth century, the world has become a much smaller place. Today 'no country, however powerful in terms of its economy or population, can any longer get by completely on its own. Transnational problems – whether they be environmental, cultural or economic – can no longer be solved at the national level' (Mayor, 1998). Thanks to the invention of aeroplanes, satellites, the Internet, e-mail and other means of communication, a country's problems are no longer simply its own. The 'knock-on effect' on people's lives is clear. Within this wider arena, people are looking at the whole globe as their home, with environmental, social and political issues being part of the greater whole.

Because national governments acknowledge the emerging interdependence of different countries, national educational systems around the globe are starting to pay more attention to international education both in their mission statements and in their curricula and assessment systems.

The Arab world and Western perceptions

Throughout the world, there are many Moslems who oppose the spread of Western secularism. They see the breakdown of the family, the rise of violence, the 'drug culture' and the relaxation of traditional Christian values of morality as the products of this secularism and as the offerings of the West to their children. They reject it because they have a fundamental belief in their own society and its values, which they wish to see maintained. Too often, such people are branded as 'fundamentalists' and labelled with all the negative connotations of this emotive term. Frequently also, their fears are played upon by those seeking to develop their own political agendas.

Many people in Jordan and in the Arab world more widely, including highly educated individuals, perceive internationalism as a threat, as an invasion by Western culture in particular. It reminds them of the hegemony of colonization from the days when they were occupied by the British or the French. They see it as a threat to their identity and cultures. Others, however, perceive internationalism as a must, an important necessity if one is to be able to survive, succeed and excel in life. For some, internationalism means globalization. Others see it as a means used by rich countries to control poorer ones, especially when 80 per cent of resources of the world are utilized by the rich countries.

It is, I believe, just as important to examine the Western image in the Arab world as it is to consider the Arab image in the West, and to consider what the term 'Arab' actually communicates in such circumstances. Does it mean Arab governments, Arab peoples or both? There seems often to be a confusion in Western minds between Arab states and Arab citizens. The Arab image might be associated with a particular nationality, or with Arab people overall. It is interesting to reflect on the extent to which the image of a particular group or government affects the image of Arabs in general. It seems to some Arabs that when Arab individuals are successful, such as in writing a book, or performing in sports competitions, they are identified in the West with their particular nationality (such as Egyptian, Lebanese, Moroccan), while when they are associated with a negative phenomenon they are identified by the general term 'Arab'. This may be because Arabism and Islam are seen as a threat (Tarbush, 1998):

The Arab image overlaps with the image of Islam and Moslems, and it is probably impossible to disentangle the two. In the minds of many Westerners, Arabs and Moslems have become interchangeable terms, despite the fact that the majority of Moslems live outside the Arab world, while there are many Christian and other non-Moslem communities living in the Middle East. This perceived inter-changeability of the terms 'Arab' and 'Moslem' means that prejudices against one become transferred to the other.

According to Tarbush (1998), the Arab world continues to be viewed with mistrust by Western public opinion. As recent events have shown, Europeans and Americans associate the Middle East with some of their greatest fears, relating to terrorism, dictatorship and weapons of mass destruction. These perceptions have served to justify the severance of diplomatic relations, the application of economic sanctions and even the use of military force. Largely, such perceptions may be attributed to existing preconceptions and prejudices.

Such an Arab image seems to be more deeply entrenched in the USA than it is in Europe. Given the position of the USA as the global super-power, the negative Arab image there has particularly serious implications both for the Arab community in the USA and for US foreign policy in the Middle East. Western perception of Arabs tends to be more negative than it is positive; Moslems, too, are viewed in a generally negative way. These negative perceptions are seen daily in the Western media, in books, in statements by politicians, in Hollywood films, and in the behaviour and views of members of the public. Negative perceptions have unfortunately become part of a wider package of attitudes, policies and strategies.

Amongst Arabs and their sympathizers, the distorted images often found in the West create a sense of injustice and anger. Owing largely to ignorance of Arabic and Islamic cultures, there are undoubtedly groups with a particular interest in promoting negative images of Arabs in general. Biased Western media play a crucial role in doing that. Fortunately, the negative Arab images are not a barrier to generally good relations. The Arab world is strategically important to Western interests for several reasons, some of which are proximity to Israel, large oil supplies and political Islam. Despite its negative images of Arabs and Moslems, in fact the West enjoys good relations with the Arab world (Tarbush, 1998).

There is clearly a need to promote Arab–Western mutual under-standing, and schools such as the bilingual Amman Baccalaureate School in Jordan have a part to play in this respect through their endeavours to promote international education.

Internationalism and Islam

The Arabs have always been international travellers and traders. From the earliest days, records show how they reached, settled and lived peacefully in countries as far afield as China, Indonesia and West Africa. Long before Marco Polo ventured across central Asia and 'discovered' China, Arab traders had been moving up and down the 'Silk Route', bringing the silks and spices of the Orient to the Middle East and on to Europe. This early exposure to the world is my heritage.

The media frequently present internationalism as something new, an invention of the late twentieth century, born of the Second World War and the globalization of world economies. For a Moslem, however, the concept of internationalism is not new, nor is it an option. Verse 13 of the Holy Qu'ran, speaking of creation, tells us 'Oh you human beings! We have created you from a male and a female, and we have made you peoples and tribes in order to know one another.' This clear directive from God makes an international outlook a requirement in our lives: Moslems and non-Moslems need to be aware of this requirement and interact more with no hesitation.

Jordan and the Amman Baccalaureate School

Jordan is about the size of the American state of Indiana, having a population of more than 4 million people, including 98 per cent Arabs (Moslems and Christians) and a 2 per cent Armenian, Circassian and Kurdish minority. The religious sectors comprise 92 per cent Sunni Moslem, 6 per cent Christian and 2 per cent others.

The Amman Baccalaureate School (ABS) was established in 1981 by the Hashemite Society for Education, a charitable society registered with the Jordanian Ministry of Social Development. The school is a non-profit organization whose educational and administrative policies are set by the school's Board of Trustees, chaired by Her Royal Highness Princess Sarvath El Hassan. It is a day national school with an international dimension. ABS has 912 students, of whom 86 per cent (788) are Jordanian and 14 per cent (124) are of other nationalities. Religious groups consist of Moslem (68 per cent: 621), Christian (31 per cent: 288) and others (1 per cent: 3). We have a teaching staff of 128 from 10 different nationalities (Jordanian, Lebanese, Iraqi, Algerian, Syrian, American, British, Australian, Canadian and New Zealander), broken down as follows:

Expatriates	Local/bilingual	Local/monolingual/semilingual
20%	60% (bilingual at cognitive level)	20% (basic interpersonal competence)

I have been fortunate to work in two of the leading national schools of the Middle East, the Al Bayan Bilingual School in Kuwait and now the Amman Baccalaureate School in Jordan. By some definitions neither of these schools can be considered an 'international school' as they were founded with the express purpose of providing an education for the national community. I would, however, contend that both are international in spirit, in philosophy and in their educational practices.

The ABS philosophy statement says 'While a national school with a predominantly local student body, ABS provides an education of high quality by incorporating the influences and elements of the best educational practices within the Kingdom, the Middle East and internationally. These are reflected in the aims, content and skills of the curriculum, the approach to teaching and the expectations of students and staff. They are mediated by maintaining a teaching staff representing different cultures, language backgrounds and outlooks' (Amman Baccalaureate School, 1994). Like Al Bayan, ABS is a bilingual (Arabic/English) school and it is my belief that a bilingual education is one of the cornerstones of international education. This belief is reflected in the citation for the European Council of International Schools (ECIS) Award for International Understanding which is presented annually to a student in each of ECIS's member schools on the recommendation of the staff of that school. The citation reads (ECIS, 1999): 'Awarded to a student who is a good representative of his/her own country, with a positive attitude toward the life and culture of others, able to converse in at least two languages, a contributing force in the life of the school, with the ability to bring differing people together into a sense of community, thus furthering the cause of international understanding.'

I believe that if the goal of promoting internationalism is to be achieved, all schools should have statements to this effect built into their philosophies/mission statements. Otherwise, it is too easy for a school to pay lip service to the concept of internationalism without having to make its practice a fundamental part of the education it offers.

ABS gained joint accreditation from the New England Association of Schools and Colleges and the European Council of International Schools in 1997. One of our objectives in undertaking this exercise was to increase the awareness of staff, students and parents of the place of the school and its curricula in the wider international setting. My belief is that for schools offering an education that claims to be international, it is necessary that the affirmation of this claim comes from the international education community. It is through this process, and particularly through a self-appraisal process, that members of staff are supported and groomed to be more international in their outlook.

Like many schools that promote international education, ABS is committed to the professional development of staff and to increasing involvement in international curricula. We realize it is essential that our teachers are exposed to programmes and good practices operating in other parts of the world. For schools such as ours with a significant proportion of host country nationals on its teaching staff, I believe a commitment to send staff abroad, for example, is particularly important. I do not, however, limit this expectation of such commitment to national schools in the developing world. I believe it is equally important for international and 'first world' schools, whose teaching staff are often monocultural, to expose their teachers to the problems and practices of the less privileged.

As a school, we are members of international organizations such as the International Baccalaureate Organisation (IBO) and its regional body the Middle East International Baccalaureate Association (MEIBA), of the International Schools Association (ISA), the European Council of International Schools (ECIS) and the Near East South Asia Association of Schools (NESA). We are acutely aware of our responsibility, as one of the leading schools in the Arab world, to ensure that the Arab Islamic point of view is represented in the deliberations of international education. We feel strongly that a danger exists that international education could become 'Western education' unless those of us from other cultures and other ideologies participate fully in deciding the paths that curriculum development and other initiatives affecting the future of international education should follow.

Characteristics of international education

What, therefore, are the fundamental characteristics of international education? Is international education synonymous with global education? Where does the balance lie between national needs and culture, and internationalism? Can an individual be international if he or she does not have a firm footing in a national culture and values system? Is the perception of these issues different in the developed world from that in the developing world? Do different areas of the world have different agenda in their promotion of international or global education? Is there a global culture with values that can form the cornerstone of international education?

If international education is limited, as is sometimes implied, to what are referred to as international schools, then it will only be available to a very small and non-representative proportion of each generation. It is, however, I believe, essential that international education reaches beyond such a limited context and, through promotion also in national schools, into every classroom and every home on this planet.

In definitions of education a reference to the concept of culture often appears, and it is clear that, as Malcolm McKenzie (1998) reminds us, 'all education systems have their underpinning values'. Hence a clear view of the concepts of culture and values is crucial in understanding the concept of education and, subsequently, of international education.

Cambridge (1998) refers to a view of culture as 'the way in which a group of people solves problems and reconciles dilemmas… Culture is the way we do things here', while Stenhouse (1967) tells us that the classical anthropological definition of culture is that of E B Tylor, who referred to it as 'that complex whole which includes knowledge, beliefs, art, morals, law, custom and other capabilities acquired by man as a member of society'.

What culture and what values, therefore, does international education represent and promote? Is there an 'international culture' that can be reflected in international education? Abuashaikh and Tamimi (1996) see international education as related to the concept of global education: 'a modern response to the urgent need of today's children for living in an interdependent, rapidly changing world, in which economic, political and social systems are getting more complicated, and cultural pluralism prevails'. They refer to 'the curricula of environmental, gender, human rights, multicultural, anti-discrimination, and peace education, as well as education for individual and social development' as being important concepts of education.

In my own country, Jordan, most national private schools demonstrate the features of an international education referred to by Walker (1995), which are:

- use of communications technology to access information;
- negotiating skills;
- understanding of other nations' priorities;
- awareness of different national 'mind sets';
- study which crosses national frontiers; and
- ability to perceive distinction between truth and falsehood.

Promotion of such features was clearly evident in the interviews I conducted as part of a piece of small-scale research with five Heads of such schools. One of them, in fact, stated that she opposes international education being the preserve of international schools only as she feels this can lead to an invasion of culture rather than to enrichment in diversity.

Esther Lucas (1998) talks about the International Schools Association (ISA) Pilot Project, of which my own school, the Amman Baccalaureate School, is a member. Criteria for membership include: 'the school should provide an education which should be directed to the strengthening of respect for human rights and fundamental freedoms. One of the aims should be to promote understanding, tolerance and friendship among all people of all nations.' The ISA Pilot Project's philosophy focuses on the equality of human beings, educational opportunities for all, human unity through diversity, responsibility, peaceful conflict resolution, and the maintenance of a sustainable future. In describing the outcomes of a survey she had undertaken, Lucas (1998) promoted the concept of an 'internationally-minded school', which she suggested 'is not an international school, though it may have many factors in common with international schools', before going on to suggest that:

> It may be a state or municipal school, a private school, a day or boarding school. The school population is basically national, but there may be a small percentage of foreign students and/or teachers. Virtually all internationally-minded schools are affiliated to international or regional organizations which encourage interest and involvement in global or community issues. Twinning is one of the most significant characteristics of an internationally-minded school. A school may be twinned with several other schools. Contacts may be maintained for many years.

Lucas also highlighted some additional characteristics of such schools, as follows:

> Other activities include exchange programmes for students and teachers, often in connection with foreign language learning. There are contacts through e-mail and the Internet, and various educational visits abroad. Internationally-minded schools are involved in a vast number of projects dealing with many international and humanitarian problems. The projects are often ongoing and involve whole school participation; the Heads of the schools are always involved. Almost all schools have credos, ranging from a short motto to a longer mission statement. Credos refer to all aspects of school life. In internationally-minded schools the emphasis is most often on international understanding.

It is clear from Lucas's descriptions that many national schools may exhibit such characteristics, acknowledging the importance of a holistic well-rounded education and employing teachers to promote that kind of education. While there may be a tendency to think of 'international education' as being something that takes place in international schools taught by expatriate teachers, there is evidence that examples exist of international education being promoted in national schools, by local teachers as well as by expatriates.

Many of our bilingual teachers possess the frame of mind necessary to promote the principles of international education as stated by the International School of Geneva (1994):

- encouraging important international values;
- supporting the student's language development;
- ensuring an international dimension to the curriculum;
- recognizing the importance of global issues;
- providing a breadth and balance of education experience;
- adopting an innovative approach to learning and teaching;
- providing appropriate student services; and
- showing respect for, and integration with, the host country.

The promotion of international education involves, for me, what might be referred to as 'internationalism', involving skills, attitudes and values. It includes freeing oneself from prejudices, stereotyping and bigotry, understanding value systems different from one's own, and empathizing and sympathizing with them. It is moving beyond tolerance to commitment, respect and appreciation for humanity. It is the promotion of peace and prosperity in spite of borders, colours, creed or beliefs.

Internationalism can never be measured in degrees on a continuum. It is an absolute; either you have it or you don't. It is about moving horizontally across cultures and focusing on similarities rather than on differences. It is present when one has the same feeling towards the suffering of children, whether they are of Bosnian, Iraqi, Palestinian or Rwandan origin, and when one works actively and diligently to stop that suffering. It is an integrating, rather than a differentiating, relationship. Internationalism is about feeling the need to preserve and protect the environment, wherever it is, and instilling a love for Mother Nature in the hearts and souls of future generations. It is about a lifelong interest in current affairs, global issues, human rights, democracy and the welfare of humanity. It is about breaking down the concepts of 'us' and 'them', and about seeking the 'others' because we cannot be without them. It is a state of being, not of having.

The translation of such intentions into national schools will require major efforts on the part of all those involved in such institutions, not least on the part of teachers themselves. International education teachers may be expatriates or local nationals. Teachers recruited directly from the neighbourhood of the school will be most aware of the domestic beliefs and value system locally. Expatriates, meanwhile, might bring with them prior perceptions of this value system, and even old prejudices, and may thus be challenged with a cultural adjustment process. We at the Amman Baccalaureate School have both. Many teachers joining ABS from other parts of the world tell me that they arrive with many misconceptions about Arabs and Moslems, which they change after living in Jordan for some time.

As for local teachers who are open to internationalism, their continuous participation in and exposure to good practice from different cultures helps them to be more international in their outlook, widens their scope professionally and broadens their understanding of the 'different': how different people from different parts of the world do things differently. This group of 'international education teachers' benefit noticeably from attending international conferences and from visiting various schools in different countries. In other words, they share and benefit from 'good practice around the world'. If we are to support 'international education' teachers at our schools, operationally we must allocate resources annually for staff development, exposure and interaction with colleagues from all over the world. The potential for national schools in Jordan to become more international is great, with national schools promoting international perspectives 'mushrooming' since the late 1980s.

Conclusion

International education offers, I believe, potential solutions to many of the world's problems. As we enter the twenty-first century we must start redesigning our national schools in order to create institutions with international outlooks where more attention is given to the curriculum, to students, and to the teachers and administrators on whom the system depends. International education teachers will continue to need financial support, resources, and continuous exposure to other ideas in order to be encouraged to do their job better. They must be provided with sufficient incentives to encourage them to pursue further international education opportunities. Policies should be developed which acknowledge relevant skills, vision and expertise. The speed at which life is changing around us is amazing, and international education teachers who, because of their open-mindedness, should be better equipped to communicate with and relate to the new generation, are the ones who have the potential to make this world a better place, encouraging students to reflect and then to act. It is important that we invest in these teachers, since staff development is school development.

I believe that international education does exist, not only as a set of curriculum documents with topics referring to literature or history from different parts of the world, nor because of the numbers of different nationalities represented among the student body or staff. I believe it exists in the hearts and minds of its practitioners, educators and learners, in the classrooms of both national and international schools. The promotion of internationalism in the world's national schools remains one of the major challenges to which it is essential that we respond.

References

Abuashaikh, M and Tamimi, S (1996) The impact of global education on developing teacher trends towards world civilization, in *Teacher Education and School Reform: International Yearbook on Teacher Education 1996*, Ministry of Education, Jordan

Amman Baccalaureate School (1994) *Handbook for 1994–1995*, Amman Baccalaureate School, Jordan

Cambridge, J (1998) Still on the crest of a wave, *International Schools Journal*, **XVII** (2), pp 68–72

ECIS (1999) *Award for International Understanding*, ECIS, Petersfield

Holy Qu'ran, Sura 49 (Al Hujurat), Verse 13

International School of Geneva (1994) *Principles for an International Education,* International School of Geneva, Geneva

Lucas, E (1998) Report on the issue of 'What is an internationally-minded school?', unpublished paper

McKenzie, M (1998) Going, going, gone… global!, in *International Education: Principles and practice*, eds M C Hayden and J J Thompson, Kogan Page, London

Mayor, F (1998) A shared future or no future, *The UNESCO Courier*, May

Stenhouse, L (1967) *Culture and Education*, Thomas Nelson and Sons, London

Tarbush, S (1998) *The Arab Image in the West,* Royal Institute for Inter-Faith Studies, Amman, Jordan

Walker, G R (1995) International School of Geneva pamphlet

Chapter 6

The politics of international education

Peter Zsebik

The political basis of international education

A considerable amount of intellectual perspiration has dripped from the foreheads of educators in their attempt to determine the best curricular structure for the student, and to achieve quality in the process. Concepts such as what material should be taught, how much time should be allotted to each area of the curriculum, and what is the most effective way of delivering the espoused curriculum have attracted a substantial slice of educational attention. One aspect that appears not to have gained the same recognition, however, is the political nature of the curriculum or, to be more precise, the elucidation of the political implications arising from the curriculum that has been put in place.

Perhaps there are a number of reasons for this seeming lack of lucidity. Educators on the front line may find the concept burdensome and unnecessary. After all, what can possibly be political about 2 + 2, or that the water molecule is comprised of two hydrogen atoms and one oxygen atom? Yet we are already faced with political decision-making aspects from these two simple examples, especially within the international context. At what age, for instance, should such concepts be taught? Should the teaching be through exploratory, Socratic or traditional (a politically sensitive word) methodology? In what language are we going to teach the material? Do we use computers to teach the concept? Do we have the resources to buy computers? The list is seemingly endless, and these questions are only focused at the micro-level.

Governments, too, by their very nature have often seen education as a source of political motivation. It is interesting to note that the majority of individuals in the world who were fortunate enough to attend high school had probably attended a government school where the curriculum was approved by governmental authority. When governments make themselves responsible for education (an already political decision), it is always interesting to consider whether there are any ulterior motives behind their educational programme. Examples can be seen through the forced language learning of Nazism and Communism to more present concerns such as having a properly educated workforce that will give the nation a competitive business, scientific or technological edge over other nations. For national governments then, there appear to be strong reasons for those governments to develop their educational planning from essentially a political arena. Yet there appears to be no conflict of interest. It may be this way because society in general has traditionally given little or no thought to the political undercurrents of education, and the political basis for educational provision is unchallengingly accepted, not disturbing what has already been inculcated into the populace. Perhaps there is also an unwillingness to acknowledge that politics exists in education.

These perceptions and more, however, may have clouded the necessity for educators to contemplate the political focus of their activity. Daily we are saturated with information, techniques, methodologies, appraisal schemes and new material that purport to supply us with the right answers. But do we really know what comprises these right answers? Are these answers actually right? Are we as educators aware of what we are feeding our students politically? Are we aware of what we ourselves are being fed? How do we ensure quality?

Suppose for a moment we were to contemplate the idea of having a non-political educational structure. If we were to divorce politics and education, then some or all of the following things might happen. There would be no standards by which to measure academic progress. Tasks as simple as the daily routine of the school would be difficult to implement owing to the lack of an administrative framework, which requires leadership. Perhaps we would have difficulty knowing what to teach because there would be no curricular motivation. In short, there would be very little recognizable structure, and this would transmit itself readily to all facets of the educational programme, resulting in a complete lack of process – an aspect that current educational practice is loathe to do without. Interestingly, however, even if we were successful in developing a curriculum that lacked any political motivation, that thought in itself could be construed as a political statement.

In his preface to Paolo Freire's book *Pedagogy of the Oppressed* (1990), Richard Shaull states:

> There is no such thing as a neutral educational process. Education either functions as an instrument which is used to facilitate the integration of the younger generation into the logic of the present system and bring about conformity to it, or it becomes the practice of freedom, the means by which men and women deal critically and creatively with reality and discover how to participate in the transformation of their world.

It is worth noting here that, although Freire's book dealt primarily with the teaching of language to illiterates, the implications that arise from his writings are much more far-reaching. As Shaull (1990) aptly points out, '[our] advanced technological society is rapidly making objects of most of us and subtly programming us into conformity to the logic of its system. To the degree that this happens, we are also becoming submerged in a new culture of silence.'

In effect, Shaull is observing the perils of too much information or, as it has been termed, information overload. As in an electrical circuit that is overburdened, there is also the danger of the human being losing his or her identity owing to the overpowering influences which are in this case riding on the coat-tails of the technological revolution. This submergence of personal identity, however, is replaced by images and conceptions portrayed through technology. Unfortunately, these technological images and mindsets are mass-produced and experienced on a global scale, and there is little regard for the individual. This conception is echoed by Appadurai (1990), who argues that society is formed by specific cultural flows, of which technology is only one. Shaull has demonstrated the possible result from these cultural flows, and that is the development of a culture of silence brought on by an inability to understand daily experience. This culture of silence can be seen in people's daily decision-making processes, where decisions are being made based neither on personal knowledge nor on experience, but on readily accessible information.

In every case, from an international education perspective, the implications may surpass even those already stated by Shaull; international schools may also be suffering from this culture of silence, not because of an inability to read (as in Freire's experiences), but from an inability to decipher the conflicting messages found within the school and its adjoining community, creating a less than satisfactory philosophical and ideological focus for the school and its curriculum. This tension, which is transferred to the student through various curricular and extracurricular channels, may be exacerbating an already complex situation, resulting in the development of our very own hybrid of cultural silence.

There is therefore a danger in an international context (Zsebik, 1997) that the components of the school (including students, parents and administrators), together with the curriculum and the whole environment of the school, will perpetuate the hegemonic perspective outlined by Freire. The term 'hegemonic' refers to the situation in which an environment is alienated from change or compromise to appease the dominant party and maintain the status quo. It is perpetuated by decision-making processes that promote a cultural silence within specific, usually non-dominant, members of a given population segment. This cultural silence may be observed where the rich and privileged remain unaware of their position, or are taught to take their educational experience for granted. Perhaps more importantly, this cultural silence may take on a form where minority groups within an institution intentionally lose their own specific cultural identity in an effort to avoid possible ostracization from the dominant group. It may be that these political inequalities are unknowingly built into the curriculum, which, in turn, lessens the chance for the institution to promote a true international education.

Traditional school establishments have generally led to what Freire describes as banking education. In this case, education becomes an act of depositing, in which the students are the depositories and the teacher is the depositor. Instead of communicating, the teacher issues communiqués and makes deposits which the students patiently receive, memorize and repeat (Freire, 1990). From an academic curricular perspective, this may no longer be the case, but what of other aspects of the curriculum, chiefly the pastoral and hidden curricular structures? If we as educators have been charged with preparing the student to enter society, then should we not also address those issues that are confronting not only our students but the entire world with ever-increasing complexity? Especially in educational environments of an international context, where the scope and variety of an international situation pose more opportunity accurately to reflect current and future society, the need for addressing these issues becomes even more important, not least because what we teach students today will have great bearing on tomorrow's decision-making practices.

Transformative and hegemonic intellectualism

It is my belief that a school, especially one in an international context, should promote a transformative intellectual environment. The term 'transformative intellectual environment' refers to the notion that the individual is given the opportunity not only to think critically about the concept being presented, but also to have the ability to take the basic concept and transform it for positive implementation into the current social environment. An intellectual environment such as this will allow the student to realize the full implications of the society to be entered and, more importantly, to enact change where he or she feels it is necessary. The school, however, must provide more than just token opportunities for students to develop and evaluate their powers of constructive re-creation. The school must also be aware that it needs to pay more than lip service to the ideological implications it espouses in its statements of philosophy and, perhaps most importantly, that time must be taken to ensure that the transformative concepts underpinning this ideological focus are developed in all aspects of the school. Failure to develop these concepts in just one part of the school community will corrupt any headway made in other areas.

The outcome resulting from this paradigmatic shift in the fundamentals of the educational process will result in a more proactive stance that will give empowerment to all involved. A focus such as this will give those individuals concerned a direction in which to dedicate their collective energies – a direction in which everyone is contributing to the positive development of the student, who will adopt these ideological qualities and use them far beyond the time spent in a primary or secondary educational environment. In an international educational context it becomes an imperative for the student to appreciate that the future decisions he or she will make may have global implications and, if not, it would still be amiss not to teach that same student those values which in themselves are necessary for successful integration into a global village environment. The hidden, academic and pastoral curricular structures will all have vital roles to play in establishment of the socio-cultural structure of the school, the culmination of which is the learners' tendency towards a certain type of intellectual determination.

It is here suggested that an international education, and *ipso facto* an international school, should, in part, be able to justify its classification as international by placing itself on the intellectual spectrum illustrated in Figure 6.1. It may well be thought that this particular spectrum has a limitation in its generalization, placing the local perspective with hegemonic intellectualism, and the international perspective with transformative intellectualism. In fact, the concepts of local and international outlined above are not based on physical/geographical boundaries, but on intellectual/abstract boundaries which humans create for themselves. These boundaries are just as imaginary as the ones

| Transformative | Critical | Accommodating | Hegemonic |
| intellectual | intellectual | intellectual | intellectual |

```
-------------------/-------------------/-------------------/-------------------
```

| International | | | Local |
| perspective | | | perspective |

Figure 6.1 Transformative vs hegemonic spectrum

that divide our nations. In today's world, however, both sets of boundaries, the physical and the mental, are no longer serving their purpose, and are in fact acting as an impediment for a society which attempts exploration and understanding beyond such artificial boundaries. The time has passed when we can safely assume that all we need to worry about is our own backyard. As a society we are confronted daily with problems and opportunities from the entire world, and to ignore these aspects only enforces a culture of silence. The world, through technology and invention, has indeed become a very small place, and there is no sign of this progress abating. If we as educators do not take the time to prepare the student properly, then we are not fulfilling the obligations that we accepted in making education our vocation. The essence of being an international school, therefore, rests not with the nationalities of the students, nor with the makeup of the teaching staff, and certainly not with the location of the physical plant. The concept of an international school rests in the ability of the individuals in the school community to prepare the student successfully to integrate, and to provide a positive transformative contribution to the global environment. In effect, an international school can call itself an international school because it has achieved a paradigmatic stance based on its political convictions that its curricular output will produce individuals of a transformative intellectual variety. This approach would represent an important contribution to setting a framework for quality provision in international terms.

The concept of culture in education in an international context

Closely related to the political nature of education in an international context is the culture of the environment. It may be surmised that the political nature of an educational setting is derived from cultural influences on the setting, with the resultant outcome usually determined by the dominant or most powerful cultural influence.

Several models have already been devised to explain the phenomenon of cultural influence. One particularly interesting approach is the analogy of the iceberg (Fennes and Hapgood, 1997). As in the actual physical iceberg, only a small portion of the whole is visible above the surface. In cultural terms, that which is visible may include the arts, cooking and clothing: things that are easily experienced through everyday interaction. Under the surface, however, lies a plethora of cultural biases, which may perhaps be determined from the parts that are visible, but in all likelihood are more clearly understood through a series of complex relationships to the visible links, and are likely to remain out of everyday awareness. Levi-Strauss, the famous anthropologist, was concerned with determining the underpart of this cultural iceberg through his use of structuralist methodology, and his concept of binary oppositions. Such binary oppositions were also the impetus for transformations which occurred within a specific cultural context (Lane, 1970); these transformations are in essence changes in the relationship between the two objects or bodies of concern, reached perhaps through compromise or the laws of the society.

Another interesting aspect that may be helpful in determining the importance of culture in the political landscape of the international school is defined by Hofstede and Bond (1988), who suggest that culture can be considered as mental programming. In this particular instance they are referring to the idea that patterns of thinking, feeling and potential acting are learned through a lifetime as mental programmes. They further make the point that since such programming is at least partly shared with people who live or who have lived within the same environment, culture is a collective phenomenon. There are three levels of mental programming; the first level is human nature (the operating system), the second level is learned culture which is specific to a certain group or category, and the third level is the personality of the individual.

We can now begin to see some interesting notions coming to light. In the case of an international school, for instance, we find a number of binary oppositions which need to be resolved on a daily basis through the structures or ideals that have been put in place within the school context; this in effect produces a micro-culture. As Hofstede and Bond point out, however, there are still a number of cultural conditions that directly influence the outcome of this micro-culture in an institution that has been labelled an international school. The complexity of the international school is largely a result of its abundant cultural influences, all of which contribute to the school's cultural outcome. The resultant difficulties must be resolved, however, in order to maintain a smooth operating procedure for the environment, and the resulting political orientation brings with it the danger of the institution being dominated by the most powerful group in the micro-culture.

It is at this point that diversity becomes particularly important. The most powerful group can now decide which action to take. In essence, this group has the opportunity to implement the type of educational outcome that is consistent with the political focus it has embraced, and this focus is determined by the additive experiences of the dominant group on all three levels of programming as described above. The main question for the dominant group to decide is whether it should promote a perspective that is hegemonic in character, or promote a perspective that is transformative in character. In the case of an international school, a transformative focus would facilitate the concept of intercultural learning (Fennes and Hapgood, 1997) which is, in my opinion, a more appropriate road for international education to take.

The very nature of an international school means that the decisions being taken in all areas of the school, be it curriculum writing or the type of food served in the cafeteria, all lead to an underlying conception of the political environment that is in existence at the school. There is very little choice but to ensure an environment where transformative instruction via the curriculum provides a basis for an intercultural learning experience, and this can only be accomplished through the careful and constructive coordination of the various political-cultural influences within the micro-culture we call an international school. Achievement of quality for the whole school can then be pursued within a political framework to which each component (curriculum, human resources, organizational style) can relate with confidence.

References

Appadurai, A (1990) Cultural flows, in *Disjuncture and Difference in the Global Cultural Economy*, ed M Featherstone, Sage Publications, London

Fennes, H and Hapgood, K (1997) *Intercultural Learning in the Classroom*, Cassell, London

Freire, P (1990) *The Pedagogy of the Oppressed*, Continuum, New York

Hofstede, G and Bond, M H (1988) The Confucius connection: from cultural roots to economic growth, *Organizational Dynamics*, **17**, pp 4–21

Lane, M (1970) *Structuralism: A reader*, Jonathan Cape, London

Shaull, R (1990) Preface in P Freire, *The Pedagogy of the Oppressed*, Continuum, New York

Zsebik, P (1997) *The SPACE Factor: An explanation of the elements within the micro-culture labeled school*, unpublished paper

Part B

THROUGH HUMAN
RESOURCES

Chapter 7

Student mobility and the international curriculum

Anne McKillop-Ostrom

As international educators, it is essential that we understand that the psychological needs of international students are as critical to their success at school as are the academic needs. We as educators must share this understanding with others within the international school community to ensure that structures are created within the curriculum framework that enhance the experiences of these students. It is only then that these young people will be able to make long-term adjustments and fully benefit from their international upbringing.

International curriculum

In some international schools around the world, students are offered an international curriculum, the most well established of which is the International Baccalaureate (Hayden and Wong, 1997). While the concept of an international curriculum in general terms has yet to be well defined in the academic community, it is usually understood to be a curriculum which is not based on any one national educational system or one teaching approach, but which draws on educational philosophies and methods from a range of sources. The goal of the international curriculum is to enable students from a variety of national backgrounds to study together and also to provide an education that would be acceptable to higher education institutions worldwide (Hayden and Wong, 1997).

Beyond this fairly structural description of an international curriculum, however, the author argues that for a curriculum to be considered international it must meet the specific academic and emotional needs of its international student body. In order to achieve this goal, an international curriculum should have two main facets. First, it must be considered to be the total programme of an educational institution. This is a curriculum that incorporates all aspects of the planned academic curriculum (what is written down on paper), all aspects of the hidden curriculum (the social, cultural and political messages which are transmitted through the materials and lessons provided), the informal curriculum (extracurricular activities which occur on a voluntary basis) and the actual or received curriculum (the 'reality of the pupils' experiences') (Kelly, 1999).

Second, an international curriculum must challenge and allow the child 'to see the world from a much wider perspective than is generally required in national systems' (Gellar, in Hayden and Thompson, 1998). Reading and listening to a variety of texts and perspectives, interacting with students from different national groups, and experiencing food, music, celebrations, religions and values of different cultural representatives are essential for the students to be able fully to understand other cultures and to live in a culture quite different from their own. The extent to which the curriculum is judged to be international may also be dependent on variables such as the mix of nationalities within the school, the location of the school, the mix of teaching practices and the degree to which the programme is recognized by other schools and institutions.

The internationally mobile child

Children and adolescents who move between cultures and live out of their home country for extended periods of time have been referred to as global nomads, third-culture kids (TCKs), transnationals/transculturals and internationally mobile children. They portray characteristics that transcend a single culture and nationality, and experience a particular stress as a result of their mobility. Through their experiences, TCKs adopt aspects of not one but many cultures into their sense of self, and relate to others who have a similar family upbringing and life experiences (Pollock, 1988). They feel most like themselves in a culture all of their own, a 'third culture' (Useem and Downie, 1979).

In order to meet with the complexities, as well as the demands, of an international upbringing, most internationally mobile individuals consistently make four adaptations to mobility. They show forced extro-version by going out of their way to get to meet new people and form friendships quickly. They tend to mesh and mimic, which cuts down on the need to gain acceptance. They travel lightly, entering relationships that are typically short-term and intense, and they develop ease in saying goodbye, leaving very few people from whom they cannot walk away (Wertsch, 1991; Gerner, 1993).

The nature of transition

Change and adaptation to change are constant features of the lives of internationally mobile individuals. Every physical move, like every developmental move from one life stage to another, forces an individual to face challenges of transition. Transition is different from change. Whereas change is an external process, transition is internal (Bridges, 1995). Transition is a psychological process that an individual goes through in order to come to terms with a new situation. According to Bridges, it is the letting go of an old reality and an old identity that existed before the change took place. Transition periods offer great potential for personal growth and development; however, they may also be quite unsettling and trigger a great deal of psychological and physio-logical pain (Adams, Hayes and Hopson, 1976).

The important outcome of research into transition has been the development of numerous models to describe the process. Although the descriptors and the number of phases may differ between the models, all models describe the experience of the individual as he or she moves through a series of emotional stages. Bridges points out that the phases of a transition model are not separate stages with clear boundaries. The phases overlap, and an individual may be in one or more phases at the same time. The 'movement through transition is marked by a change in the dominance of one phase as it gives way to the next' (Bridges, 1995). Transitions can be geographical, relational or professional and it is important to understand that a transition is 'the psycho-social process one goes through when changing jobs, losing a loved one, learning a new sport, developing a spiritual practice' (Schaetti, 1996). Such models help to predict human responses to transitional events, and suggest ideal ways in which people may endure and ultimately gain from their transi-tional experiences.

Individuals need to be aware of the process that they are experiencing and of the importance of managing this adjustment. Adams, Hayes and Hopson (1976) classify an event as transitional only when the individual is personally aware of both the change and the need for new behavioural responses to the new situation. Since all transitions encountered, negative or positive, result in some degree of stress, we need to focus on managing the degree to which it impacts on our lives (Adams, Hayes and Hopson, 1976). Immaturity may make young people more vulnerable to the psychological impact of transition, and at the same time make it difficult for them to manage their experience of transition on their own. Just like adults, children who move feel a sense of loss. Their loss will be related to both general and specific areas, for example, familiar surroundings such as school and community and, more specifically, close friends. The losses brought about by moving can result in various forms of grieving.

For a child who is in the process of developing his or her sense of self, frequent international moves can have a particularly powerful influence on his or her psyche. Walling (1970) claims that a child's perception of self emerges through interaction with other children in a cultural context. When moving displaces the familiar culture, there will be a disruption in the sense of belonging and the sense of self. The confusion resulting from the demands of adaptation may in fact be more than the child can contend with independently. Here, the parent and the school should be taking on shared responsibility for presenting their understanding of transition in ways that make sense to a developing child.

Sojourner adjustment is the psychological adjustment of relatively short-term visitors to new geographic areas where permanent settlement is not intended, and where assimilation into the host culture is not expected (Berry et al,1992; Church, 1982). Various models of adaptation have been developed to study sojourners' psychological adjustment, such as Oberg's '4 stages' (Church, 1982), Adler's '5 phases' (Adler, 1975), Lysguaard's 'U-Curve' (Church, 1982) and the 'W-Curve' of Gullahorn and Gullahorn (Church, 1982). All models point out and describe different phases through which individuals pass; some suggest lengths of time and most portray characteristic behaviours for each phase. Like other transition models previously discussed, these models indicate a period of trauma: a time of extreme discomfort and dissatisfaction. This was recognized as part of the standard process of 'adapting to and coping with various types of unfamiliar cultures' (Taft, 1977). It was termed 'culture shock' in the 1950s by Oberg, who stressed that it is 'precipitated by the anxiety that results from losing all our familiar signs and symbols of social intercourse such as customs, gestures, facial expressions or words' (in Church, 1982). Culture shock is one type of trauma that is experienced by individuals to varying degrees and according to the demands of the situation. If the trauma is managed successfully, the individual should eventually grow from his or her experiences. This process of coping with a new culture requires that the individual learns new responses and skills and acquires new information (Taft, 1977).

Culture learning

Culture learning is seen as part of the process of adaptation that people experience when they enter into a new culture. The aim of culture learning derives from an interest or necessity to gain an insight into how others live or behave. If done properly, it requires cognitive, affective and behavioural knowledge (Hess, 1994). Richard Pearce (1998) argues that it is imperative that as educators we understand how children carry out culture learning in order to be able to support the adjustment process.

In order for individuals to adapt to a new school culture, a minimal level of culture learning must take place. If the process of fitting in is seen as desirable to the student, he or she will be motivated to get to know the new culture. Since young children learn culture much faster than adults do, they may adopt a new culture much faster and more easily than their parents may. While adults are expected to have problems adapting because they may be set in their ways, in contrast children may not share the same values or reactions to the new culture. Adults who are not as motivated to adapt to the new culture may have a negative effect on their children's overall adjustment process.

Culture is defined by Berry *et al* as 'the shared way of life of a group of people' (in Pearce, 1998). If this is the case, then a school culture should be identified as the way in which its members, students, teachers, support staff and parents behave. Thus, all communication and expectations should adhere to the school's norms. Individuals who do not initially behave or communicate accordingly will need to adapt by learning the culture in order to fit in. Difficulties arise for children who had previously adapted to a particular culture of a school and developed a set of appropriate cultural norms, only to find themselves suddenly and completely turned around when entering a new type of school. This process may bring about a clash of 'old and new norms', with some students exhibiting extreme culture shock and others showing signs of indifference (Pearce, 1996). What sets off a particular reaction to a new environment may be hard to pinpoint. Differences between cultures will create challenges, as will an individual child's reactions to the support (or lack of support) provided by the new school.

In order for individuals in a school to recognize why some students may be delayed in their adjustment or exhibit signs of adjustment stress, these individuals need to be able to identify and understand their own school culture. This type of understanding requires careful, and at times painful, reflection and analysis. Those in schools need to be shown how to step back and determine what their school culture is. Strategic planning sessions and accreditation processes provide opportunities for schools to examine themselves and define their school culture. Looking at important issues such as the school's ability to celebrate and allow for diversity, how the school accommodates students from other school systems, the degree to which the school's values reflect an understanding of other cultures, systems and adaptation patterns, and the extent to which the school expects students to conform to their particular type of school must also be taken into consideration. Schools that take the opportunity to learn from new students can gain a clearer view of themselves and in turn use this information to facilitate an appropriate system of culture learning (Pearce, 1996).

Mobility in international schools

A high turnover rate in a school's community is a distinctive characteristic of international schools. A large component of the population of these schools comprises international students who are on the move, relocating from country to country or international community to international community. The very nature of their internationally mobile lives causes international students to face transition repeatedly, whether it is in response to their own movement from location to location or to the movement of their friends and teachers.

International schools cannot ignore the specific nature of their students; nor can they fail to address the transition-related issues, which are so much a part of each student's life. In order to help students cope with their mobile lifestyle, the teachers, administrators and policy makers at international schools must also understand the psychological phenomena of moving. Learning how to recognize transitional stress and manage transitional events will lessen the impact on the school's emotional and learning environment and help to create a more stable environment.

Studies in areas related to cross-cultural adaptation and transition share a general consensus that cross-cultural contact is inherently stressful. There is, however, substantial disagreement on how it may be alleviated (Walling, 1970). The focus on the psychological functioning of the individual recommends a clinical approach to dealing with problems of cross-cultural adaptation involving therapy and counselling. Later models, however, liken cross-cultural exposure to a learning experience and propose programmes of preparation, orientation and the acquisition of culturally appropriate social skills (Church, 1982). Klinberg (in Furnham and Bochner, 1986) points out that pre-departure experiences, levels of competence and degree of preparation will affect what happens to a person while abroad and at a later stage have an impact on the individual's life after returning to the home country.

A model discussing the transition cycle of the internationally mobile child must reflect both frequent mobility and transcultural experience (Larson, 1998). In conjunction with a child's own mobility is the mobility of other children and adults with whom they are associated – individuals who may be at a different stage in a transition process. Larson stresses that the high frequency of mobility of these children produces a continual need for readjustment in order to cope with this 'kaleidoscope of change' (Larson, 1998). Social relations strongly influence children's feelings of well-being and have a direct influence on their stability. Although it may be argued that this is similar in adults, it is perhaps more critical for children.

The Transition Experience Model

David Pollock developed a five-phase transition model after many years of working with third-culture missionary kids (MKs) around the world. His Transition Experience Model outlines experiences that children and adults encounter while facing transitions. Pollock's model describes the characteristics of each of five phases in terms of three variables: one's social status (how one is perceived by others), one's social posture (how one presents oneself to and interacts with others) and one's psychological experience (how one typically feels inside) (Schaetti, 1996). Each phase describes the mental activity of the participants in transition. They may be, for example, engaged in and thinking of the present, or they may be more oriented towards, and thinking about, the future (Larson, 1998). Pollock's transition model can be used to incorporate transition support activities and transition education, both academic-based and non-academic-based, into the school programme in order to augment the students' ability to manage the transitions positively.

In the involvement phase, the first of Pollock's five phases, the child indicates feelings of belonging, commitment and intimacy. This leads to an anticipation phase called leaving, which is characterized by feelings of celebration, distancing and denial. During the third phase, the transition phase when the individual is physically between moves, the child experiences feelings of 'statuslessness', chaos and anxiety. The fourth, the entering phase, is characterized by introductory-type frustrations, superficial attempts to settle in, and a feeling of vulnerability. The model indicates that this is a disappointment phase. Following this phase is an involvement phase where the individual experiences a sense of belonging, commitment and intimacy more or less similar to the first stage. Unlike other earlier models, Pollock's model describes the first, second and third phases as starting before entry into the new culture.

Supporting transition in international schools

Researchers such as Schaetti (1996), Walling (1970), Langford (1997) and Pearce (1996) have identified and emphasized the necessity for international schools to provide a holistic form of education and support to members of their entire school community.

To meet the needs of the student body, the school must also communicate with and support the parents. The teachers and administrators need to appreciate the importance of both the child's and the parents' attitudes towards a move. 'If the move is seen as positive by the parent, then children usually feel less anxious' (Walling, 1970). It is important that the parents understand the goals and values of the new school. Any conflicts and confusion regarding expectations of parents, students, teachers and administrators need to be communicated and resolved as soon as possible.

Some international schools, such as the United Nations International School of Hanoi (UNIS-Hanoi), have already developed transition programmes which recognize the importance of involving the whole family and address conflict resolution, stress management and the management of grief and loss as recommended by Schaetti (1996). A transition resource team can be an effective means of delivering a successful transition programme, helping individuals to understand and support the transition process. The formation of a team ensures that transition education and programming does not fall on any one individual and allows for a variety of ideas and expertise to be shared. Transition resource teams generally consist of a group of 7 to 10 volunteers representing a cross-section of teachers, administrators, counsellors, parents and students. Leadership of the team is provided by a 'transitions resource coordinator'.

Drawing primarily from the work of Schaetti (1996, 1998), but also from Langford (1997), Pearce (1996) and from the author's personal experience and research (McKillop-Ostrom, 1999), transition teams can be involved in the following activities:

- Consolidation of transition efforts: Assessing the different ways in which a school currently serves internationally mobile pupils helps to identify programme strengths and weaknesses, and set priorities. Developing programmes that incorporate all age levels and areas of the curriculum and integrating support in different areas of the school will serve to create a framework for creating a transition programme (Langford, 1997). From here a school can develop strategies to ensure that programming eventually becomes part of school policy. How and to what extent a school goes about this task will vary according to the mission statement of the school and the expertise available within the school.

- Increased transitions expertise: The provision of transitions-related professional development for team members and then other members of the school staff will ensure that members of the school staff develop a good understanding of transition-related issues and processes. Once an awareness of issues and concepts has been reached, the school will be in a better position to implement programmes, modify curricula and address issues of school culture.

- Transition education and cultural awareness: Careful preparation of guidance support and advisor/advisee-type programmes that focus on a variety of transition-related areas should be developed. These should address the following issues: the management of stress, grief and loss, conflict resolution, an analysis of characteristics of internationally mobile children, and cross-cultural awareness. Schaetti (1996) recommends that schools develop opportunities for students to learn more about managing transitions through a reworking of the curriculum. Writing activities, discussion groups and the analysis of relevant pieces of literature are some examples of how teachers can incorporate activities into their lessons. Implementing school-based or division-based programmes set up with the purpose of promoting an understanding of issues surrounding student mobility will also help to provide transition education. Some schools have adopted the International Baccalaureate programmes, which teach students 'to equate classroom experiences with the realities of the outside world by placing an emphasis on the ideals of international understanding and responsible citizenship' (International Baccalaureate Organisation, 1997).

- Transition-related activities: The orientation of new students regardless of when they arrive at the school, and the provision of departure programmes for students who are leaving, is essential. The transition resource team, in conjunction with other staff, can also provide activities to support those students who must continually adjust to the comings and goings of those around them. The provision of orientation and counselling support, as well as programmes for departure and re-entry, and orientation programmes for those entering mid-year, should be part of the support programme that takes place throughout the year.

- Customized transition services: Schools should modify transition programmes carried out at other schools so that the needs of the particular school can be met. Instead of buying handbooks, each school could prepare its own to suit the school culture and needs.
- Institutionalized transition programming: Transitions programming should be part of Board policy and be supported by standard budgets to ensure continuous support.
- Year-round transition support: Langford (1998) highlights four main forms of support, as follows:
  - Teacher support: Support should be provided throughout the year. In order to ease the students' adjustment, the school should implement strategies that will help students to adapt academically. For example, teachers should include a means for helping students with gaps in particular subject areas as a result of their mobility and exposure to different teaching techniques and curricula. English as a Second Language (ESL) programmes should be provided for non-native speakers, as well as counselling regarding the importance of mother-tongue literacy. Wherever possible, schools should provide mother-tongue instruction. Teachers should encourage culture learning and sharing in their individual classrooms, and schools should assess how the overall curriculum meets the needs of their internationally mobile pupils.
  - Peer support: The importance of peer support for helping with social and academic integration is paramount, and opportunities for social interaction need to be provided. Student groups, such as a student council, can work to organize events and buddy programmes. Students can also be involved in writing handbooks for new pupils. Other students can be resources for sharing information about their home countries or countries in which they have lived previously.
  - Administrative support: Administrators can support the successful transition of students by the hiring of teachers who are internationally oriented, providing support for newly arrived teachers, providing in-service training related to understanding and meeting the needs of pupils in transition, and ensuring that appropriate and ongoing programmes are in place. Forums for discussing students who are suffering extensively with transition stress can be built into regular staff meetings.

- Parent support: Parents also have a role to play in supporting the transient population. Measures such as the provision of volunteer opportunities at the school and regularly scheduled social and other gatherings for parents, as well as formal orientation programmes for families, can support both parents and children.
- Cost reduction: Developing expertise within the school, as well as preparing handbooks and support materials by members of the transition team and other staff members, will significantly reduce costs without compromising the transition programme.
- Enhanced public relations: Efforts to demonstrate that transitions education is being addressed will help promote the school as one that is sensitive to a mobile community. Including materials relating to the transition programme on the school's Web site will create a positive initial impression.

Conclusion

All newcomers to a school will undergo a transition experience, something once thought best minimized but now recognized as an essential component of adapting to a new environment. International educators have a responsibility to use their knowledge of transition issues wisely in order to provide a programme that addresses the needs of students and families in a quality manner. As we learn more about internationally mobile children, we will realize how important it is to develop a well-rounded curriculum of both an academic and a pastoral nature. In doing so, international educators will help to ensure that their students have opportunities to grow from their experiences and, in return, become well-rounded and better adjusted individuals.

References

Adams, J, Hayes, J and Hopson, B (1976) *Transition: Understanding and managing personal change*, Martin Robinson, London

Adler, P (1975) The transition experience: an alternate view of culture shock, *Journal of Humanistic Psychology*, **15** (4), pp 13–22

Berry, J, Poottinga, Y, Segall, M and Dasen, P (1992) *Communication and Training. Cross-cultural Psychology: Research and applications*, Cambridge University Press, Cambridge

Bridges, W (1995) *Managing Transitions: Making the most out of change*, Nicholas Brealey Publishing, London

Church, A I (1982) Sojourner adjustment, *Psychological Bulletin*, **91** (3), pp 540–71

Furnham, A and Bochner, S (1986) *Culture Shock: Psychological reactions to unfamiliar environments*, Methuen, London

Gerner, M E (1993) *Understanding Developmental and Personality Differences in Internationally Mobile Children and Adolescents*, On-site consultation at the Jakarta International School, Jakarta

Hayden, M and Wong, C (1997) The International Baccalaureate: international education and cultural preservation, *Educational Studies*, **23** (3), pp 349–61

Hayden, M C and Thompson, J J (eds) (1998) *International Education: Principles and practice*, Kogan Page, London

Hess, D J (1994) *The Whole World Guide to Culture Learning*, Intercultural Press, Yarmouth

International Baccalaureate Organisation (1997) *IBO*, IBO, Geneva

Kelly, A V (1999) *The Curriculum: Theory and practice*, Paul Chapman Publishing, London

Langford, M (1997*) Internationally Mobile Pupils in Transition: The role of the international school*, unpublished MA dissertation, University of Bath

Langford, M (1998) Global nomads, third culture kids and international schools, in *International Education: Principles and practice*, eds M C Hayden and J J Thompson, Kogan Page, London

Larson, J M (1998) Transitions and the TCK, in *Raising Resilient MKs: Resources for caregivers, parents and teachers*, ed J M Bowers, Association of Christian Schools International, Colorado Springs

McKillop-Ostrom, A (1999) *Addressing Transition in International Schools: Learning from the experiences of internationally mobile children*, unpublished MA dissertation, University of Bath

Pearce, R (1996) Kipling's cat: learning from the new student, *International Schools Journal*, **XV** (2), pp 23–30

Pearce, R (1998) Developing cultural identity in an international school environment, in *International Education: Principles and practice*, eds M C Hayden and J J Thompson, Kogan Page, London

Pollock, D C (1988) *TCK Definition*, copyrighted, unpublished lecture notes

Schaetti, B F (1996) Transition programming in international schools: an emerging mandate, *Inter-Ed. Association for the Advancement of International Education*, **24**, pp 12–19

Schaetti, B F (1998) Transitions resource teams: a good answer to an important question, *International Schools Journal*, **XVII** (2), pp 52–58

Taft, R (1977) Coping with unfamiliar cultures, in *Studies in Cross-Cultural Psychology*, N Warren, Academic Press, London

Useem, R and Downie, R D (1979) Third-culture kids, *Today's Education*, **65** (3), pp 103–05

Walling, D R (1970) *Meeting the Needs of Transient Students*, Phi Delta Kappa Educational Foundation, Bloomington

Wertsch, M E (1991) *Military Brats as Nomads. Military Brats: Legacies of childhood inside the fortress*, Harmony Books, New York

Chapter 8

Recruitment of teachers for international education

Brian Garton

The context

Curriculum innovation, implementation and control, assessment structures and the impact of computer technology are all playing a major part in changing the nature of schools and therefore the education of children, but 'nothing yet looks like killing off the method tried and tested long before the millennium began: a teacher standing before a group of pupils and imparting wisdom by word of mouth' (*The Economist*, 1999). How can schools recruit the best teachers for their context, and is there something different about teachers who need to be recruited for international education and for international schools?

This brief review will focus on the recruitment of teachers to those schools that are generally referred to as 'international schools'. Hayden and Thompson (1995) noted that 'for the most part the body of international schools is a conglomeration of individual institutions which may or may not share an underlying educational philosophy'. Similarly, Kevin Bartlett (1998) writes: 'With the exception of isolated clusters such as the United World Colleges, international schools share no recognized philosophical foundation. There are no deeply held, publicly declared beliefs and values to bind them, to bond them into a coherent global system.' In recent years the number of such schools has continued to expand significantly, in terms both of overall student enrolment (albeit with some dramatic 'dips' due to economic and political crises, as well as natural disasters), and of geographical range, notably in Eastern Europe and the former USSR. The overall sentiment remains valid, however, even though there are increasingly strong influences moving towards the creation of more 'bonds' between such schools.

The challenge to identify the best teachers

Forrest Broman (1999) writes: 'The international school Head's best possibility to influence learning is through the teacher he/she hires. Thus no stone should be left unturned in the search for the best possible candidates.' In 1991, however, he had made the comment: 'Yet...very few Heads have ever received any kind of formal training on teacher selection procedures, techniques, interview skills etc' (Broman, 1991). In general terms, though the training of Heads of international schools, as of most other schools, has improved over the past decade, the situation is today perhaps not radically different from what it was in the early 1990s.

In all these schools, there can be no doubting the paramount emphasis given to effective teacher recruitment. It is probably the most important and time-consuming single activity that the international school Head undertakes in the course of the year. Even in many of the large schools where there is significant delegation of administrative roles, it is still usually regarded as being within the sphere of the Chief Executive Officer's direct responsibilities. In a number of schools its importance is further recognized, since it is also formally, and often also in practice, an area in which the Board seeks to take an active part. This can be a cause of some frustration and friction at the highest administrative level. There may also be a number of problems in trying to reconcile practicalities with vision. As Joe Blaney (1991) wrote: 'Staff should be carefully recruited so as to represent, without an unreasonable financial burden being placed upon the schools, the major culture areas of the world, and as many nationalities as feasible. This... will also provide the students with a variety of racial, ethnic, and national role models.'

Institutions such as the United World Colleges do indeed aim to be consistent with such a focus, but for most schools it is not likely to be the dominant factor in determining the very practical arrangements that the Head must make for effective teacher recruitment in international education.

How to identify the 'best' teachers

For many international schools the pragmatic approach to teacher recruitment is accentuated by the widespread practice of having a teaching staff that can be grouped into three distinct categories. These are:

- host-country nationals;
- 'local hire' expatriates;
- 'overseas hire' expatriates.

The grouping of teachers into these three categories is inevitably an over-simplification of the situation. Teachers in the first two categories probably form the majority of teachers in international schools, although this is not always an obvious inference from general descriptions of teachers in international schools. The remarkable contribution made by such teachers is a topic that still requires extensive research. Sadly, but understandably, the very existence of these categories has also been a cause of serious and unproductive tension in a number of schools. Parental and community opinion is frequently a factor of importance here, as there is plenty of anecdotal evidence to suggest that it is often the case that a number of parents would 'prefer' their child to be taught by a native-English-speaking 'Western-trained' overseas-hire expatriate, for reasons that may be founded rather more on prejudice than on a well-informed evaluation.

Host-country nationals

Host country national teachers are usually recruited for a variety of reasons, including those that relate to the school's mission statement, the legal requirements – and especially the work permit requirements – of the host country, and financial expediency. Some schools would regard it as axiomatic for their international aspirations that they should have a number of faculty recruited from the host country. Without such an element in their staffing they would, arguably, only be 'overseas' schools, displaced from their national, 'home' contexts. A number of these schools may also have significant numbers of host-country nationals enrolled as students, and the recruitment of host-country national teachers can be perceived as an appropriate complement to that situation. In some countries, the labour laws relating to the issue of work permits may make it necessary to recruit from the local population for at least some teaching positions. This may itself be a factor which affects the overall 'quality' of the faculty, as it may have both positive and negative effects.

In other circumstances, and in countries whose economic development lies well outside G7 criteria, host-country nationals may be recruited because they can also reduce costs, and this obviously raises an additional 'quality' issue. It is unlikely that this last reason would be publicly acknowledged, but there does seem to be sufficient anecdotal support for this interpretation of a situation whose existence is well documented. The quality of faculty can also be affected by the fact that in a number of situations such teachers can, by virtue of the local laws, attain 'tenure' status and so may cause problems for the school in the future if they are deemed to be unsatisfactory from the school's perspective, but are not necessarily so within the terms of the local legal system. Any overall approach to quality assurance will need to take such circumstances into account.

Local-hire expatriates

Local-hire-expatriate teachers regularly play a vital part in the staffing of international schools, especially in capital cities or in other large centres where there is a large resident expatriate population. Their availability for recruitment is almost always dependent on the fact that they have spouses or partners who work for embassies, aid agencies or multi-national companies in that particular country, or who are host-country nationals or residents of the country in question. The same criteria for recruitment can be used as for overseas-hire expatriates (see below), and their contribution to the school is often very difficult to distinguish from teachers in that category; they may often, however, be recruited at considerably less cost, as it is perceived that they do not require housing, flights or most of the other fringe benefits regarded as axiomatic for overseas-hire recruits. They may also provide very important bridges with the host country, as they may already have been living there for some time.

The actual process of recruitment can also be made easier as there may be opportunities to employ local-hire expatriates as 'substitute' teachers, allowing the Head the opportunity to see how they perform in the classroom and how they work with the rest of the team. On the negative side, it has to be recognized that they may have to leave the school at an inconvenient time owing to the posting of the spouse elsewhere. The potential for cost-saving, and the pressure on a Head to appoint 'almost anybody available' when faced with a major vacancy on the first day of the school year, can also have an impact on the 'quality' issue.

Overseas-hire expatriates

As regards the recruitment of overseas-hire expatriate teachers, a significant caveat has been recorded by Peter Gummer, the Director of Gabbitas

Educational Consultants: 'First, ensure breadth in the search process. We need constant new blood in the international sector, so schools should be trying to access as wide a range of potential candidates as possible, rather than dipping only into the pool of existing international staff. This means the press, the web, and probably several agencies, as well as any recruitment fairs you may choose to attend' (Gummer, 2000).

The general pattern of recruitment

Over the years, a general pattern of recruitment has developed which creates a sequential framework within which three main stages can be perceived. These three phases extend over the whole year and for schools operating a northern hemisphere timetable have a peak of activity for the middle phase in the month of February related to the recruitment fairs organized by the major recruitment agencies. The three phases are as follows.

(a) The preparation and advertising phase

Martin Skelton (Director of the British-based organization Fieldwork Education) makes a pertinent comment when he writes (Skelton, 1999) that the process of recruitment is almost the end of the line and not the beginning. Schools which recruit most effectively seem to me to be those schools which:

1. have already clearly defined what they stand for;
2. have clearly defined what their students should learn and how they should learn it;
3. have defined their particular 'act' through clear policies;
4. analyse their strengths and weaknesses every two years or so rather than assume that everything is all right;
5. from the above, produce good job descriptions for staff which help them to be clear about what they are supposed to do, and allow the possibility of staff review;
6. from the above, define as clearly as possible what they need [The process of recruiting teachers for international schools often has to be done at a distance. Poorly defined criteria can ruin the process before it has begun.];
7. define the requirements clearly in any advertisement or supporting documentation so that inappropriate candidates have a chance to filter themselves out of the process; and
8. devise an interview process which actively seeks information focussed on the criteria which have been established.

The work of the Head during this phase is complicated by the fact that in many schools it is not until quite late in the academic year that contractual conditions make it clearly apparent just which of the current staff will be leaving, and yet there are great advantages to be gained by advertising vacancies well before that time. Not surprisingly, it is usual for the major recruitment agencies to identify vacancies as either 'provisional' or 'definite'.

There are also budgetary implications, often requiring Board approval, which need to be considered at this stage, not only in terms of the actual numbers of posts which may be available, but also with respect to salary levels and conditions of service; these all have to be clearly agreed, at least in a reasonably definite format, before interviews can be arranged and contracts offered. Yet many school budgets are not formally agreed until the second half of the school year, by which time enrolment predictions can more confidently be made. Thus there is a significant element of stressful guesswork at that time of the year.

The advertising dimension of this phase is more easily undertaken. It involves updating previous literature and data for the recruitment agencies and, which is even more time-consuming, the preparation of online information and media presentations such as videotapes, CD ROMs and PowerPoint presentations. One positive aspect of this phase is that the Head can involve a number of colleagues on the faculty in the presentation of these information packages, and especially on those parts of them that deal with the crucially important but essentially nebulous question 'What it is like to be a teacher at the... school?'. It is precisely because it is so difficult for candidates to find answers to this question that this part of the process is so important.

(b) The interviewing and contract-offering phase

This is undoubtedly the most stressful and critical phase, although it would be rash to predict that the advent of online teacher recruitment will not have an effect on this situation. One of the consequences of the increasing use of e-mail and the Internet is that it has become possible to set up very useful contacts between candidates and recruiters long before the 'initial' interview. There is, however, a significant 'weariness' factor that has arisen from the sheer volume of the e-mail traffic generated by the recruitment season. It is very difficult to delegate the scrutiny of the flood of e-mail messages that a Head receives once the vacancies have been posted online, and even for those that arrive when no vacancies have been posted, or an online information site has incorrect information. Yet if a Head tries to read them all, then other work will suffer. The sheer volume of information itself is potentially a negative factor, and this is undoubtedly an advantage for the major recruitment agencies, which can make much more appropriate use of the technology than could a single Headteacher.

Jim McKay, the Executive Officer for ECIS Staffing Services, has made a case for the existence of his and other organizations very succinctly:

> At typical international recruitment centres, an international school Head can screen and select from hundreds of candidates all of whom have a minimum of two years previous teaching experience in the subject areas they are applying for, current teaching certification and three highly supportive references. Technology has made selection of candidates much easier as we can quickly and accurately screen large pools of candidates selecting only those matching our specific criteria which allows much more time for the ever important candidate/recruiter interview. Technology, properly harnessed, will continue to make significant contributions to the recruitment process.
>
> (McKay, 1999)

The juxtaposition of interviewing and contract-offering creates a particular opportunity and challenge for those interviewers who are in the position to offer contracts on the spot. This is not the case in all schools, as a number of Heads have to refer the results of their interviews to their Boards, and it is only after referral has been made and discussed that formal contracts can be offered. The challenge is one that involves some ethical considerations, as Heads with good packages to offer and freedom of action as regards offering contracts may be tempted to 'pressure' candidates who are perceived to be among 'the best' just because so many schools appear to be interested in them! The major recruitment agencies go out of their way to state a clear code of ethical conduct for such situations.

Ideally, all recruiters and candidates would have as many initial interviews as they think desirable, and then proceed to more detailed and usually longer second and third interviews so that, on the last day of a Recruitment Fair, offers can be made and considered, accepted or rejected. In practice this creates great difficulties, as the recruiters are understandably anxious to close a deal with those candidates who are regarded as outstanding, but the candidates may not have had sufficient time or opportunity to meet with all the recruiters they would wish to see before they are effectively asked to make a choice. The scenario itself creates major pressures on time which could lead to a negative outcome just because there are not the opportunities for reflection and discussion that could apply to interviews in a national context.

Alan Travers, Placement Coordinator for the Queen's University, Kingston, Ontario, Faculty of Education, in Canada, after noting the importance of the preliminary screening work that is so essential before a candidate is seen, goes on to comment that, in his view, 'the edge in recruiting goes to those with the ability, both innate and cultivated, to listen to and "read" people. This intuitive sense can facilitate the optimum matching of teachers with the culture and needs of a particular school community' (Travers, 1999). This emphasis is reinforced by Jane Larsson, Director of Educational Staffing for International Schools Services (Princeton, USA), who writes: 'School Heads are interested in hiring the person first and the teacher second, when examining those who present themselves for overseas employment. Over and over again, we see personal qualities counting just as much as educational credentials in the selection process. Those most successful in making the transition to an overseas career are people who can take the unexpected in their stride, adjust to changing circumstances and enjoy the ride' (Larsson, 1999). Similarly, from the other side of the Atlantic we find Therese McNulty, Team Manager of CfBT (UK) writing: '... probably more importantly (than just appropriate qualifications and experience) are teachers who are flexible, adaptable, realistic and have a good sense of humour. International schools offer their own challenges, and teachers who have a "can do" attitude and can deal positively with the unexpected are always an asset to any organization' (McNulty, 2000).

Assuming that the recruiter can gain a clear picture of the academic stature and pedagogical expertise of the candidate, and in many cases this can be ascertained successfully through the preliminary screening process, what are likely to be those desirable personal qualities that will make all the difference? This will inevitably be different for different schools. One factor which can assist the recruiter in assessing these qualities will be a consideration of the likely motivation of the candidate. This can be relatively easily assessed by a careful scrutiny of the documentation and a few leading questions in the interview. The most likely determining influences on such motivation will be one or more of the following:

- personal, and often family, considerations affecting working in that particular city/school;
- the financial package, and especially the potential for saving;
- the location of the school and the likely lifestyle in that location, combined with the potential for travel in the country or the region;
- frustration and dissatisfaction as a result of working in a national system or another school;
- a temperament that is most comfortable with a lifestyle and professional focus that regards employment periods of more than two or three years as limiting of personal and professional development;

- the programme offered by the school's curriculum, especially through the International Baccalaureate; and
- the reputation of the school itself, or even of its Head.

The first five of these factors are potentially capable of having a negative impact on quality, but this is not necessarily the case. The notion that international school teachers should be primarily concerned to 'serve' would not appear to have much relevance now, but an undue focus on the 'package' should also lead to some reservations. Similarly, many parents and Board members appear to favour teachers who have a commitment to 'stay' and so apparently offer some stability, but this may well be more to do with their own 'guilt' feelings about always moving their children around, than a quality issue as such. The 'best' teachers in international schools will be those who, in addition to meeting all the screening requirements, also have the personality to deal with a wide range of practical and human challenges, and to work collegially with the rest of the staff. At the end of the interview the Head should have some confidence that the candidate will 'fit in'.

(c) The follow-up and settling-in or orientation phase

The orientation phase should be regarded as an important aspect of the overall recruitment process. Candidates may be elated by the prospect of a job in a potentially exciting location, but the initial euphoria can soon be dissipated if effective communications are not carefully maintained between the new recruit and the school. Speed and efficiency in concluding contract details are always important factors. General contacts with the school can now more easily be maintained by the use of e-mail, and by the regular updating of school Web pages. There is always a wide range of questions relating to the practicalities of living and of the curriculum. With a significant number of international school teachers only staying in one place for a two-year period (and some countries will not allow more than one-year contracts, although usually with the option of renewal), it is very important that the settling-in process is effectively accomplished as quickly as possible. Thus the follow-up and orientation programme plays a crucial part in determining not only the immediate effectiveness, but also the overall effectiveness, of such appointments.

Online recruitment of teachers in international education

All the major agencies now use the Internet for advertising vacancies and providing much more information about schools than it is possible to provide in a single page of one of the standard directories. Setting up communication links between a Head and potential candidates before a Recruitment Fair can be a very positive experience, and it is also possible for Heads to customize their reference requirements by using e-mail. There are also now some agencies that seek to operate entirely through the Internet. It is likely that this will be particularly advantageous for those schools that are not necessarily regarded as major attractions by teacher candidates. As Broman writes: 'Schools with less attractions will and must increasingly recruit outside and before the major Fairs; here their offers get accepted' (Broman, 1999).

It would be foolish to predict anything about the future role of the Internet for recruitment purposes. The Internet agencies are unlikely to be able to have the facilities to provide the rigorous screening that is perceived to have such an important role for the major traditional agencies, nor can they conveniently provide the crucially important face-to-face interview opportunities that take place at the Fairs. On the other hand it is true that a number of appointments are made as a result of telephone interviews, and there are increasingly sophisticated possibilities available through video-conferencing. Research into the 'success' of such appointments in comparison with those made through the more traditional methods would be helpful. The Internet can certainly, however, play a very important part in supporting the more traditional procedures and also, because of its speed and flexibility, offer a number of last-minute opportunities for schools and candidates, which may well have very positive outcomes.

Conclusion

The key to quality in the recruitment of teachers for international education would seem to be careful preparation, rigorous screening, sophisticated and effective recruiting techniques and positive follow-up and orientation procedures. High professional and pedagogical standards are axiomatic for quality teachers but, in international education especially, the ability to play as a full member of the 'team', to adapt to a range of different cultures, and to have at least some sense of adventure are also vital.

References

Bartlett, K (1998) International curricula: more or less important at the primary level?, in *International Education: Principles and practice*, eds M C Hayden and J J Thompson, Kogan Page, London

Blaney, J J (1991) The international school system, in *World Yearbook of Education 1991: International schools and international education*, eds P L Jonietz and D Harris, Kogan Page, London

Broman, F (1991) *Effective Strategies, Practices and Techniques in Recruiting Faculty for International Schools: A handbook*, Macmillan/McGraw-Hill International, New York

Broman, F (1999) Personal e-mail communication, 14 December

The Economist (1999) *The Economist,* Millennium Special Edition, January 1st 1000–December 31st 1999, p 94

Gummer, P (2000) Personal e-mail communication, 11 January

Hayden, M C and Thompson, J J (1995) International schools and international education: a relationship reviewed, *Oxford Review of Education,* **21** (3), 327–45

Larsson, J (1999) Personal e-mail communication, 14 December

McKay, J (1999) Personal e-mail communication, 15 December

McNulty, T (2000) Personal e-mail communication, 26 January

Skelton, M (1999) Personal e-mail communication, 23 December

Travers, A (1999) Personal e-mail communication, 22 December

Chapter 9

Professional development and reflective practice

William Powell

A basis in reflective practice

While few educators or policy makers would argue that planning for professional development is unimportant, and while considerable lip service is paid to teacher in-service education, the facts of the matter suggest a different picture. When student enrolment falls and the budget is stretched, professional development is one of the most likely targets for the financial pruning shears. The suggestion is clear – when hard priorities are assigned, professional development is often still perceived as a frill, as something outside and beyond the essential core activities of the school. Like most misperceptions, the vision of professional development as an add-on has numerous antecedents, among them the grand promise of an educational panacea and the admittedly poor track record of traditional models in effecting the improvement of instructional practices.

One is reminded of H L Mencken's caustic comment that there is 'no sure-cure so idiotic that some superintendent of schools will not swallow it. The aim seems to be to reduce the whole teaching process to a sort of automatic reaction, to discover some master formula that will not only take the place of competence and resourcefulness in the teacher, but will also create an artificial receptivity in the child' (in Postman, 1996).

In this chapter, I will argue for a reconceptualization of the purpose and structure of professional development, as a contribution to raising the quality of educational provision in international schools. I will describe some characteristics of effective professional development, and will offer some specific suggestions for activities that might be included in a professional development framework. I will also argue that the purpose behind an effective programme of professional development is to engender a school culture that encourages and celebrates the reflective practice of teachers.

Traditional professional development programmes have either taken place at universities during school holiday periods or have been comprised of imported experts who spend brief periods of time in schools in order to transmit knowledge and information to relatively passive recipients. For international schools these models are very expensive but, more importantly, neither importing experts nor sending teachers to conferences has shown itself to be particularly effective in improving instruction within the classroom (Sparks and Hirsh, 1997). Eisner (1998) points out that many times the outside experts decontextualize the in-service education and, as a result, weaken its potential usefulness: 'The assumption on which such in-service education is based seems to be that once teachers are exposed to such wisdom [from external experts], they will implement the practices suggested in their own classrooms. The situation is much like a voice coach giving advice to a singer whom he or she has never heard sing. One does not need to be a specialist in learning theory to know that for complex forms of human action, general advice is of limited utility. Feedback needs to be specific and focused on the actor in context.'

For the most part, and in some specific areas of training, the influence of outside experts in terms of effecting lasting school improvement often disappears as soon as they do. There are exceptions, and there are times when short-term, external consultants can be useful. However, the transmittal model of professional development, wherein the goal is simply the transfer of information or the acquisition of skills, has shown itself to be generally ineffective in promoting desired change in instructional practice (Sparks and Hirsh, 1997). From our experiences in the classroom as teachers, we know that mere transmittal of information is not the way in which conceptual understanding is constructed (Brooks and Brooks, 1993); nor is it influential in the development of positive learning attitudes and dispositions. Therefore, it is little wonder that this model has been only marginally successful in school reform. Ann Lieberman (1995, in Sparks and Hirsh, 1997) points out the ironic contradiction of the traditional, transmittal approach to professional development: 'What everyone appears to want for students (a wide array of learning opportunities that engage students in experiencing, creating, and solving real problems, using their own experiences, and working with others) is for some reason sometimes denied to teachers when they are learners.'

I am arguing for a broader vision of professional development that is not limited to a specific time, place or consultant, but rather pervades the entire life of the organization. The objective behind this broader vision of professional development is to build a culture of reflective teaching practice, so enhancing the quality of education provided within the school. Reflective practice is the hallmark of self-perpetuating quality instruction as it is not something that happens by imposition on teachers, but rather it represents the professional growth that teachers increasingly provide for themselves through collaborative reflection on teaching and learning.

Traditionally, teaching has been a very lonely profession. Someone once described schools as collections of highly educated professionals linked by a common parking lot. Teachers frequently have very little contact with other adults in the course of the school day and the resulting isolation makes it extremely difficult for teachers to learn about what they actually do in their classrooms when they teach. Caldwell (1999) perceives such isolation as incompatible with the new professionalism, and Eisner (1998) writes that 'classrooms, unlike the rooms in which ballerinas practice, have no mirrors'. While some schools have embraced collaboration and teaming, many teachers, perhaps even most, continue to teach behind closed doors in isolation from their colleagues. Professional isolation perpetuates professional ignorance. Without adult-to-adult reflective interaction it is almost impossible for a teacher to learn whether his or her class climate promotes risk taking, whether his or her use of humour is appreciated or whether he or she is asking too many low-level questions.

Reflective teaching is the practice of colleagues joining together to observe and analyse the consequences for student learning of different teaching behaviours and materials in order to gain insights that will result in the continuous evaluation and modification of pedagogy. We need to create in international schools an organizational structure that will make it possible for teachers to observe how colleagues teach. We need to mould and nurture a professional climate in our schools in which teachers learn how to observe and how to critique teaching.

Reflective teaching practice is essential to the inclusion of the diverse learners that we find within international schools because it:

- embraces a willingness to alter both content and practice in the pursuit of individual meaning;
- focuses on learning theory, cognitive psychology, developments in brain research and special education;
- provides a powerful framework for ongoing, fault-free assessment of pedagogy;
- relies upon the teacher developing knowledge about how specific students learn;
- depends on colleagues giving and receiving professional help; and
- models the metacognition we would want for our own students.

I find it difficult to conceive of reflective practice as a frill or a desirable, but dispensable, add-on. Roland Barth (1990) links the very survival of the profession of teaching to reflective practice: 'How can a profession survive, let alone flourish, when its members are cut off from each other and from the rich knowledge base upon which success and excellence depend? Not very well. Professional isolation stifles professional growth. There can be no community of learners when there is no community and when there are no learners.'

Characteristics of professional development programmes that improve the quality of classroom instruction

Effective professional development improves schools by supporting planned change. If this is the case, then the evaluation of professional development must be linked to school improvement. It is no longer acceptable to assess professional development activities on their respective popularity or entertainment value. The so-called feel good factor is simply not an acceptable instrument of evaluation. Staff development success will be judged not by how many teachers and administrators participate in staff development programmes or how they perceive its value, but by whether it alters instructional behaviour in a way that benefits students. The goal is improved performance by students, staff and the organization (Sparks and Hirsh, 1997).

In our work both at the International School of Tanganyika (IST) and with the Association of International Schools in Africa (AISA), we were able to identify five common characteristics of effective professional development that could be directly linked to school improvement. These are:

- a team approach;
- strong leadership and active administrative support;
- sustained focus;
- modelling what is to be achieved;
- keeping current.

A team approach

There are several important reasons why using a team structure in professional development is effective in generating positive change. First of all, professional opportunities that require collegial collaboration, such as Team Teaching or Cognitive Coaching, break down teacher isolation and create an expectation for reflective practice. We agree with Barth (1990) and with Costa and Garmston (1994) that insufficient attention has been given to the important relationship among adults within the school. Barth would place the development of collegiality at the top of the American national agenda of school improvement, because 'the relationships among adults in schools are the basis, the precondition, the *sine qua non* that allow, energize, and sustain all other attempts at school improvement. Unless adults talk with one another, observe one another, and help one another, very little will change.' For Barth, collegiality is the bedrock of reflective practice.

Needless to say, collegiality is a great deal more than teachers merely being pleasant to each other. Little (1981, in Barth 1990) offers an excellent definition of collegiality and shows explicitly how it serves as a cornerstone of reflective practice. She perceives collegiality as comprising four specific teacher behaviours, as follows:

- Teachers talk about teaching and these conversations are frequent, continuous, concrete and precise.
- Teachers observe each other engaged in the practice of teaching and administration.
- Teachers work on curriculum together, designing, researching and evaluating the substance of what is taught.
- Teachers teach each other what they know about teaching and learning. Craft knowledge is revealed, articulated and shared.

Collegiality does not just happen and teachers need to be trained in techniques of professional observation and in strategies for giving and receiving supportive, but also probing, feedback.

Second, there is something in schools that is profoundly resistant to change and to overcome the leviathan inertia, a critical mass of practitioners must come to share a vision and an enthusiasm for specific change. The critical mass does not need to be a majority; in fact the threshold can be a significant minority so long as it includes both formal and informal leadership. A team approach to professional development is often helpful in fostering this critical mass. A team approach can depart, on occasion, from conventional administrative wisdom. For example, concern for conserving our financial resources might result in us selecting only one individual to attend an external conference or workshop. The plan might be for the individual to collect the information, learn the knowledge and skills, and then return to the school to provide similar workshops for the colleagues who remained at home. The problem with this model is twofold. First of all, it is based on the transmittal model that simply treats professional development as the movement of information and the acquisition of skills. There is little emphasis on the development of relationships, attitudes and dispositions, all of which are necessary for significant change to occur. Secondly, a single individual, no matter how enthusiastic he or she may be upon returning to the school, cannot carry the heavy mantle of change responsibility in isolation.

An excellent example of a team approach to professional development was employed when the American International School of Lusaka (AISL) determined that it wanted to become more inclusive in meeting the needs of exceptional children. The Director and his administrative team did their research and located a school in a neighbouring country that had an established inclusion programme. A consultant from that school was requested under the AISA Consultant Pool Scheme who subsequently spent a week at AISL working with their teachers and administrators. Next, the Director sent four of his staff members, including an administrator, to spend a week at the school with the established inclusive programme. The visiting teachers were able to observe classes; study resources; discuss challenges and opportunities with special educators, class teachers and administrators; and engage in guided teaching practice with subsequent reflective debriefing sessions. The visitors were also able to reflect among themselves on what was and what was not appropriate and transferable to their own school in Lusaka. Through this collegiality and reflection a shared vision emerged for programme development at their own school.

Strong leadership and active administrative support

Strong leadership and active administrative support are not necessarily the same thing, but both are vital to the development of a culture of reflective practice. 'Effective professional learning assumes effective leadership to create the motivation and commitment to change and improve. It also involves intensive, sustained, theoretically-based yet practically-situated learning, with opportunities to observe good practice, to be involved in coaching and mentoring processes, and to take time for reflection' (Hill and Crevola, 1999).

Too often in the past strong leadership has been perceived as synonymous with either autocratic edicts or wily manipulation. Neither the former nor the latter equates with the strong leadership that produces reflective practice. Autocracy and manipulation create an organizational climate of fear and mistrust, which precludes the risk-taking that is inherent in giving and receiving collegial help. Effectively strong leaders do not follow established formulae for task accomplishment, but are careful diagnosticians, problem solvers and leaders of others in order to identify needs and create solutions (Joyce, Wolf and Calhoun, 1993). The purpose of strong leadership is to generate a collaborative and trusting community in which individuals join together to meet the needs of diverse students. The importance of administrative support is to a large extent self-evident. However, such support should not be seen as limited only to advocating with policy makers and providing material and financial and human resources. The symbolic leadership of the effective school principal or director cannot be underestimated as a change agent. Perhaps the most powerful reason for principals to be learners as well as leaders is the extraordinary influence of (their) modelling behaviour (Barth, 1990). It is the modelling behaviour of principals and directors that creates the implicit expectation for reflective practice. When administrators model learning in the workplace, they set a powerful public example for students and teachers to follow. They give a clear message that professional development is so important that there is room for it even in their own busy schedules.

The reflective administrator manages to keep the torch of change and innovation burning even in the face of challenges and frustrations. For example, the physical presence of the principal or school director at a mathematics or social studies workshop provides a clear and unambiguous message that the leadership values learning. A principal who reads and shares current research about pedagogy gives a straightforward message that in this school everyone is a learner. And adult learning is the essence of reflective practice.

Sustained focus

Too much educational reform and concomitant professional development has been of the smorgasbord kind in which schools have sampled a wide variety of innovations, have enjoyed the novelty, but have seen very little lasting change or improvement. Fullan (1991) writes that 'the greatest problem faced by school districts and schools is not resistance to innovation, but the fragmentation, overload and incoherence resulting from uncritical acceptance of too many different innovations'.

Change in schools tends to happen slowly. We know from both research and first-hand professional experience that new programmes take between two and three years to be established, but these are still very fragile entities. Such programmes easily wither on the vine when the leadership for the change initiative departs from the scene – regrettably, an all-too-common occurrence in international schools where relatively high staff turnover creates an ongoing lack of continuity.

We also know that new programmes take between three and five years to be institutionalized (ie self-perpetuating even following the departure of the original change agent). In addition, it may take between five and ten years for the core values of a new programme, such as the reflective practice, to become part and parcel of the ethos of the school. It is when such core values become embedded in the identity of the organization that a culture of adult learning can be said to be genuinely self-perpetuating, and the quality of the teaching process is enhanced.

Thus, the focus of professional development needs to be sustained over a significant period of time. Because of the length of time required to initiate and manage complex change in schools, I would argue for transforming annual goals into multi-year initiatives (perhaps three to five years in duration) with regular (annual or even bi-annual) assessment/progress reports.

Modelling what is to be achieved

Too many times schools fall foul of Ralph Waldo Emerson's adage that 'what you do speaks so loudly that no one can hear what you are saying' (in Eisner, 1998). If we want to produce articulate and literate critical thinkers, we need to be sure that we have teachers in classrooms who model those behaviours. If we want our students to become skilful problem solvers, we must provide the adult models for young people to emulate. 'When students work with adults who continue to view themselves as learners, who ask questions with which they themselves still grapple, who are willing and able to alter both content and practice in pursuit of meaning, and who treat students and their endeavours as works in progress, rather than finished productions, students are more likely to demonstrate these characteristics themselves' (Brooks and Brooks, 1993).

This same modelling of what we hope to achieve is equally important in the professional development of adults. I once attended a workshop entitled New Trends in Instructional Design. The person who led the workshop lectured virtually non-stop for over two hours, stressing the need for participatory and engaging lesson strategies, relevant project work and, above all, cooperative learning! In the transmittal model, excessive teacher talk and over-reliance on textbooks are employed almost exclusively in an attempt to cover vast content landscapes which, because there is no link to the student's prior knowledge, often lack relevance for the passive recipient. Rather than receiving knowledge from experts in isolated and fragmented training sessions, teachers and administrators need to be provided with opportunities to collaborate with colleagues in continuous, job-embedded reflection on learning and teaching. Effective professional development models what it hopes to achieve.

Keeping current

In the field of education, more is unknown than has yet been revealed. In the next decade or two, scientific breakthroughs in our knowledge about cognition, the significance of emotions for learning and the biology of how the brain works will almost certainly have a profound effect on the way in which we think about education. If this is true, the importance of staying current with developments in educational research and practice becomes axiomatic.

The historical isolation of some international schools, particularly those in remote locations in the developing world, is rapidly becoming a thing of the past. As fraught with problems as local telephone services may be, electronic mail and the Internet now provide almost instantaneous access to the latest educational research. Within only a few years, even the most remote and isolated international schools will be linked by the cyber-revolution.

But will schools avail themselves of this resource? Will teachers become widespread consumers of educational research simply because it is now easily available to them? I believe that the answer is probably no. Teacher aversion to much educational research is understandable. In the past, research was something undertaken, for the most part, in a laboratory or university, not in the classroom, and therefore the subsequent findings of such studies were seen by many to be not immediately relevant to the classroom practitioner. Some of the research was disorganized, some was used out of context for political ends, much was contradictory and almost all underwent rapid revision. In addition, much of the research has been born out of dissatisfaction with the educational status quo and implicitly or explicitly criticized what teachers were doing in their classrooms. Why should an overworked and stress-ridden teacher take time out of his or her already overcrowded day to read such research? It is a fair question with a disturbingly simple answer. We need to stay current with research because we do not have a choice. We simply do not have the answers to pressing questions. The current scope of our knowledge and understanding about learning and teaching can be likened to what a mid-20th-century mailman, bicycling his way through sleet and snow, could then envision about e-mail, the Internet and the other cyber marvels that we presently enjoy. Obviously not everyone can keep current with every development. That is not the point. The central issue is for school leaders visibly to show that current research is welcomed and valued. This demonstration of adult learning is an essential building block of reflective practice.

Some practical suggestions for a framework for professional development that supports reflective teaching

The following is a brief account of a range of approaches to the quality provision of professional development activities which have recently been implemented at the International School of Tanganyika (IST) in order to further a school culture that encouraged teachers to become reflective practitioners.

Cognitive Coaching

Developed by Costa and Garmston (1994), Cognitive Coaching is an intellectually stimulating framework for promoting and improving adult-to-adult reflective professional interaction. The principles upon which Cognitive Coaching is based are drawn from recent developments in learning theory, cognitive and social psychology, and research on how the brain works. Teachers are provided with training and practice in peer observation and with strategies that build rapport and enable them to give and receive non-threatening, but probing, feedback.

Individual reflective practices

Over the past decade, teachers at IST have been encouraged to engage in individual reflective practices such as keeping a professional journal or portfolio and periodically sharing selected contents with a trusted colleague. In 1996, the school formalized the expectation that all teachers would develop and maintain a professional portfolio. The initial reaction to this initiative was mixed, with a number of early problems attributable to a lack of clear guidance. During the second year, a working party of teachers and administrators was established which wrote definitions of crucial terms, developed a clear set of portfolio objectives and devised a recommended portfolio structure and format. A major milestone was reached when the working party defined the three dimensions of portfolios at IST as focus, organization and growth. 'Portfolios', the committee wrote, 'are focused and organized collections of artefacts that demonstrate the professional growth of the teacher or administrator.' It is worth dwelling for a moment on these three dimensions. It became abundantly clear that a portfolio was not a grab-bag assortment of classroom flotsam and jetsam. The teacher was responsible for selecting a focus for the portfolio. Some teachers targeted generic areas such as lesson pacing or checking for conceptual understanding, while others selected content-specific topics such as Using Graphing Calculators in the IB Mathematical Studies programme. Once the focus had been selected, the teacher then organized the artefacts in such a way as to demonstrate adult learning and professional growth. Portfolios that merely showcased a teacher's accomplishments did not meet the growth expectation.

After four years, a number of teachers were producing exemplary portfolios. (They tended to be the younger teachers who were already familiar with portfolios from their teacher training at university.) Some other teachers and administrators continued to go through the motions of portfolio development without engaging in significant or meaningful reflection. The most commonly cited impediment to the development of professional portfolios was a perceived lack of time. As Eisner (1998) writes: 'Efforts to encourage teachers to engage in reflective teaching are likely to be feckless if teachers have no time during the school day for reflection.'

Co-taught graduate level courses

It is fairly common to find American and British universities providing support on site for teachers in international schools to study graduate-level courses. However, at IST we perceived such a model as having a tendency to perpetuate the visiting expert syndrome that characterized the transmittal model of professional development and lacked the external feedback loops that serve to improve the quality of the programmes in both institutions (Lambert, 1998).

Our thinking was significantly influenced by Barth's (1990) excellent book *Improving Schools From Within*, particularly the chapter entitled 'Between School and University'. Barth criticizes most so-called university-to-school partnerships as not real partnership at all, but rather mono-directional transmittal of information from the university to the school. In this model the university is seen as the domain of theory and the schoolhouse the arena of practice, and Barth argues that 'to suggest that theory is the province of the university, as practice is of schools, sets up a caste system that, by anointing some, insults all of us'. In wrestling with the question of how schools and universities can become more genuinely collaborative, Barth proposes that 'a more promising means for academics to contribute to the improvement of schools is by helping school teachers and principals to clarify and to reveal their own rich thinking about good schools. Making craft knowledge visible dignifies and benefits the individual, other school people, and the schools themselves.' Barth challenges us to remove school teachers and university professors from the 'typecasting that so severely limits and strains our work together'.

In order to move in the direction of a more genuine partnership, IST entered into a relationship with The State University of New York College at Buffalo (Buffalo State). Buffalo State would send a visiting professor to IST to teach a graduate-level course and IST would provide a teacher volunteer who would co-plan and co-teach the course. The IST co-teacher would receive all course material and readings at least three months in advance and then the co-planning would proceed by e-mail. The professor would bring to the course a thorough grounding in relevant content and research, while the IST co-teacher would bring an intimate knowledge of our specific school environment and first-hand classroom experience. While the university-to-school partnership with Buffalo State is still in its infancy, the model appears to offer considerable promise.

Action research

In 1996, IST implemented a teacher action research programme. Such action research is designed to encourage teachers to collaborate with other teachers in order to undertake research in their own classrooms. The purpose of the project was to stimulate professional reflection by encouraging staff members to take on a more intellectual role in understanding and improving their own teaching practice.

In the IST Research Fellowship Programme teachers at the school can apply for fellowships to conduct research in their own classrooms and up to four are awarded each year. The fellowships carry with them financial support for the individual. The fellowship applications are screened by an Editorial Board of teaching and administrative colleagues against pre-determined criteria (quality, relevance, value to the school, international context, feasibility and originality). The approved Research Fellows are then assigned two coaches from the Editorial Board who provide support and guidance throughout the course of the project. More often than not the coaches had been through Costa and Garmston's Cognitive Coaching workshops. The Research Fellows are required to prepare a research report on their findings which is then edited for publication in IST's professional journal *Finding Our Voices: A Journal of Effective Teaching Practice*. Research projects varied enormously, ranging from a case study of an exceptional child in an inclusive elementary setting to an analysis of the emotional impact of expatriation in secondary school students to a full-blown, experimentally designed evaluation of a morphographic spelling programme. The Editorial Board has received increasing numbers of applications and each year the professional journal has grown in length, quality, number of contributors and readership.

Innovative teaching grants

IST also offered up to a maximum of 10 small, innovative teaching grants each year. The grants were offered to encourage, support and recognize creativity, imagination, research and appropriate risk-taking in the delivery of the educational programme in the classroom. Funds could be used for special materials, equipment, in-service activities and/or workshops. These small grants were a source of enormous creativity and produced outstanding results. For example, a fourth-grade class studied and then actually constructed the houses of different tribes in Tanzania and the entire seventh grade created an original opera company.

Professional Book Club

In order to promote the idea of teacher learning teams (Hill and Crevola, 1999), IST initiated a professional book club in which any teacher could purchase books related to the field of education at a significantly subsidized price. The only condition on the purchase was that the teacher agreed to join a discussion/study group of colleagues on that particular book. The uptake for the Professional Book Club was such that in the second year of its existence a request had to be made for increased funding.

Visits/consultancies to other schools

As one of the larger international schools in Africa, IST was often called upon to share its expertise with smaller schools in more remote locations. This sharing often took place under the AISA Consultant Pool Programme or the AISA Teachers-Helping-Teachers Scheme. The consultant services covered a broad range of topics including Early Childhood programme development, special education initiatives and writing specific content curricula. Each consultancy provided a rich opportunity for our teachers to gain distance from their daily work and to reflect upon both content and craft practice. The same holds true for having teachers serve on Visiting Accreditation Teams to other schools, a practice we openly encouraged at IST.

Publication of a professional journal

Elisabeth Wiig is fond of saying: 'If your thoughts are not in writing, they remain in the ether.' Eisner (1998) agrees:

> First it is important to recognize that there is nothing so slippery as a thought. The great articles and books I have written on my way to work or just before rising in the morning come and go with a flick of an eyelid. The process of externalization is a process of stabilization. Working with a form of representation provides the opportunity to stabilize what is ephemeral and fleeting. It gives students (and teachers) an opportunity to hold onto their thinking. This holding onto provides a second important benefit. Thoughts in one's head are difficult to edit, but thoughts on paper can be edited. Editing allows one to refine one's thinking, to make it clearer, more powerful, and, not least, to appreciate the happy results of creativity. It allows one to confer a personal signature to a public product.

Simply put, no professional development activity has as much potential for promoting reflection as writing. The business of translating the wonderful cacophony of our thoughts to crafted, clarified and refined prose and then sharing that writing through publication is professional development at its greatest maturity. At the same time, there is probably no activity in all the repertoire of adult learning that is as risky. (An excellent analysis of the obstacles and rewards of professional writing is contained in Barth's (1990) chapter entitled 'Practice to Prose'.) Nevertheless, the process of encouraging teacher reflective writing is manifestly worth the effort. The professional satisfaction that it brings, on both a personal and a professional level, is nothing short of transformational.

Initially as part of the Research Fellowship Programme, IST launched the publication of an annual journal of teachers' professional writing.

The journal was not limited to the research reports of the Fellows but also included other reflective and anecdotal pieces on craft practice and pedagogy. The response from the teachers was unequivocal. In the first year of publication, the Editorial Board received more submissions than it could publish and they have increased in each subsequent year. Even more exciting was the fact that most of the submissions were of a very high standard. It was as though a significant number of teachers had just been waiting for an opportunity to write and share their wealth of experience and insights. The journal is entitled *Finding Our Voices: A Journal of Effective Teaching Practice*, and it is distributed annually to international schools and educational organizations worldwide. Copies can be requested from The International School of Tanganyika Ltd, PO Box 2651, Dar es Salaam, Tanzania.

Conclusion

Traditional professional development programmes that rely solely upon the transmittal model have not always served international schools well. They can be expensive and have an inconsistent track record of bringing about lasting school improvement. Instead, effective teaching is nurtured where teachers are given opportunities for critical contemplation of their beliefs about content, their observations on instructional practice and their thoughts about learning itself. Quality adult learning flourishes when professional development is embedded in the daily collaborative interaction of colleagues, when there are continuous and meaningful conversations about learning and teaching; and when the responsibility and leadership for adult learning comes from the individuals most concerned, the teachers themselves.

References

Barth, R (1990) *Improving Schools from Within*, Jossey-Bass, San Francisco

Brooks, J G and Brooks, M G (1993) *The Case for Constructivist Classrooms*, Association for Supervision and Curriculum Development, Alexandria, VA

Caldwell, B J (1999) Education for the public good: strategic intentions for the 21st century, in *Preparing Our Schools for the 21st Century, ASCD Yearbook 1999*, Association for Supervision and Curriculum Development, Alexandria, VA

Costa, A L and Garmston, R J (1994) *Cognitive Coaching: A foundation for renaissance schools*, Christopher-Gordon Publishers, Norwood, MA

Eisner, E W (1998) *The Kind of Schools We Need: Personal essays*, Heinemann, Portsmouth, NH

Fullan, M (1991) *The New Meaning of Educational Change*, Teachers College Press, New York

Hill, P W and Crevola, C A (1999) The role of standards in educational reform for the 21st century, in *Preparing Our Schools for the 21st Century: ASCD Yearbook 1999*, Association for Supervision and Curriculum Development, Alexandria, VA

Joyce, B, Wolf, J and Calhoun, E (1993) *The Self-Renewing School*, Association for Supervision and Curriculum Development, Alexandria, VA

Lambert, L (1998) *Building Leadership Capacity in Schools*, Association for Supervision and Curriculum Development, Alexandria, VA

Lieberman, A (1995) Practices that support teacher development, *Phi Delta Kappan*, **76** (8), pp 591–96

Little, J W (1981) *School Success and Staff Development in Urban Desegregated Schools: A summary of recently completed research*, Center for Action Research, Boulder CO

Postman, N (1996) *The End of Education: Redefining the value of school*, Vintage Press, New York

Sparks, D and Hirsh, S (1997) *A New Vision for Staff Development*, Association for Supervision and Curriculum Development, Alexandria, VA

Chapter 10

The role of women in senior management in international schools

Carol Thearle

The statement that women are under-represented in senior management positions in international schools is rarely greeted with surprise. The response varies from a resigned 'What's new?' to a diatribe on the unfairness of the structure of society. Neither of these responses is particularly helpful, and I believe that those of us who are involved in international education should be examining this issue and addressing it in practical ways. Much work has been done in 'internationalizing the curriculum' and creating an atmosphere of intercultural awareness in our schools, but we still offer our students and our colleagues stereotypical role models in terms of who runs the organizations. The creation of a predominantly female management team in an international school still causes more eyebrows to be raised than does the creation of an all male team: this in spite of the fact that more than 60 per cent of the workforce in international schools is female (ECIS, 1997).

Under-representation of women in school senior management positions

The evidence that women are under-represented in senior management positions in schools within national systems throughout the world is overwhelming (Ozga, 1993; Strachan, 1993; Taylor, 1995): 'It is well documented that women are under represented in senior management in all areas of work. In education, women are over represented at the levels where status, power and salaries are lower' (Freeman, 1993).

Most of the research in this field has been concentrated on studies of women in national school or university systems. Shirley Randell addressed the issue of women in senior management positions in schools in Australia:

In 1983 Chapman (1984) undertook two major studies in relation to Australian school principals which provided benchmark data on the personal and professional characteristics of principals, and detailed information on the procedures adopted in principal selection. The data showed that only 23 per cent of Australian school principals were women. Women were least likely to be principals in government schools: only 15 per cent in primary, 9 per cent in secondary and 7 per cent in schools combining both primary and secondary levels.

(Randell, 1991)

Although the situation in international schools is better balanced than in national systems, women are, nonetheless, seriously under-represented in senior management. The European Council of International Schools (ECIS) *Statistical Survey 1997* included, for the first time, data regarding the sex of both teachers and senior administrators: 'The survey showed that women accounted for 66% of all full- and part-time teaching posts and, of a total of 1,242 senior administrators, 43% were women. However, only 20% women held the most senior position in a school – that of Director/Head.'

The literature concerning national systems, higher education and management in areas of work other than education identifies three significant areas for women:

- career paths;
- mentors, role models and networking;
- domestic responsibilities and support.

Each of these I will consider in more detail below.

Career paths

In his research concerning teachers returning to the United Kingdom after a period of employment overseas, David Black pointed out that the career paths of women teachers, particularly those who took time out to have children, were referred to in much of the literature as 'deviant'

(Black, 1995; Black and Scott, 1997). This confirmed Randell's (1991) suggestion that 'broken career paths and family leave are frequently described as barriers to women's progress'.

According to Rosemary Grant (in Acker, 1989), gender differences were ignored in early research into teachers' careers unless it was to explain them in terms of women's deficiencies. In tracing the history of research into the career structure of teachers, Grant commented that early studies suggested that:

- career disadvantage was particularly evident for women in primary schools;
- men applied for more jobs and were more persistent in their applications;
- women have been found frequently to perceive themselves to be disadvantaged on account of their sex.

She went on to say that: 'In comparing the career patterns of women with those of men there is a danger of presenting men's experiences as the norm against which, correspondingly, women's experiences are defined as deviant.'

Through interviews with practising deputies in a city in the north of England, Grant (1989) set about constructing an alternative concept of 'career' which 'fits more readily with the realities of women's lives'. She rejected Lyons' description of the career-oriented teacher as one who is 'single-mindedly purposeful in the pursuit of career goals', which she found to be inappropriate. Grant's interviewees achieved their success in spite of the traditional constraints of family and other domestic responsibilities and without a definite career plan.

McGrath (1992) suggested that 'lack of qualifications' was a reason often given for women not being successful candidates for senior positions, and that one desirable qualification often seems to be a track record of successively more responsible management positions, commenting that: 'Women have not been aware of this, nor have they known which career paths lead upwards as opposed to those which are dead-end.' McGrath went on to say that: 'Women who do achieve top level positions have career paths that resemble those of males.'

My own experience suggests that, in general, women in international education do not have a long-term career plan. I have moved from country to country during the past 20 years, sometimes taking a sideways move in terms of seniority, but to larger schools where there might be opportunities for promotion. Job applications have often been the result of expediency rather than planning. As opportunities arose I considered whether or not I could (and wanted to) do the job, rather than whether or not this would be an appropriate step up the career ladder. This experience reinforces Coleman's (1996) findings in a study of female Headteachers that: 'All five of the Headteachers interviewed had developed career plans as their careers progressed, rather than aiming for a Headship from the start.'

Mollie Roach, when writing from the perspective of a Secondary Deputy Head (in Ozga, 1993) began her contribution as follows: 'Analysing my career for the purpose of this book, I am forced to realize that much of what has happened has been reactive and unplanned. In retrospect I realize that there has been, over the years, a gradual strengthening of purpose and resolve, but perhaps this too has been reactive, in that ambition – always a powerful motivator – has been strengthened and reinforced by increasing success and job satisfaction.'

There has also been the notion, referred to by Albino (1992), that having a career strategy was considered by women somehow to be cheating and that 'men admire strategy, but women perceive it as shady business', although such a perception may be more of a stereotypical myth than actually based on research.

Conclusions drawn from the literature are that most women do not plan their careers carefully, and that most career progress is largely opportunistic. My own research findings (Thearle, 1998) indicate that the situation for women involved in international education is no different. They do not embark on their international teaching careers with a view to making steady upward progress until they achieve senior management positions. Rather, they tend to change jobs as opportunities arise and as their circumstances or interests change.

Mentors, role models and networking

According to Burke and McKeen (in Davidson and Burke, 1994), organizational support for aspiring managers could include the setting up of a mentoring system. They reported that the careers literature suggested that while mentors played a crucial role in the career development and success of both men and women, they might be even more critical for women. However, the evidence indicated that women had access to a smaller supply of available mentors than men: 'Women may have trouble finding mentors because they are different from men in senior positions, they occupy a token status and there may be potential discomfort in cross gender relationships.'

In the same collection of papers, Parker and Fagenson (1994) revealed evidence which contradicted this stance and argued that research into women in corporate management showed that 'people who are protégés of powerful people secure more promotions and power themselves, have greater job mobility, recognition, satisfaction, and easier access to powerful individuals than do non-protégés, and that women become protégés at the same rate as men. At the same time, women perceive that they face greater barriers to obtaining mentors.'

Adler, Laney and Packer (1993) supported the notion that one way to get to the top was with the support of mentors. However, they suggested that this was a concept alien to many women. The women in their study had differing views on the role of mentors, although they did talk about the importance of friendship from other women and support from men. Three out of the five women whose responses formed the basis of the study referred to the fact that they had been encouraged and been given guidance by influential individuals who could have been described as mentors, although 'Unfortunately for women, mentors tend to choose protégés who are like themselves, so men choose men.'

Burke and McKeen (1994) also suggested that, as well as their role in encouraging career success, mentors may have had a special role in enabling women to deal with work-related stress by improving their confidence and self-esteem. This was particularly the case in a female–female mentoring relationship because female mentors could more easily relate to the stresses that young women faced in terms of stereotyping, discrimination and the balancing of family and career.

One of the functions of a mentor is that he or she can be instrumental in helping the protégé gain access to the formal and informal network of power relations within the organization or professional associations. Hall (1996) identified two roles which mentors could fulfil, both of which were influenced by the fact that in most secondary schools the mentor is likely to be male: 'First, mentors may act as a guide to an unfamiliar male dominated organization culture. Secondly they provide sponsorship and legitimate access to power.'

According to Hall (1996) the exclusion of women from 'old boy' networks has largely deprived them of mentors and, although the individuals in her study exploited the opportunities afforded by their career moves, their use of networks of any kind was limited. However, all of them described a variety of role models as having had an influence on their work behaviour, either positive or negative: 'From a Head who refused to delegate and rarely encouraged, she learned what she did not want to do when she became a Head herself.'

Perry and Sedgwick in Ozga (1993) referred to the importance of female role models. Perry, who was Director of a polytechnic at the time of the study, emphasized the importance of women in positions such as hers being role models for other women: 'I... do not believe that any woman should take men as role models. It is vitally important for future generations of women that those of us who have taken on senior roles occupy them in ways that provide female role models.'

According to Parker and Fagenson (in Davidson and Burke, 1994) many studies have indicated that women had been largely excluded from networks which included those who had traditionally held power in an organization. This perception was confirmed by Adler, Laney and Packer (1993), who found that 'When men create networks these often exclude women – the "locker room syndrome".'

Although women can successfully form their own networks, these do not necessarily afford women the same visibility and access to the power bases that the traditional 'old boy' networks afford to men. Such exclusion has tended to perpetuate male customs and traditions and negative attitudes towards women. Burke and McKeen (in Davidson and Burke, 1994) cite Ibarra's study in which women's networks were found to be differentiated. Their female networks provided social support, while 'instrumental access' was sought from men. Burke and McKeen conclude that 'Managerial and professional women are still less inte-grated with important organizational networks, and it is these internal networks that influence critical human resource decisions such as promotion and acceptance.'

Much of the literature suggests that, for women, the importance of mentors lies in the support they can give in enhancing self-esteem (Burke and McKeen, 1994). The evidence I have gathered for my own research in the context of international schools has supported this perception. The women I interviewed spoke of individuals who encouraged them to look beyond their immediate circumstances and made them aware that they were capable of greater responsibility than they had envisaged; this gave them the confidence to take positions that they might otherwise have deemed beyond their reach. Professional role models tend to be of either sex, but personal role models are likely to be female, although not exclusively so. Such relationships often start as professional and then move to the personal.

The exclusion of women from organizational networks cited in the literature surveyed was also confirmed by my own research. One of the ways in which individuals can develop networks is by attending confer-ences or workshops such as those run by the European Council of International Schools (ECIS) and the International Baccalaureate Organization (IBO). Although a large number of women included in my study agreed that attendance at such events gave them an oppor-tunity to meet new people, very few women saw this as a benefit in making contacts that could be instrumental in their promotion.

Domestic responsibilities and support

Randell (1991) found that, for women, there was incompatibility between career progress and domestic responsibilities. Not only were they expected to put family commitments ahead of their careers, these responsibilities were not valued by institutions which see 'time out for child rearing as divorced from the workforce rather than contributing to experience'. Even as recently as the early 1970s, Randell points out, pregnant academics were being fired by Flinders University in Australia.

According to Lewis (1994) research indicates that while there is a greater tendency for women than men in management positions to be single, when women are married or in long-term relationships they are much more likely to have partners with professional or management careers. While both men and women in dual-career partnerships confront the issues of management of two careers and family life, the impact is greater on the women's careers than on the men's. Lewis points out that, in spite of women's increased involvement in paid work, management of the household still seems to be viewed largely as a female responsibility, even in relationships with modern ideologies and in countries with a commitment to gender equality at home and at work. Even when dual-career couples move towards an equitable allocation of tasks and responsibilities, men are more likely to share in the performance of domestic tasks rather than in managing the household. This view is supported by the findings of Adler, Laney and Packer (1993), who reported in relation to women interviewed in their study that 'A few mentioned caring male partners who took some responsibility for childcare but it was clear that childcare is still regarded as primarily a woman's issue.' Such extra responsibilities for women 'can create role conflict and overload and can spill over to affect a woman's experience of work, reducing the satisfaction and achievement in their careers' (Lewis, 1994).

The maintenance of traditional roles may be due in part to women's low expectations of their partners to contribute on the domestic front. As a result, male contributions may be overvalued. My own father, for example, washes the dishes every night after supper and is lavishly praised by my mother, both in public and in private, for this one instance of domestic activity. Lewis (1994) also suggested that, in some cultures, men are considered inept at domestic work. Although such a situation implies dependence of men upon women, it can be socially acceptable for men to be dependent on women for domestic services.

Parenthood brings further pressures to men as well as women, but because of the way society is constructed, the impact of parenthood on a career is greater for most women than it is for most men, as Lewis points out: 'In the UK, the return to employment after maternity leave is socially constructed as a choice, even in the context of economic need.'

Having 'chosen' to carry the dual burden of motherhood and career, many women are faced with the necessity of changing their work patterns to fit in with their family responsibilities, often at considerable cost to their career advancement. In addition, it is sometimes assumed that a woman's attachment to her career will decline with motherhood, resulting in her being faced with identity dilemmas and difficult career decisions.

Al-Khalifa (1992) suggests that the dual role that women have had to face has deterred some of them from applying for senior positions. The balancing of different roles and expectations is achieved through considerable organizational expertise but is also experienced as a source of pressure. Classroom teaching and curriculum-linked posts offer a degree of flexibility in terms of time management which can accommodate the different demands on a working mother's time, but this contrasts with the perception of greater inflexibility and restrictiveness associated with management responsibilities. The existence of such a tension is supported to some extent by the findings of Adler, Laney and Packer (1993), who point out that 'The pressure of working in education places women in a position where they are forced to devote more and more time to the job. ... It is ironic that teaching, seen as a "good" job for working mothers, demands extremely long hours.'

In a study of seven female educational managers in Trinidad and Tobago, Morris (1993) found that the women who had families were able to pursue further studies or succeed in management positions because of domestic support given by husbands, friends or neighbours. In two cases, mobility was possible because husbands had bought cars, and in another case a neighbour stepped in to look after a child with special needs. Although the women interviewed did not believe that marriage and family responsibilities had seriously hindered their careers, clearly such levels of support had eased their domestic responsibilities. Strachan (1993) found in her research when interviewing women in New Zealand that there was an interweaving of their family and working lives such that the two were inseparable. She found that these women's experiences were supported by other studies carried out in New Zealand (Neville, 1988 in Strachan, 1993) in that professionally successful women were either single or had a very supportive partner. In her examination of barriers to career progress for women, Coleman

(1996) found that each of the Headteachers she interviewed had domestic arrangements that reflected a partnership rather than the stereotypical approach to household management and child care. Coleman went on to cite Ruijs (1993), who suggests that, for most women, the choice of a management position means choosing not to have a family. Finally, Coleman quoted Acker (1994), who argued that 'For family-career conflicts, a helpful partner, clever manoeuvring, luck and money might provide a nanny or other solution. But... these are individual solutions and not open to all. One woman finds a way, but the same problem is there for the next.'

Almost all the women who were the subjects of my own research were responsible for the management of their households, whether or not they had a partner. In order for the women to pursue their careers effectively, the domestic tasks were either shared (with a partner) or taken over by hired help. My findings confirmed the evidence cited in the literature that working women are expected to occupy the dual role of worker and household manager.

The next steps

It is clear from the literature reviewed, and from my own personal observation, that there is a need to find ways in which women can play a greater role in the management of international schools. If, as I believe, there are many women who are potentially capable of performing effectively at senior management level in the international school context, then a higher proportion of female senior managers in evidence will act as encouragement to those women who initially lack confidence in their own abilities – a lack of confidence which can only be exacerbated by any implication that only men can operate effectively in such positions. In terms of issues of quality in the context of international education we have also, I believe, a responsibility as international educators to provide positive female – as well as male – role models for all our students. What price the explicit spoken and written commitment to equality of opportunity for men and women espoused in the majority of international schools worldwide if the 'hidden curriculum' operating within the school perpetuates a perception that such equality of opportunity is a phenomenon that applies only up to middle-management level?

One of the routes through which the appointment of a higher proportion of female senior managers can be encouraged is recruitment. Recruitment for international schools is often through the 'job fairs' organized in the UK, the USA, the Far East and elsewhere by organizations such as the European Council for International Schools (ECIS) and Search Associates. Administrators from international schools sometimes travel from fair to fair during the recruiting season in order to fill their schools' staffing needs for the coming academic year. Although Chief Executive Officers are generally not recruited in this way, some senior positions such as Assistant Principal or Head of Section, as well as the majority of teaching positions, are certainly filled as a result of attendance at a recruitment fair. Having attended three such recruitment fairs (two as a candidate and one as a recruiter), and having heard colleagues' comments on their return from such fairs, it seems to me that this system might discriminate against women. Securing interviews is often a competitive and public process; it can involve standing in line for some time and then persuading the recruiter that you are worth interviewing, while being conscious all the time that he or she has only a limited number of time slots available in which interviews can be conducted. Attendance necessitates at least four days away from home and school, meaning that arrangements have to be made, not only for classes to be covered, but also for children to be cared for. It would be interesting to know what proportion of candidates at these fairs are women, and what their success rate is, particularly in terms of securing posts that might lead them eventually to senior management positions.

Every year there are a number of conferences organized specifically for international educators by organizations such as ECIS and the International Baccalaureate Organisation (IBO). It would be interesting to see if the attendance at such conferences reflects the make-up of the workforce in international schools, and to establish the reasons for teachers' attendance (or non-attendance) at such events. A quick look at the participants list for recent IB Middle Years Programme workshops revealed that about 50 per cent were women. However, the list of presenters indicates that the *minority* of these are women.

The International Baccalaureate Organisation has become increasingly conscious of the need to widen its cultural base in order truly to 'internationalize' the curriculum. In its search for representatives of different cultures to serve on various committees, it also seems to have taken the opportunity actively to seek out women for this purpose. In addition, several key positions at the IBO's Curriculum and Assessment Centre in Cardiff have gone to women who are outstanding in their fields. If this is a deliberate policy, rather than a fortuitous accident, it would be encouraging if the IBO would publish and disseminate the policy to member schools.

Women themselves should be encouraged by senior colleagues to seek out advisers to help them with career planning, and career-planning sessions could be made available at some of the large professional conferences run by organizations such as ECIS. Finally, if women are to play a significant role in the management of international schools, they must find ways of helping themselves and each other. They must use the new technologies to create their networks and support systems. They must share domestic responsibilities without experiencing accompanying guilt. Most importantly, they must be visible!

References

Acker, S (ed) (1989) *Teachers, Gender and Careers*, Falmer Press, Lewes
Adler, S, Laney, J and Packer, M (1993) *Managing Women*, Open University Press, Buckingham
Albino, J E (1992) Strategy: the dirty word that women must learn, *Educational Record*, Spring
Al-Khalifa, E (1992) Management by halves: women teachers and school management, in *Managing Change in Education*, eds N Bennett, M Crawford and C Riches, Paul Chapman Publishing, London
Black, D R (1995) *Factors Affecting the Employment of Teachers Returning to the United Kingdom after Teaching Abroad*, unpublished MPhil thesis, University of Bath
Black, D R and Scott, W A H S (1997) Factors affecting the employment of teachers returning to the United Kingdom after teaching abroad, *Educational Research*, **39** (1), pp 37–63
Burke, R and McKeen, C (1994) Career development among managerial and professional women, in *Women in Management*, eds M J Davidson and R J Burke, Paul Chapman Publishing, London
Coleman, M (1996) Barriers to career progress for women in education: the perceptions of female headteachers, *Educational Research*, **38** (3), pp 317–32
Davidson, M J and Burke, R J (1994) *Women in Management*, Paul Chapman Publishing, London
ECIS (1997) *Statistical Survey 1997*, ECIS, Petersfield
Freeman, A (1993) Behind every successful woman is a man who's amazed: ambition and stress, *Educational Change and Development*, **14** (1)
Grant, R (1989) Women teachers' career pathways: towards an alternative model of 'career', in *Teachers, Gender and Careers*, ed S Acker, Falmer Press, Lewes
Hall, V (1996) *Dancing on the Ceiling*, Paul Chapman Publishing, London
Lewis, S (1994) Role tensions and dual career couples, in *Women in Management*, eds M J Davidson and R J Burke, Paul Chapman Publishing, London
McGrath, S T (1992) Here come the women, *Educational Leadership*, February
Morris, J (1993) Women and educational management: a Trinidad and Tobago perspective, *British Educational Research Journal*, **19** (4), pp 343–56
Ozga, J (ed) (1993) *Women in Educational Management*, Open University Press, Buckingham
Parker, B and Fagenson, E (1994) An introductory overview to women in corporate management, in *Women in Management*, eds M J Davidson and R J Burke, Paul Chapman Publishing, London

Randell, S (1991) *Not Advancing Equally: Women in educational management in Australia*, The Council of Adult Education, Melbourne

Strachan, J (1993) Including the personal and the professional: researching women in educational leadership, *Gender and Education*, **5** (1), pp 71–80

Taylor, A (1995) Glass ceilings and stone walls: employment equity for women in Ontario school boards, *Gender and Education*, **7** (2), pp 123–41

Thearle, C D (1998) *Women in Senior Management Positions in International Schools*, unpublished MA in Education dissertation, University of Bath

Chapter 11

The international school and its community: think globally, interact locally

Keith Allen

Schools and communities

Some years ago, I worked in a school in Latin America situated in a walled paradise of leafy luxury with armed security guards separating it from the economically impoverished *pueblo* outside. Students were bussed in from affluent suburbs. What signal does this give about the school? Certainly not one of relating to the local community – except in the very narrow sense of the cluster of grandiose mansions within the walled village. Such separation is far from unique. Mitchell (1989) points out that the architecture and location of schools often reveal their original attitude to the community. He states that many schools are like 'monasteries, mansions and prisons: institutions designed to keep safely separate the dedicated, the privileged or the vicious'. Now, writing this chapter in Oxford, I cannot help but match this view with the cloistered tradition of several of the older colleges that were constructed specifi-cally to reinforce the separation of town and gown.

Such a picture, though, is far from uniform. Thailand has seen a boom in the construction of new international schools in the 1990s. Some have incorporated wonderful architectural features that reflect the culture of the host country and are 'open' in their design, while others have taken a different direction. One has buildings that proudly mimic a private school in south London, another's architecture is strongly redolent of a leading

THE INTERNATIONAL SCHOOL AND ITS COMMUNITY   125

Australian school. Both are proclaiming their 'foreignness' and, in doing so, promote the idea of difference rather than communality.

Moving from architecture to attitudes, Bush (1999) argues that, before the 1990s, 'it was rare for schools, in particular, to accord centrality to relationships with bodies and individuals beyond the boundary', although he does acknowledge a growing recognition of the importance of the external dimensions of school management during the past decade. Other authors have suggested that schools have historically been related in some way to the local community. McDill and Rigsby (1973) note that 'external values affect the culture of the school, shaping what goes on inside'. They go on to refer to research linking the orientation of the community to student performance, although they relate the concept of 'community' more to the sector that produces their student enrolment than to the wider community.

I would suggest that schools have frequently been aware of the community around them, but their reactions to these communities have been (and continue to be) far from uniform. Some have developed barriers, whether structural or cultural, to preserve their airy academia or to retain their sense of privilege; a few have embraced the local community with open arms. Many, however, have taken a stance some-where in the middle of these two approaches, being attentive to market forces from outside, but seeing education as a process distinct from the business of the community. Overall, there is a suggestion that schools are becoming increasingly aware of the need to build links with their communities. This raises the question of what we mean by 'community' and what the nature of those links might be.

Traditional views of the community refer to the 'commonality' found within it. Dewey (1916), for example, stated that people live in communities because of the things that they have in common: 'aims, beliefs, aspirations, knowledge, a common understanding, and likemindedness'. More recent analyses have been less simplistic and acknowledged the diversity within 'community'. Others have stressed the importance of interactions. Eggleston (1967) states that the traditional concept of community has been replaced by association: 'a complex network of contractual agreements or collaborations for specific tasks in modern industrial societies'. Thus, the community can be viewed as a network of reciprocal social relationships within a complex, diverse and changing collection of individuals and interests.

Schools as communities

If communities are presented in this organic manner, what of schools?

Interestingly, a comparable concept of international schools is suggested by Jim Cambridge (1998). He presents schools as 'open systems'. Like living organisms, they take in raw materials, process them and have recognizable outputs. Also, like living entities, schools interact in multiple ways with their environment. Cambridge argues that the barriers between each organization and its surrounding environment are permeable and permit a dynamic, two-way exchange. Finally, Cambridge argues that the internal and external actions of international schools, like organisms, are regulated by feedback loops to make them adaptive. The model is appealing. Cambridge goes on to emphasize further the nature of the relationships between international schools and their local communities, as follows:

> International schools are organizations located within communities of stake-holders and others with diverse interests that may be in competition. The students and their parents, and the teaching staff, may come from a number of different countries and, depending on the school and its location, there may be either intimate or distant relations with the host country community... The school will be profoundly influenced – either positively or negatively – by the host environment within which it operates.

With communities that are diverse, dynamic and pluralistic, and schools that are equally diverse but adaptive to their environment, it is not surprising that mapping out the links between school and community is far from simple. In attempting to do so, Bush (1999) lists five varieties of relationship: formal, funding, client, inspection and community relationships. In the context of international schools and local communities, and quality issues relating to their interaction, client and community relationships are of greatest importance and will be discussed further.

In addition to links between school and a number of different constituencies, another variable to be considered is the intensity of the relationship between the school and the constituency. Skrimshire (1981) identifies three broad categories of local community links. In the first, a school typically develops home–school links or encourages community use of facilities when not required by the school. The second category is when parents and other adults come into the school to help in either the educational process or its management, or school facilities (such as the library and canteen) are made available to the community throughout the school day. The third requires the totality of school-based enterprises to be planned and coordinated in a way that maximizes the school's contribution to improving the quality of life in the community.

A third dimension is the purpose of the links. While Martin (1987) recognizes that many schools are motivated to build school–community links for market reasons, he argues that the development of links should be motivated by educational rather than economic imperatives. In reality, the motivation for linkage is likely to be a combination of educational reasons, economic drivers and ethical considerations. In analysing the practice in UK national schools, Martin identified different models of practice in school–community links. Three are relevant here:

- Community service model: in this model the school provides resources to meet local needs. In return, educational benefits are reaped by the school.
- Awareness-raising model: the school acts as a catalyst for community involvement through classroom analysis of key issues within the community.
- Ideological approach model: the school develops, as part of its mission, social action designed to change the community.

Effective schools have organizational characteristics that are fed by a particular culture. This culture influences the behaviour of the 'administration', teachers and students. It affects the perceptions of the community and the confidence of the parents. It also determines the school's links with its community (Bell, 1988). For international schools, there are economic, educational and ethical issues associated with the range of relationships, their intensity and their purpose. However, the organic nature of both the school and its community serve to warn us about generalizations. Furthermore, we are reminded that the body of international schools is a 'conglomeration of individual institutions which may or may not share an underlying philosophy' (Hayden and Thompson, 1995a). If we also recall that international schools operate within very different host cultures, it is clear that there is no single path. Nevertheless, some issues will be explored further in this chapter. On a number of occasions, I will refer to developments at the New International School of Thailand (NIST), which was founded in 1992 with community links at the heart of its philosophy.

Client relationships: students

Although some schools may bristle at the concept of 'clients' or 'consumers', the use of the terms here is not an indication of the primacy of market forces, but rather represents the sectors of the community that are in the most intimate relationship with the school without being employed by it. The key players are students and their parents.

Typically, international schools have students from a diverse range of cultures and, apart from in the case of the small proportion of residential (boarding) schools, these students are from the local community. The nature of this intake is one of the features that distinguishes international schools from their national counterparts. In fact, Michael Matthews (1989a) argued that neither the pedagogy nor the curriculum of most international schools is particularly unusual. In contrast, it is the student body that *is* distinctive. Matthews went on to categorize the student body into three sub-groups:

- expatriates who are native speakers of the language of instruction (normally, but not exclusively, English);
- expatriates who are not native speakers of the language of instruction, but want to learn it; and
- local students who want to learn the language of instruction, *or* who are attracted by the prestige of an international school, *or* who do not fit into the local system.

Some may debate whether expatriate families should be considered as part of the 'local community'. The division of 'expatriate' from 'local' is far from clear. Pollock (1998) identified four categories of 'expatriates', which he described as follows:

- Look like host – think like host (strong physical and cultural similarities).
- Look different – think like host (cultural similarities, but physically different).
- Look like host – think differently (physical similarities, but culturally different).
- Look different – think differently (distinctive in all manners).

It clearly does not help to think of expatriates as a single group. More helpfully, they can be considered to fit on a scale related to the extent to which they are distinct from the host community. This scale intermeshes with the length of time they have lived in the country and their cross-cultural skills. Even characteristics such as 'nationality' are far from distinct. Many individuals are bicultural or have multiple nationality. Evidently, 'globalization of culture is not the same as homogenization' (Willis, Enloe and Minoura, 1994).

Catering for the needs to which this diversity gives rise is not a simple task. Schools that define themselves as British, French or American may choose to continue to provide a British, French or American culture abroad, or they may 'abjure national identity' and develop a culture which clearly demonstrates each individual's value (Pearce, 1998). Fully international schools will, hopefully, already have structures in place to minimize the influence of any one culture over others.

But what about host country nationals? Matthews' suggestions as to why they attend international schools are echoed by Pearce (1998). Through attending 'the local American, British, French, or international school', children in less-developed countries may gain access either to the economies of more-developed countries or to the socio-economic elite of their nation. But, as Wilkinson (1998) points out, students from less-developed nations can find access to an international school impossible unless they are *already* part of the socio-economic elite. This suggests that international schools are often reinforcing the stratification of the host-country by accepting host nationals. Is this what they want? It is arguable that the host-country elite have encouraged the opening of international schools to accept host nationals so that they can maintain their distance from the majority of the population and gain further advantages for their children. I suspect, however, that such a stance sits awkwardly with the philosophies of many international schools. At NIST, it was perhaps inevitable that our host-country students were disproportionately from sectors of Thai society that were separated culturally (such as the Thai Indian population) and/or economically from the majority of the population. In discussions with Thai parents it was clear that they saw an international school as reinforcing privilege, even though many of our other aims were developed in order to try to 'level the playing-field'.

This relationship with the host nation presents a dilemma for those international schools that have 'inclusive' missions and are, ostensibly, 'open to all constituencies' (Sylvester, 1998). They *want* host nationals to attend, just as they want to extend the best qualities of international education as widely as possible. They are aware, however, that in providing access for host nationals they are encouraging non-inclusivity within the host community and are reinforcing socio-economic strata. Wilkinson (1998) suggests that one solution to such a dilemma is through the provision of scholarships, but this can be a difficult path to take.

A second issue relates to the proportion of host nationals in the school. Having a school with a large proportion of host-country nationals raises specific problems: expatriates, for instance, could view the school as 'local' rather than 'international'. There are also educational implications. Large proportions of any cultural or linguistic group affect the operation of the school. A school that proclaims itself to be 'British' and has a significant proportion of UK citizens may be fine. But for an 'international' school to have a bias towards one group is problematic. As Pearce (1998) points out, the result can be 'an institution whose ethos contrasts with its operating system'.

What proportion of the student population of an international school should be from the host culture? The United World Colleges aim specifically for about 25 per cent of their student body to represent the host nation (Wilkinson, 1998), and at NIST we had the same target figure. I know of schools with much higher proportions (up to 90 per cent) and they found it hard to attract expatriates. On the other hand, I also know of several schools with lower 'quotas'. In many cases, these seem hard to justify as the schools enrolled high proportions of other nationals. In a few cases, the school admitted a carefully selected handful of host nationals in order to gain influence within the host community. NIST had a policy of limiting the proportion of *any* national grouping. Owing to market forces, the largest sector was Thai, with no other nation comprising more than 15 per cent. This created an inclusive culture, while also recognizing the importance of the host community.

Other issues also arise in relation to host nationals. Education relates to culture and its action implies change (Hayden and Thompson, 1995c). International education is dynamic and inevitably influences change in the culture of the students who participate. That change may be positive or negative. 'Ana Koloto relates an example on the negative side within the Kingdom of Tonga. She describes the change from an education system that was 'informal, flexible and based on the family and the environment', arising from the influence of imported 'formal education'. She reports that Western educational systems became valued because they helped youngsters to obtain jobs but, she adds, such systems resulted in the breakdown of traditional culture (Koloto, 1998). Her example is not based on international schools *per se*, but there are strong resonances with the situation in many such schools.

Another issue is presented by Phillipson (1992). He argues that the global emphasis on teaching and promoting the English language causes cultural, social and psychological damage: 'Fallaciously identified with modernity, progress, freedom, civilization and reason, English commands monumental financial, official and popular backing in parts of the globe where its role is dubious.' As a result, he suggests, indigenous languages 'are not accorded enough resources to develop so that the same functions could be performed in them'.

The argument here is that the inclusion of host nationals in an international school can negatively influence the culture of the host country. The Singapore government, for instance, recognized these problems, which led to Singaporeans being prevented from attending international schools. In Tonga, Koloto (1998) sees the challenge as keeping the balance between 'education for cultural development' and 'education for economic development'. The balance is precarious. Within international schools we need to ensure that the educational experiences the students enjoy are challenging and, wherever possible, are related to the 'real' culture of the host nation, not just to the elite. Referring back to Martin's model (1987), our school–community links should include 'awareness raising'.

Client relationships: parents

Parents are clearly another client group. Parents have many potential roles in schools and there are several different types of parent–teacher partnership. In discussing these, Hornby (1999) identifies the following models:

Model	Features
Protective	Teachers teach; parents do the parenting; their roles are separate
Expert	Teachers are experts in child development; they advise parents
Transmission	Teachers are experts; parents are extra resources to help teachers
Curriculum-enrichment	Teachers use parental expertise to improve student learning
Consumer	Teachers provide information; parents decide what to do
Partnership	Teachers are experts on education; parents are experts on children; they work together

Which model operates in any school relates to issues of formal power (authority) and informal power (influence). Many teachers and administrators feel that they have the expertise and experience to make valid educational decisions. However, owing largely to their socio-economic background, many international school parents expect to be empowered. This wish for empowerment is heightened by the high fees required for most international schools, and the situation becomes even more critical with parents who have extra time on their hands, as is often the case for non-working spouses of expatriate families. In Africa, Asia and Latin America, maids, gardeners and chauffeurs reduce the normal family commitments for parents and a significant proportion of expatriate families fail to find a social 'niche' that matches the time they have at their disposal. These 'expatriate mums' (as they often are) are willing and able to devote their time to the school, but will usually expect this devotion to be rewarded with influence.

Such a situation is not true of parents from all cultures. McLean (1995) argues that culture affects the attitudes of parents to their partnership with the school: 'parent participation is culturally specific'. In a 'collectivist state' parents accept, and obey, the demands of the school. In a 'communalist-localist culture' parents control schooling. But in 'democratic-participatory collectivism', parents expect to be represented in decision-making, while accepting that the broad ideology of the school is not in their hands. In other words, they have significant influence, but not overall authority.

Issues such as these become crucial in international school communities. 'Inclusive' international schools need to build partnerships with parents, while taking care over issues of influence to ensure that this is not skewed in favour of those groups with the time, the interest or the cultural background to become involved. It is essential, therefore, that the school strives to engage *all* parents in meaningful, cooperative partnerships. Two-way communication, mutual support and joint decision-making are imperative. At the same time, there needs to be a clear indication of *who* has authority (such as the governors, or the Chief Executive Officer) and how others can have influence. As Bacharach (1988) states, 'educational organizations must be seen as political entities that shape and are shaped by their environmental and organizational context'. At the same time, however, international schools can encourage 'expert', 'transmission' and 'curriculum-enrichment' relationships with those parents who have the appropriate time and skills. In reality, the school needs to establish a range of structures for parent–school interactions.

Most international schools have a population made up of children of a diverse and changing group of parents. If the school is 'inclusive' in its aims, it must strive to involve them all, regardless of cultural traits. In particular, an effective international school needs to ensure that parents are not disenfranchised by their language or culture. On the first point, schools need to consider mechanisms for ensuring that effective two-way communication occurs between the school and all parents. On the second, the school must clarify its expectations for partnership. In my experience in Argentina, many parents wanted their children to attend a particular school specifically for the prestige it created. Their interest in the progress of their son or daughter was minimal: the key was that they remained at the school. For the benefit of the students, inclusive schools need to set in motion policies and procedures to combat this 'hands-off' attitude.

The fluidity of the expatriate population can also be problematic, although the impact of this fluidity can be reduced by having a significant student body from the local community, whether host country nationals or long-term expatriates. Again, the school must be aware of the dangers of influence skewed towards these sectors solely because of their 'permanence'.

Community relations

Research suggests that links with the local community have not been seen as important for either international school students or teachers. In surveys that asked respondents to rank the key features of international education, three groups of students at different stages of secondary school placed 'exposure to others of different cultures/links with the local community' last, while the cohort of teachers ranked it one before last (Thompson, 1998). It is mildly encouraging that alumni from international schools ranked the same facet significantly higher, but the majority opinion is clear. While international education aims to expose students to 'culture, language and people in a way which engenders the ability to judge and understand others by their standards rather than one's own' (Hayden and Thompson, 1995a), it is all too frequently the case that the school sees these aims being fulfilled *within* its own student body, rather than by interaction with the external community. Although international schools typically have students with high 'national' diversity, they are generally uniform in their socio-economic origins. In many schools (especially those with a low percentage of host nationals), the student body can easily become focused on the life of the expatriate community. If we are to utilize the possibilities of *real* cross-cultural fertilization, international schools need to look outside their walls. As McKenzie (1998) reports, however, 'so few schools... have any genuine or sustained contact with their ambient society'.

Jeff Thompson has provided a useful classification of models for the development of international curricula (Thompson, 1998). Within his four models, those that have evolved from 'Integration' or 'Creation' are much more likely to incorporate community links than those in the categories of 'Exportation' and 'Adaptation'. But, just because a school has been involved in curriculum design, it does not necessarily follow that this design will have a local focus. Once again, I would expect that local relevance would be much more likely amongst those with 'inclusive' missions (Sylvester, 1998), although the rationale for its inclusion may also be in response to national regulations. For example, the government of Thailand requires international schools to include Thai Studies in their curriculum. How this operates and the degree of importance it is given in schools is variable. In the best cases, it encourages and facilitates interaction with the host culture, mapping onto Martin's 'awareness raising' purpose for school–community links (Martin, 1987).

Fletcher (1987) has described three ways that schools can help young-sters to understand their 'community', as follows:

- by looking at social conditions in a scientific manner or by surveying the community;
- by sharing people's meanings in a realistic way, through participatory observation; and
- by learning through social movements, being political and involving participatory action.

If international schools choose to study the host culture only in a 'scien-tific' manner, learning will be sterile and academic. Schools that find ways to promote the second purpose will be encouraging interaction, while any programme that corresponds to the third will be akin to Martin's category of the 'ideological approach': an approach which might be seen as dangerous territory for many schools. There are, never-theless, arguments for encouraging the *emotional* involvement of students in what is happening in the world around them (Apple, 1996). As he argues, for international schools in the more economically disadvan-taged areas of the world, there are real and valid opportunities for students to learn through interaction with their local environment. Such interaction is likely to lead to actual 'involvement'.

The New International School of Thailand was founded on beliefs related to such an approach. Its original philosophy statement included the following memorable words: 'Some elements of the curriculum are designed to promote individual development, others to encourage cooperation, because personal satisfaction does not have to be at the expense of society's needs, and self-esteem can flower alongside social responsibility' (Blaney and Thomas, 1992).

Although social responsibility can certainly be encouraged within a school, as Colin Jenkins has argued, the achievement of certain fundamental education goals (establishing a sense of values, coping with change, developing a sense of belonging and identity, developing a sense of usefulness, and learning to recognize the value of cooperation and teamwork) can best be supported through participatory action. Jenkins (1998) writes, 'the commitment to community service does all of these things more powerfully than any form of education'. With the environmentalists' maxim of 'think globally, act locally' ringing in our ears, we, as international educators, are derelict in our duty if we do not develop effective community service programmes. 'If students and teachers learn interdependence through community service in their local contexts a genuine feeling for global interdependence is just a short step away' (McKenzie, 1998).

At NIST, we first developed close links with the Karen refugee communities on the Thai–Burmese border. This was a whole-school enterprise, embraced most fully by the Elementary School. Subsequently, we established relations with Nang Rong, a rural community to the north-east of Bangkok, while maintaining the Karen links. In Nang Rong, older students worked *with* the local people to encourage both education and economic self-sufficiency in the region, with the assistance and cooperation of the Thai Population and Development Agency. In the third year we worked to add another project to our repertoire. This time, our focus was Bangkok and the programme was for Middle School students. Students met with the Governor to discuss ideas and the teachers liaised with local schools. This led to plans for NIST to assist in training local teachers and for the school to host 'fun days' for local youngsters ('community in-reach', as advocated by McKenzie, 1998). Our aim was to utilize our skills and resources to improve the local community *and*, at the same time, to develop social responsibility in our students. This ideological approach seemed essential in the light of the school's mission.

An ideological approach to community involvement contrasts with the involvement identified in a limited survey of undergraduate students by Hayden and Thompson (1995b), who asked students whether their schools had overtly encouraged the development of international attitudes outside the formal curriculum. Two-thirds of those who had experienced 'international education' said they had. Further questioning revealed that nearly half of these saw the development of international attitudes through sporting contacts. Others recalled the influence of 'International Evenings' and 'Culture Days'. Only one or two mentioned 'community service/charity work in the local community'. Hopefully, this low priority is changing – not least as a result of the 'Community' aspects of all three International Baccalaureate programmes. We must hope that schools are bold enough to develop meaningful community action so that students can gain the greatest benefit from their local community, while giving back as much as possible. Youngsters from the more privileged sectors of society must be encouraged to understand interdependence and social justice. The most powerful way of encouraging such understanding is through meaningful social action.

Even for those international schools that do not see the need for social involvement with the local community, there are economic factors that link school to community. One of these is staffing. All international schools will have non-teaching employees from the host culture and a key indicator of the school's relationship with the local community is the way that they are treated. Inevitably, many of those support staff will be the lowest-paid employees. There will often be linguistic, as well as socio-economic and cultural, differences between them and expatriate members of the school. Fletcher (1987) warns of the 'danger of a two-tier system of white "qualified" teachers and other ancillaries'. This is, unfortunately, too much of a reality in many international schools in the developing world. The school needs to combat this apartheid. Without clear, positive practices for acknowledging and integrating such employees with the remainder of the school, any inclusive mission will be seriously damaged. Throughout my experience in international education, the host nationals on the staff have been proud and highly supportive of 'their' school. This attitude *must* be reciprocated.

Local community as a source of teachers

The local community can also be an important source of teachers. Matthews (1989b) suggested that the teachers were a key factor in distinguishing international schools. He identified five categories:

1. teachers attracted to the country specifically to work at the school;
2. teachers who have settled in the host community;
3. teachers who are *from* the local community;
4. expatriate wives; and
5. other transients (often seeking short-term experiences and adventure).

All but the first category can be said to come from the local community.

Some international schools argue that teachers hired through competitive international recruiting will be the best resource for the school. However, it can also be argued that 'local' teachers are likely to be more stable (especially if they come from categories 2 or 3 above) and are well attuned to the nuances of the local community. I have found these colleagues to be of outstanding value: within the classroom, in the wider school community and, most particularly, in the development and sustenance of 'community links'. If you want an inclusive school, include local teachers.

Some schools may hire local teachers because they are 'cheaper'. This is certainly the case – teachers who are more stable do not incur hiring, or counselling, costs; if they are local, they will not require relocation costs. Differentials in pay and/or benefits between 'overseas hired' and 'locally hired' teachers, however, create a more difficult area. As suggested previously, international schools are expensive and this makes them inaccessible for many host country (and some expatriate) families. The greatest factor in the cost is the salaries and benefits of the teachers, especially in less-developed countries, where the expatriate teachers' salaries are frequently aligned with salaries 'back home'. Many schools want to keep their fees low (if they are targeting a population beyond those on 'expatriate packages'), so employing a greater number of 'cheaper', local, teachers might be appealing. At NIST, we deliberately changed the proportion of locally hired teachers from 40 per cent to 55 per cent. At the same time, we reduced differentials in benefits (pay was never different between the two categories). The end result was only a small reduction in the salaries and benefits budget, but a significant increase in stability. This policy was especially effective in Bangkok, as the local community was diverse, and gave us a broad pool of qualified teachers to select from, many with extensive knowledge of the country. It also allowed us to recruit teachers from many different cultural backgrounds.

More problematic is the hire of host nationals as teachers in an international school. Some suggest that the idea of an 'international school' is that the teachers are from 'abroad'. Others argue that 'host nationals' are usually not as well qualified as expatriates. If, however, one of the aims of the school is to develop awareness and value of the host culture, it seems essential for a proportion of the teachers to represent that culture. Luckily, internationally accessible staff development programmes can help to reduce distinctions in expertise (Richards, 1998), although there are still battles to be won in defeating the educationally imperialist notion that 'West is best'. At NIST I had several rather heated discussions with parents, often host nationals, who did not like the idea of an 'Asian' teacher for their child. Fortunately, I was able to take a firm line. As an international school in Asia, we were determined to have a diverse, talented and hard-working teaching body that included a significant proportion of Asian professionals – and not only as teachers of Asian languages.

Conclusion

International schools are not ivory towers. They are learning institutions with the potential for facilitating the development of a better world. They are blessed with young people with great talents and tremendous opportunities. They have skilful and dedicated teachers. To deny those opportunities to members of the host culture would be unfortunate, but one of the most important roles of an international school is to encourage its privileged students to develop an appreciation of, a respect for, and an empathy towards, their world. Such objectives cannot be achieved through isolationism. The most effective tactic is to embrace, as fully as the constraints of the host country allow, the local community: in that way, an opportunity will be taken, not missed, for the enhancement of an international education that is of international quality, delivered locally. To engender global thinking, we *must* interact locally: the nature of that interaction should be driven by our ideologies.

References

Apple, M W (1996) *Cultural Politics and Education*, Open University Press, Milton Keynes

Bacharach, S B (1988) Notes on a political theory of educational organisations, in *Culture and Power in Educational Organizations*, ed A Westoby, Open University Press, Milton Keynes

Bell, L A (1988) The school as an organisation: a reappraisal, in *Culture and Power in Educational Organizations*, ed A Westoby, Open University Press, Milton Keynes

Blaney, J J and Thomas, P (1992) *Philosophy Statement for the New International School of Thailand*

Bush, A (1999) The vanishing boundaries: the importance of effective external relations, in *Managing External Relations in Schools and Colleges*, eds J Lumby and N Foskett, Paul Chapman, Sage Publications, Thousand Oaks, CA

Cambridge, J (1998) Investigating national and organisational cultures in the context of the international school, in *International Education: Principles and practice*, eds M C Hayden and J J Thompson, Kogan Page, London

Dewey, J (1916) *Democracy and Education*, Macmillan, Basingstoke

Eggleston, S J (1967) *The Social Context of the School*, Routledge, London

Fletcher, C (1987) The meanings of 'community in community education', in *Community Education: An agenda for educational reform*, eds G Allen, J Bastiani, I Martin and J K Richards, Open University Press, Milton Keynes

Hayden, M C and Thompson, J J (1995a) International schools and international education: a relationship reviewed, *Oxford Review of Education*, **21** (3), pp 327–45

Hayden, M C and Thompson, J J (1995b) Perceptions of international education: a preliminary study, *International Review of Education*, **41** (5), pp 389–404

Hayden, M C and Thompson, J J (1995c) International education: the crossing of frontiers, *International Schools Journal*, **XV** (1), pp 13–19

Hornby, G (1999) *Improving Parental Involvement*, Cassell, London

Jenkins, C (1998) Global issues: a necessary component of a balanced curriculum for the 21st century, in *International Education: Principles and Practice*, eds M C

Hayden and J J Thompson, Kogan Page, London

Koloto, 'A (1998) Issues for education in the South Pacific: education and change in the Kingdom of Tonga, in *Education and Change in the Pacific Rim: Meeting the challenges*, ed K Sullivan, Oxford Studies in Comparative Education (series editor: David Phillips), Triangle, Wallingford

Martin, I (1987) Community education: towards a theoretical analysis, in *Community Education: An agenda for educational reform*, eds G Allen, J Bastiani, I Martin and J K Richards, Open University Press, Milton Keynes

Matthews, M (1989a) The scale of international education: Part I, *International Schools Journal*, **17**, pp 7–17

Matthews, M (1989b) The uniqueness of international education: Part II, *International Schools Journal*, **18**, pp 24–34

McDill, E and Rigsby, L (1973) *Structure and Process in Secondary Schools*, Johns Hopkins University Press, Baltimore

McKenzie, M (1998), Going, going, gone... global!, in *International Education: Principles and practice*, eds M C Hayden and J J Thompson, Kogan Page, London

McLean, M (1995) *Educational Traditions Compared*, David Fulton, London

Mitchell, G (1989) Community education and school, in *Educational Institutions and Their Environments: Managing the boundaries*, ed R Glatter, Open University Press, Milton Keynes

Pearce, R (1998), Developing cultural identity in an international school environments, in *International Education: Principles and practice*, eds M C Hayden and J J Thompson, Kogan Page, London

Phillipson, R (1992) *Linguistic Imperialism*, Oxford University Press, Oxford

Pollock, D C (1998) Lecture to New International School of Thailand on *Third Culture Kids*

Richards, N (1998) The emperor's new clothes? The issue of staffing in international schools, in *International Education: Principles and practice*, eds M C Hayden and J J Thompson, Kogan Page, London

Skrimshire, A (1981) Community schools and the education of the 'social individual', *Oxford Review of Education*, **7**, pp 53–65

Sylvester, R (1998) Through the lens of diversity: inclusive and encapsulated school missions, in *International Education: Principles and practice*, eds M C Hayden and J J Thompson, Kogan Page, London

Thompson, J J (1998) Towards a model for international education, in *International Education: Principles and practice*, eds M C Hayden and J J Thompson, Kogan Page, London

Wilkinson, D (1998) International education: a question of access, in *International Education: Principles and practice*, eds M C Hayden and J J Thompson, Kogan Page, London

Willis, D B, Enloe, W W and Minoura, Y (1994) Transculturals, transnationals: the new diaspora, *International Schools Journal*, **XIV** (1), pp 29–42

Part C

THROUGH SCHOOL
MANAGEMENT

Chapter 12

Moving from school effectiveness to school improvement in international schools

Michael Fertig

Introduction

The history of school effectiveness research is a distinguished one, dating as it does from the late 1960s and the intense interest generated by the question 'Do schools make a difference?' Out of the investigations emanating from this question has emerged a picture of the 'effective school', a detailed portrait for schools that desire to become 'effective'. This work initially attempted to identify the factors that can be said to bring about 'effectiveness' at the whole-school level. Other, more recent, research has sought to identify factors at the levels of the classroom and the individual teacher. In addition, considerable energy has been expended on examining ways in which schools can use the information emerging from this research to improve themselves and aim to become more effective.

Investigating school effectiveness

The purpose of this chapter is, firstly, to present a brief synopsis of the key areas of school effectiveness research and then to pose some questions as to possible areas where this research could have an impact upon international schools attempting to bring about an improvement in the education of their pupils. It is important to bear in mind at the outset that this research has centred primarily on schools operating within national systems of education, with very little work having been done to date in exploring the nature of effectiveness in international schools.

It is salutary to note that less than four decades ago, the answer to the central question posed above about the value of schooling would have been delivered in the negative. In the late 1960s there seemed to be a general pessimism about the role of schools in society. At that time, the Coleman Report (Coleman *et al*, 1966) in the United States and the writings of researchers such as Jencks *et al* (1972) were suggesting most strongly that the impact of schools upon pupils' life chances was less than positive. The process of schooling, these writers argued, had only a modest impact upon children's futures, compared to factors such as family background. Some, such as Ivan Illich and the 'de-schooling' movement, went even further, arguing that schools were positively harmful to children and should, therefore, be disbanded.

It was as a reaction to such pessimistic prognostications that educational researchers began to explore issues related to effectiveness. Initial investigations, by writers such as Edmonds (1979) in the United States, concentrated upon examining the performance of different schools found within the same locality and parental catchment zone. How was it possible, researchers asked, for two schools with similar pupil characteristics and parental profiles to generate different levels of pupil achievement? The reason seemed to be located within the school, in the different ways in which schools operated. Attempts were therefore made to try to isolate those characteristics that appeared to impact significantly upon pupil achievement.

Much of the early research into school effectiveness in the United States was committed to the belief that the children of the urban poor could succeed in school, and that research could identify ways in which schools could help these children to succeed. As Sammons, Hillman and Mortimore (1997) commented: 'Early school effectiveness research incorporated explicit aims or goals concerned with equity and excellence.' There was a tendency, therefore, for much of the research to concentrate upon inner-city schools, and this was mirrored in some of the pioneering work done in the United Kingdom by research teams led by Rutter (1979) and by Mortimore (1988).

More recent research has emphasized the need to examine effectiveness in a wide range of schools. There is now general agreement about the dominant model underpinning research into school effectiveness that has emerged over recent decades. Firstly, there has been a clear focus on the concept of 'value added', with Mortimore (1991) defining an effective school as one in which pupils progress further than might be expected from a consideration of its intake. An effective school, seen through this lens, adds some extra value to the outcomes of its pupils in comparison with other schools serving similar intakes. In contrast, the reverse would be happening in a school deemed to be ineffective.

A second common focus for school effectiveness research is the use of an outcomes-oriented approach to what happens in schools. This is clearly exemplified by Scheerens and Bosker (1997), who state that: 'An important characteristic of school effectiveness is that it uses an outcome measure as its criterion, that is adjusted for prior achievement and/or other relevant student background characteristics. In this way, the added value of schooling can be separated from overall development or innate growth of students.'

This central emphasis upon the use of 'outcome measures' suggests notions of being able to observe finite behaviour which can be closely related to cognitive achievement amongst pupils. It also suggests that these achievements are susceptible to measurement. Writing in 1987, Cohn and Rossmiller commented that: 'effective schools have been defined primarily in terms of gains in cognitive knowledge rather than by broader, more inclusive, measures of the outcomes of schooling'.

What, then, have been the key findings of school effectiveness research? There is now a fair level of agreement regarding school factors that are seen to correlate with school effectiveness. It is important to stress, however, that these factors or characteristics should not be regarded as independent of each other. The exact relationship between them will be determined primarily by school context. It is argued strongly later in this chapter that these factors can act both as a useful checklist for those trying to promote improvement within international schools and as an aid in the process of school self-evaluation and improvement.

Sammons et al (1997) identified 11 factors for effective schools. The following summary offers both a glimpse of what each means in relation to school practice, and a template against which to judge the degree to which a school can be said to be 'effective'.

(i) Professional leadership

The vast majority of studies of school effectiveness portray leadership, at both primary and secondary level, as being a crucial factor. As Gray (1990) points out: 'the importance of the headteacher's leadership is one of the clearest of the messages from school effectiveness research'. Much of the research reinforces the point made by Bossert *et al* (1982), who concluded that 'no simple style of management seems appropriate for all schools... principals must use the style and structures most suited to their own local situation'.

(ii) Shared vision and goals

The overwhelming message of research into this area of school effectiveness is that schools are more effective where there is a consensus among the staff about the aims and values of the school. An allied factor emerging from the research is the need to put these aims and values into practice in a consistent and purposeful manner, both in relation to what goes on within the classroom and to what happens in other areas of the school's activities. Rutter *et al* (1979), for example, found that pupils were more likely to maintain behaviour guidelines when they saw that the standards of discipline were based upon general school expectations rather than on the whim of an individual teacher. This research also stressed the importance of teachers acting as positive role models for pupils in their relationships with their pupils and their colleagues in the school.

(iii) Learning environment

School ethos seems, according to the research literature, to be determined by more than staff working together in the school, with shared goals and vision. Another key factor is the learning environment in which the pupils are working. Central to these concerns are issues connected with an orderly atmosphere and an attractive working environment. One message emerging from the research is that successful schools are likely to be calm rather than chaotic places in which to work, both for the staff and for the pupils. Mortimore *et al*, for example, in their study of junior schools in Inner London (Mortimore *et al*, 1988), indicated that an orderly environment was seen as a prerequisite for effective learning to take place.

(iv) Concentration on teaching and learning

Given that general agreement about the primary purpose of schools emphasizes the learning of the pupils, it should come as no surprise that many research studies have indicated a strong correlation between a focus on teaching and learning and school effectiveness. Some studies have looked specifically at quantifying teachers' and pupils' use of time in the classroom, while others have focused on examining the quality of the teaching and learning process and its impact upon achievement. Linking the two approaches has been a concern to examine the extent to which the school stresses academic success, with a concentration on 'mastery of academic content' by the pupils and an emphasis upon the detailed subject knowledge displayed by the teacher. Researchers such as Bennett (1992) have seen adequate subject knowledge as a necessary prerequisite for effective teaching and learning.

(v) Purposeful teaching

Research on effective schooling makes very clear that the quality of teaching lies at the heart of the issue. Not only do effective schools ensure that the quality of teachers is given a high priority, they also lay stress upon the quality of teaching. This is seen to consist of: teachers being efficiently organized; teaching taking place with a clear purpose; teachers presenting structured lessons; and teachers being aware of the differential learning needs of pupils within the classroom. Joyce and Showers (1988), for example, concluded that more effective teachers:

- teach the classroom as a whole;
- present material or skills in a clear and user-friendly manner;
- keep the teaching sessions focused on key tasks;
- keep instruction within the lesson relaxed and simple;
- have high expectations for the achievement of their pupils; and
- relate well to their pupils, with a consequent absence of serious behaviour problems.

(vi) High expectations

This is seen as one of the central lessons to be learnt from the canon of school effectiveness research, and goes to the heart of the early attempts by researchers to identify the factors which lead to 'added value' within inner-city schools. In broad terms: 'the weight of the evidence suggests that if teachers set high standards for their pupils, let them know that they are expected to meet them and provide intellectually challenging lessons to correspond to these expectations, then the impact on achievement can be considerable' (Sammons, Hillman and Mortimore, 1997).

Clearly, high expectations alone cannot of themselves raise effectiveness within schools. Here, one can again see the importance of the interrelatedness of these factors, with 'high expectations' operating most positively in an atmosphere where there is a strong emphasis on academic achievement, where there is an orderly environment conducive to learning, and where there is regular monitoring of pupils' work.

(vii) Positive reinforcement

In this area of investigation, research has shown that rewards, clear rules and positive incentives are more likely to have an impact on learning and result in better outcomes than are negative reinforcements such as punishment. The issue of consistency was raised earlier in this chapter, and this relates to the need for clear and fair discipline within the school which emerges clearly from the literature on effective schools. Here, indeed, is an area open to fruitful investigation, in particular from the viewpoint of the pupils. Some of the work by Rudduck, Chaplain and Wallace (1996) has done much to open up this area, by examining pupil perceptions of the schooling they experience.

(viii) Monitoring progress

The frequent and systematic monitoring of pupil and class progress can be seen as a mechanism for charting the extent to which the goals of the school are being put into practice. It is seen also as a key opportunity to focus the attention of key players, such as the pupils and the parents, upon these school goals, and as a way of giving a clear message to pupils that teachers are interested in their achievements and progress. Interest in this area has centred primarily on the degree and quality of the monitoring found within effective schools. Writers such as Levine and Lezotte (1990) are keen to point out the dangers of over-monitoring, and of the time-wasting that can sometimes occur where the school emphasizes the gathering of information and neglects to think about the ways in which these data can be used to improve aspects of the school's work.

(ix) Pupil rights and responsibilities

One factor that seems to shine through the research literature is that of pupil rights and responsibilities. Investigations into schools that were seen to be effective suggest that substantial gains in effectiveness occur when:

- the school succeeds in raising the self-esteem of pupils;
- pupils are given an active role in the day-to-day life of the school; and
- pupils are given some responsibility for their own learning.

(x) Home–school partnership

Effective schools research indicates that supportive and cooperative relations between home and school have positive effects in terms of pupil learning. Studies suggest that the ways in which this positive relationship manifests itself will vary according to the age of the pupils. The work done by Mortimore *et al* (1988) into effective junior schools found positive benefits where parents helped in the classroom and with school trips, and where they attended regular progress meetings concerning their child. As the pupils get older, so the emphasis from the research studies centres on parental support and/or supervision of homework, and a regular monitoring of pupil attendance and behaviour.

(xi) The school as a learning organization

The centrality given to learning within effective schools is mirrored by the idea of regarding effective schools as learning organizations. Writers such as Senge (1992) and Southworth (1993) have identified the characteristics of learning organizations; essentially they focus on the core idea that all people within the organization need to be seen as learners. In the case of schools, this involves all teachers and senior managers continuing to be learners through keeping up to date with changes in their curriculum area and with advances in understanding effective classroom and management practice. A key indicator here would be the degree to which teacher professional development is supported by the school.

Issues emerging from school effectiveness research

Analysis of research emerging from the school effectiveness stable poses a number of interesting questions for those teaching and managing in international schools. Two that come into prominence relate, firstly, to the possibility of transfer of ideas from one type of educational context to another and, secondly, to the nature of the criteria used by many research studies to judge effectiveness. Much lively debate has taken place as to whether the lessons learnt by educational practitioners in one part of the world can be transplanted elsewhere. Whether it is possible to transfer ideas from one country to another and achieve similar results in the receiving country is a serious question in relation to the impact of specific local contexts on the ways in which educational policies operate.

In the context of the lessons that might be drawn from school effectiveness research, this question is equally evident. The vast majority of school effectiveness studies have investigated schools operating within a national educational framework. In contrast, international schools operate within the private sector, are very often fee-paying, and usually draw their pupil and teacher populations from a broader range of backgrounds and experiences than do schools found in the national system.

Such disparities will clearly need to be considered by those working within international schools when examining ways in which such schools might benefit from the work of researchers looking at 'effective schools' in other contexts.

Similarly, it is clear that the majority of school effectiveness studies have centred primarily upon explorations of pupils' cognitive outcomes in areas such as public testing and examinations. These outcomes have been used as the criteria against which to judge whether or not a school could be considered 'effective'. Few studies have paid attention to affective or social outcomes for pupils, an issue that bears heavily upon the broader aims espoused by many international schools in, for example, their mission statements. As writers such as Reynolds, Hopkins and Stoll (1993) have observed, the research into effective schools has not, as yet, provided us with much significant evidence about school and classroom processes that are important in determining the effectiveness of the school in promoting social and affective outcomes. The remainder of this chapter will focus on this area, in order to explore ways in which the knowledge gained from identifying the characteristics of 'effective schools' can be translated into practical strategies for improving the education of young people in international schools, thereby influencing the quality of their experience.

From analysis to action: improving international schools

Characteristics emerging from research into school effectiveness present us with a clear template of the features of the 'effective school', one towards which schools seeking to improve and become more effective can aspire. The process of becoming more effective, the 'school improvement' journey, has been defined by van Velzen et al (1985) as: 'a systematic, sustained effort aimed at change in learning conditions and other related internal conditions in one or more schools, with the ultimate aim of accomplishing educational goals more effectively' (in Teddlie and Reynolds, 2000).

How, then, is a school to move from an understanding of the range of characteristics that could denote 'effectiveness' to turning this knowledge into practical action that will be of benefit to the school's pupils? One approach that could be used for the type of systematic effort indicated by van Velzen et al is to start by examining where the school lies in relation to all (or some) of these 'effectiveness' characteristics.

A mechanism for doing this, for exploring what have been labelled 'ethos indicators', has been devised in Scotland (Scottish Office

Education Department, 1992), and has been used by over 500 schools since 1992. A useful way of looking at the notion of 'ethos' was provided by Rutter *et al* (1979), who suggested that: 'individuals, actions or measures may combine to create a particular ethos, or set of values, attitudes and behaviours which will become characteristic of the school as a whole'. In examining the ideas behind 'school ethos', MacBeath, McCreath and Aitchison (1995) have stated very clearly that: 'ethos is, after all, a phenomenological matter and there is, therefore, no better way of getting at a school's ethos than through subjective measures'.

International schools, in particular, can benefit from such an approach in that it enables the school to move away from the rather narrow definitions of 'added value' and 'effectiveness' linked solely to pupils' cognitive achievements into an examination of the degree to which the school is fulfilling its wider aims. This kind of broader investigation ties in with the work of researchers such as Rutter *et al* (1979) and Stoll and Fink (1996), who have laid significant emphasis upon the ethos and the culture of the school as major determining factors in aiding the school to improve.

For international schools, the idea of looking at these aspects of school experience resonates well with those who have a concern and a commitment to the holistic curriculum approach found, for example, within the range of International Baccalaureate programmes. Other connections can be made with the views expressed by writers examining the philosophy of international education. Thompson (1998), for example, has laid stress upon five central pillars to be considered by those wishing to develop programmes of international education:

- exposure to others of different cultures within the school;
- teachers as exemplars of 'international-mindedness';
- exposure to others of different cultures outside the school;
- a balanced formal curriculum; and
- a management regime that is value consistent with an institutional international philosophy.

One can see here a clear emphasis upon a curriculum perspective that encompasses much more than a concern with pupil achievement that can be measured in tests or examinations. It is in these broader areas that the 'ethos indicator' approach developed in Scotland can play a significant part in the process of self-evaluation and improvement in international schools.

The rationale behind the Scottish Office Education Department (SOED) development has been expressed clearly (SOED, 1992):

School development planning rests on the assumption that teachers and school managers want, and need, information about how they are doing their job. Some evidence for this can be found by the analysis of results of assessment, by looking at pupil, and teacher, attendance rates, or levels of participation in school events or extra-curricular activities. All of these provide some hard data for a review, or audit, of a school's effectiveness. While all of these are pointers to important aspects of school life, they do not tell the whole story about, for example, the quality of teaching and learning and relationships in the classroom.

There is also a need to consider performance indicators which tell us something about how these important aspects of school are seen from the perspectives of those centrally involved in the education process, that is pupils and teachers, and also something about the attitudes, expectations, and degrees of satisfaction of those whose attitudes play an important role in influencing what takes place in classrooms – that is, parents and other relevant interest groups.

Some work in this area has been done in relation to stakeholder perceptions of schooling by Rudduck, Chaplain and Wallace (1996) and the Office of Educational Research and Improvement (OERI, 1993a, 1993b, 1994). The ideas behind the 'ethos indicator' research from the Scottish Office present the potential for international schools to engage in a practice-oriented approach to the issue of school improvement, and the ways in which such schools can address these issues have been illustrated by some recent examples of research using, or adapting, the Scottish Office approach. Both Crute (1998) and Gray (1999) have published studies of the use of the SOED indicators within an international school context, and I am personally engaged in similar research with an international school in South-East Asia.

Crute (1998) made use of ethos indicators in his study of the ways in which an international school located in Europe prepared itself for the accreditation process of the European Council of International Schools (ECIS). His concern in embarking on the study was that there was 'some disagreement at all levels of the school community regarding the present perceived ethos of the school'. There was a desire, also, to 'assess and analyse [stakeholder] opinions in a way that will provide a reliable and valid source of data to serve as guidelines in the decision-making process' (Crute, 1998).

Gray's study (1999) examined one aspect of the ethos indicator package, that of teacher–pupil interaction, in attempting to understand the ways in which this aspect was perceived by both teachers and pupils at an international school located in Asia. Gray's focus on the practitioner level within the school arose from a belief that any improvements at this level would have a direct effect upon pupil learning. As MacGilchrist *et al* (1997) have commented: 'Our experience is that school improvement efforts that concentrate on the classroom, in such a way that teachers experience the benefits of change for themselves and their children, are the ones that are more likely to be successful.'

In contrast to Crute, who was able to draw upon the whole-school population from three stakeholder groups (pupils, teachers, parents), Gray drew upon a sample of pupils and staff at one school, while using an approach similar to that of Crute. Both studies, and that currently being undertaken by the author in South-East Asia, pose critical questions about the ways in which international schools might go about the process of school improvement, and of the potential value of 'ethos indicators' in this process. The issues raised by these pieces of research can be delineated as follows:

1. On what basis should judgements about the effectiveness of an international school be made? The emphasis which school effectiveness research has tended to place upon observable and testable achievement, and on 'added value', has already been examined earlier in this chapter. International schools share with schools operating within a national system a concern for the levels of achievement of their pupils. If international schools wish to travel along this road, and seek answers to the question: 'What difference does the school make to the cognitive achievements of its pupils?', then some degree of knowledge is implied about pupil achievement levels on entry to the school. The fluid nature of the pupil populations of many international schools poses difficult, but crucially important, questions as to the ways in which 'baseline testing' on entry might occur.

2. Allied to this, and of equally fundamental importance, is the question: 'Can criteria for effectiveness garnered from studies carried out within national educational systems be transported to schools operating within a private, market atmosphere?' Both Crute (1998) and Gray (1999) found that the original SOED questionnaires could be suitably customized to make them appropriate for use in their schools. The author, in an ongoing study of teacher attitudes at an international school, has also made use of an adapted version of the questionnaire. It is clear that, if an international school wishes to embark on its school improvement journey using this approach, it will need to examine carefully the validity of existing instruments for such different contexts.

3. Specific methodological questions are raised by the use of the SOED questionnaires as a way of opening up the doors to school

improvement, and these questions take on added significance in the context of international schools. One key issue revolves around the question of who should be asked to complete the questionnaires. Crute (1998) was able to give the questionnaires to all pupils, teachers and parents within the school. Gray (1999), on the other hand, introduced some degree of sampling because of the size of the school population, and managed to create a target group in proportion to the various nationalities and experiences within the school. A crucial area within an international school context will focus on the parental group. Given the relatively high degree of mobility of parents normally found in an international school, the question of 'which parents?' is clearly a difficult one. Such methodological questions will need to be addressed from the outset, as they reflect views about the importance, or lack of importance, of different stakeholder groups within the school.

4. Linked to such issues are questions about the process of carrying out the 'ethos indicator' audit within the school. Crute, in his study, explored whether there was a relationship between the intent of a school to embark upon the process of improvement and the nature of the leadership within the school. The study found that there was a sound degree of consonance between the espoused aims of the school regarding openness to change and responses to the questionnaire from the teachers, suggesting that: 'it does take inspired leadership to have the openness to give permission for a searching questionnaire – a section of which probes the perceived effectiveness of the school's leadership – to be administered in the school' (Crute, 1998). An allied point relates to the nature of the teaching staff and their willingness to engage with the process of school improvement. What, for example, is going to motivate teachers to look positively at this opportunity for change? What might be the impact of short-term and/or differential contracts for teachers in international schools who are being encouraged to take a degree of ownership of the change process? Gray, in his study, was mindful of the need to draw upon a representative range of nationalities in his sampling, and this indicates a further area for careful consideration. Writers such as Hofstede (1980) and Trompenaars and Hampden-Turner (1997) have pointed to the importance of understanding that people with different cultural values will view social and organizational constructs in different ways. The multicultural nature of many international school staffrooms clearly points to the need for awareness that staff may have varied perceptions related to key effectiveness indicators, with origins in their cultural background.

5. Once a decision has been taken to embark on the 'ethos indicator' approach to the school-improvement journey, the questionnaire items agreed, the target group(s) identified, and the questionnaires distributed and returned, the question then arises: 'What are we going to do once we have discovered what the data reveal?' This raises issues surrounding power relationships within the school, which bear upon international schools as much as upon those within a national system. Schools which are seen by owners or proprietors as operating solely, or even essentially, for profit will be likely to present a different view regarding the use of indicator data than those which have as their major concern the improvement of the educational process. If the whole purpose of the exercise is to act as a first step on the change journey, then there will need to be an implied, or openly stated, commitment to look on the results of the process in a positive light. International schools will need to take that commitment on board from the start of the investigative process. The alternative stance would clearly breed an atmosphere of cynicism and negativism within the school.

Conclusion

International schools, though often much more diverse in their nature than schools within a national education system, are not isolated from the currents of educational opinion swirling around the atmosphere and affecting the schooling process globally. The demands for schools to operate effectively and to become more self-evaluative and accountable are just as likely to be heard from parents of pupils in international schools as they are from those whose children attend a national school; indeed, it may be that the 'customer' relationship between parents and schools within the international school sector makes the voices of the 'customers' more strident than those of their state-funded neighbours. An approach using 'ethos indicators' does not offer any kind of panacea for international schools responding to these calls. If anything, it presents a number of urgent and searching questions that schools looking to bring about improvement will need to answer. The importance of such a broader investigation of what the school is doing cannot be overlooked. It is summarized by MacBeath, McCreath and Aitchison (1995), who have stated that schools which have used the results of the SOED questionnaires as a tool for school improvement: 'have seen them more as tin openers, revealing aspects of school life that merit closer attention'.

International schools often espouse a holistic and humane approach to the educational process for their pupils. They would seem, therefore, to be well placed to invest time and energy in opening themselves up to the kind of scrutiny that will enable them to have a clear focus on their potential for school improvement. That could only be a positive contribution to the enhancement of quality of such institutions.

References

Bennett, N (1992) *Managing Learning in the Primary Classroom*, Trentham Books, Stoke

Bossert, S T, Dwyer, D C, Rowan, B and Lee, G (1982) The instructional management role of the principal, *Educational Administration Quarterly*, **18**, pp 34–64

Cohn, E and Rossmiller, R A (1987) Research on effective schools: implications for less developed countries, *Comparative Education Review*, **31** (3), pp 377–99

Coleman, J S, Campbell, E, Hobson, C, McPartland, J, Mood, A, Weinfeld, F and York, R (1966) *Equality of Educational Opportunity*, National Centre for Educational Statistics, Washington, DC

Crute, P (1998) *Using Ethos Indicators in School Improvement*, MA in Education dissertation, University of Bath, Bath

Edmonds, R R (1979) Effective schools for the urban poor, *Educational Leadership*, **37** (10), pp 15–24

Gray, J (1990) The quality of schooling: frameworks for judgements, *British Journal of Educational Studies*, **38** (3), pp 204–33

Gray, M (1999) *Teacher/Student Interaction and School Improvement in an International School*, MA in Education dissertation, University of Bath, Bath

Hofstede, G (1980) *Culture's Consequences,* Sage, London

Jencks, C S, Smith, M, Ackland, H, Bane, M J, Cohen, D, Gintis, H, Heyns, B and Micholson, S (1972) *Inequality: A re-assessment of the effect of family and schooling in America*, Rinehart and Winston, London

Joyce, B and Showers, B (1988) *Student Achievement through Staff Development*, Longman, New York

Levine, D U and Lezotte, L W (1990) *Unusually Effective Schools: A review and analysis of research and practice*, National Center for Effective Schools Research and Development, Madison, WI

MacBeath, J, McCreath, D and Aitchison, J (1995) *Collaborate or Compete?*, Falmer Press, London

MacGilchrist, B, Myers, K and Reed, J (1997) *The Intelligent School*, Paul Chapman, London

Mortimore, P, Sammons, P, Stoll, L, Lewis, D and Ecob, R (1988) *School Matters: The junior years*, Open Books, London

Mortimore, P (1991) School effectiveness research: which way at the crossroads?, *School Effectiveness and School Improvement*, **2** (3), pp 213–29

Office of Educational Research and Improvement (1993a) *Who Runs the Schools? The Principal's View*, US Department of Education, Washington (Web site: http://ed.gov/pubs/OR/ResearchRpts/prinview.html)

Office of Educational Research and Improvement (1993b) *Who Runs the Schools? The Teachers' Views*, US Department of Education, Washington (Web site: http://ed.gov/pubs/OR/ResearchRpts/teachvie.html)

Office of Educational Research and Improvement (1994) *Who's in Charge? Teachers' Views on Control over School Policy and Classroom Practices*, US Department of Education, Washington
(Web site: http://ed.gov/pubs/OR/ResearchRpts/whos.html)

Reynolds, D, Hopkins, D and Stoll, L (1993) Linking school effectiveness knowledge and school improvement practice: towards a synergy, *School Effectiveness and School Improvement*, **4** (1), pp 37–58

Rudduck, J, Chaplain, R and Wallace, G (1996) *School Improvement: What Can Students Tell Us?* David Fulton, London

Rutter, M, Maughan, B, Mortimore, P and Ouston, J (1979) *Fifteen Thousand Hours: Secondary schools and their effects on children*, Open Books, London

Sammons, P, Hillman, J and Mortimore, P (1997) Key characteristics of effective schools: a review of school effectiveness research, in *Perspectives on School Effectiveness and School Improvement*, eds J White and M Barber, Institute of Education, London

Scheerens, J and Bosker, R (1997) *The Foundations of Educational Effectiveness*, Pergamon Press, London

Scottish Office Education Department (1992) *Using Ethos Indicators in Secondary School Self-Evaluation: Taking account of the views of pupils, parents and teachers*, Her Majesty's Inspectorate, Edinburgh

Senge, P M (1992) *The Fifth Discipline: The art and practice of the learning organization*, Nicholas Brealey, London

Southworth, G (1993) School leadership and school development: reflections from research, *School Organization*, **13**, pp 73–87

Stoll, L and Fink, D (1996) *Changing Our Schools: Linking school effectiveness and school improvement*, Open University Press, Buckingham

Teddlie, C and Reynolds, D (2000) *The International Handbook of School Effectiveness Research*, Falmer Press, London

Thompson, J J (1998) Towards a model for international education, in *International Education: Principles and Practice*, eds M C Hayden and J J Thompson, Kogan Page, London

Trompenaars, F and Hampden-Turner, C (1997) *Riding the Waves of Culture: Understanding cultural diversity in business*, Nicholas Brealey Publishing, London

van Velzen, W, Miles, M, Ekholm, M, Hameyer, U and Robin, D (1985) *Making School Improvement Work: A conceptual guide to practice*, ACCO, Leuven

Chapter 13

Long-term planning in international schools

Joseph J Blaney

Introduction

Long-term planning will be discussed in this chapter from several, inter-related perspectives:

- planning as the chief responsibility of leadership and governance;
- what planning is;
- formal, systematic planning as a way of life in effective schools;
- what promotes and what hinders the practice of planning in international schools; and
- characteristics of successful strategic planning in schools.

In the course of the discussion set out in this chapter certain problems and conditions are identified which arise *sui generis* in international schools, and which have a bearing on the planning issue. The status of the practice of planning in schools is discussed, particularly as it applies to international schools. Reasons are suggested for why effective planning is difficult to accomplish in international schools, and suggestions are made for dealing with those difficulties. The planning function is reviewed: planning as an active, dynamic process of decision-making, as the central management function and tool, as comprehensive in content and impact, as an inclusive process, and as the *sine qua non* of successful schools.

Characteristics of international schools

A visitor to the office of a Head of an international school, when asking to look at a copy of the school's long-term plan, will often hear one of the following statements:

- We do not have a long-term plan.
- Our long-term plan is outdated.
- We do not have a long-term plan but we know it's important and we've made it a priority to do one.
- We don't have time to plan around here.
- Doing a long-term plan requires too much time, effort and cost.
- It's tough enough to plan for next year, never mind for the 'long term'.

Alternatively, the visitor may be handed a plan document from the Head's credenza, probably prepared for the school's last accreditation, handsomely bound and looking very much as though it has not been touched by human hands since its publication.

In short, the visitor may well discover that strategic thinking and planning, for a variety of reasons, are not centrepieces of the school's governance and leadership activities. Foremost among the reasons is the fact that school management is highly reactive because of the nature of schools generally. Secondly, all of the factors that make this so are doubly compelling in international schools. It is for these reasons, and not incompetence or dereliction of duty on the part of Heads of schools, that their organizations may not be managed strategically. Yet if international schools with a captive clientele, or state schools which are required by law to exist, were suddenly to find themselves in highly competitive environments, they could not survive without strategic management.

International schools sometimes seem like a bewildering array of educational organizations. It has been estimated that there are approximately one thousand international schools worldwide (Hayden and Thompson, 1995). While a few are relatively old (among them the Yokohama International School and the International School of Geneva, both founded in 1924), the vast majority of international schools were established in the second half of the twentieth century. Although there is a diversity in the sponsorship of international schools, with the diplomatic and multinational corporate communities leading the way in this regard, most of the international schools are strikingly similar in the following important characteristics:

- Their essential purpose is to serve international families for whom the local state schools are not suitable, often because of the language of instruction.
- They are not-for-profit and non-sectarian.
- Their legal status was obtained and is maintained through charter or treaty with the host country or state.
- Their governance is provided by lay, self-perpetuating Boards or by democratic election.
- The language of instruction is English.
- While some offer elementary grades only, the majority are K–12.
- They are open to all students who seem likely to benefit from an international education and whose parents are able to pay the cost.
- They are academic preparatory schools for university.
- Their curriculum is adapted primarily from the educational systems of the United States and United Kingdom; more recently, the International Baccalaureate programmes are being offered as the curriculum of many international schools.
- They serve transitional, highly mobile families.
- Their governing Boards, faculties and staff also turn over frequently (it is not unusual for the membership of a governing Board to change completely within two or three years).
- They are often not housed in state-of-the-art facilities.

Of course there are international schools whose profile is different. For example, there are some that are proprietary (profit-making), that are sectarian, that are divisions of national systems such as in France, and some that are operated by business and industry, such as oil company schools in the Middle East. It is also the case that, increasingly, the share of enrolment comprising 'local' students is growing as host-country families desire, or need to find, alternatives to the state system for their children. Neither do all international schools have short-term faculty and staff. The three schools which serve large United Nations Organization populations – the United Nations International School in New York, the International School of Geneva and the Vienna International School – all have large numbers of the faculty and staff with long years of service: one would assume their location has much to do with this phenomenon. At the schools in New York and Geneva, which are older than the Vienna school, there is a significant proportion who have 20 or more years of service. These schools are not typical in this respect.

International schools are fee-based and tuition-driven with respect to the funding of their operations. Many students in international schools have their tuition fees paid by the corporation or diplomatic entity that employs their parents. In the case of students whose parents are employed by the United Nations Organization, including its specialized agencies such as UNICEF, UNDP, WHO and ILO, or by diplomatic missions to the UN, an education grant ordinarily takes care of school costs. The United Nations International School in New York is atypical in this respect in that approximately half of its 1,500 students are from non-UN families and pay all costs themselves.

Capital costs for land and buildings are ordinarily funded by grants from the host country or city government, from the multinational corporations served by the school, and/or by donations from the families – present, past and future – which are usually in the form of a one-time capital charge at the time of enrolment, by a surcharge on tuition fees, or by a mortgage fee paid when they arrive and refunded when they depart. In some cases, the host country authorities will provide land and buildings, whose ownership they retain, for use by the international school. A few international schools have been the beneficiaries of philanthropic foundation grants to assist with capital costs. It is interesting to note here that the longer-term planning associated with a capital campaign is the only experience with long-range planning that many international schools have. It is, moreover, usually well done.

Last but not least, a major characteristic that virtually all international schools share is their *raison d'être* which is not, in my view surprisingly, to provide a truly international education to their students but, rather, to cater for students cut off from their education at home by providing them with a programme of studies as similar as possible to what they left behind and to enable their re-entry to their national system, particularly at university level. The descriptor 'international school' is therefore misleading in as much as few international schools are, in fact, truly international. Even the eminent International Baccalaureate programme, which comprises as close to an international curriculum extant, is predominantly Western in its cultural optic and must continue to work diligently to acquire a global or trans-national content and spirit.

Because of the salient characteristics of international schools set out above, planning is daunting for those who are given the responsibility for carrying it out. There are challenging uncertainties and imponderables involved, including the difficulty in accurately forecasting future enrolment and not knowing when and how host country political and economic circumstances may change, and how quickly. Boards and administrations, which are themselves likely to be short term, along with faculty, staff and the parent community, are called upon to make provision for the long term. Yet, it is precisely in these circumstances that planning is essential; a powerful paradox indeed.

Planning as decision-making

Long-term (strategic) planning is a decision-making process. That is worth repeating: *planning is about making decisions*. It is not organizational day-dreaming about a pie-in-the-sky, idyllic future. It is about deciding *now* what the organization (in this case the school) will be by a specific future date and beginning immediately to take the steps that will assure the necessary development.

A classic example of planning as decision-making was the lunar-landing project of the 1960s. When the president of the United States announced the decision to put a man on the moon within a decade, that decision began a process and a period of design to produce the propulsion systems, computers, navigational systems, communication systems, heat-shield materials, and so on which did not exist at the time the decision was made. The landing the world watched on television in 1969 was the result of a decision made eight years earlier.

Nothing is more action-oriented than planning when it is done properly. Anyone surprised by this definition of planning as decision-making has a lot of company. Ordinarily planning is perceived as something that goes on apart from the daily business of the school; indeed, some schools (and other organizations as well) have a 'Planning Office' which does the planning, all too often unrelated to the real life of the school.

Those who analyse the practice of management invariably subdivide it into major functions such as planning, organizing, controlling and motivating. Each of these, in turn, has a number of subsets. Planning is the key function from which all the others follow. It determines what is to be accomplished in the way of change, the setting of goals and objectives to achieve that change, and major courses of action (strategies) to be taken. With respect to the other functions, *organizing* is ensuring that the school, its staff and its programmes are structured in such a way as to enhance the likelihood of achieving the stated goals and objectives, and *controlling* is the way in which the results are monitored, assessed and reported. The function of motivating needs no definition.

Strategic planning

It would be difficult to exaggerate the critical importance of strategic planning in schools, particularly in international schools. The plan, which is regularly updated, provides the context for dealing with unexpected developments or changing demands so characteristic of life in an international school. A plan that is the basis of all decision-making provides continuity in an unstable environment. Certainly there is otherwise little continuity in a setting where the composition of the Board, the leadership of the school and the faculty itself is undergoing constant and comprehensive turnover (Hawley, 1995). Since the value of strategic planning is clearly manifest for these schools, why is it so difficult to achieve? Why are there so few international schools with a strategic plan, which is the chief tool of management, the source of all that the school is and does? These are important questions to address.

In the first place, international schools are educational organizations, and educational organizations of all kinds seem to have a particular aversion to planning. Perhaps this is so because their experience with planning in the past has not been a positive one. Moreover, the use of business terminology in planning such as 'management', 'goals', 'objectives' and 'strategy' may be off-putting to those of an academic bent who resist the idea that education is in any sense comparable to business. There are those in universities as well as in schools who fervently believe that teaching and learning cannot be planned and measured – that it is a process 'that offers eternity', too broad in scope and too long-term in its effect to be effectively assessed.

Historically, strategic planning has been more a characteristic of the business sector, government and the military than it has been of education. In spite of fundamental shifts in these sectors in recent years, in favour of shorter planning horizons and with emphasis on more immediate returns on the investments of shareholders and officers, most of the actions taken are rationalized as necessary for the long-term stability and prosperity of the enterprise. Schools and many colleges had a history of a more hand-to-mouth existence. Yet the financial fragility and intense competition most independent schools and colleges must live with – and which distract them from managing more strategically – are ordinarily not the same kind of issue for those international schools whose funding comes in large measure from the organizations whose employees' children are served by the school, and which often do not face strong competition from other schools for their students. One suspects, therefore, that the paucity of strategic thinking and planning in a typical international school arises primarily from the heavy and constant turnover of Board members, administrators and faculty. Sadly, virtually all of the problems and shortcomings in international schools are a result of not engaging in strategic planning.

Obstacles to strategic planning

In the absence of a strategic plan as the guide for governance and management, and with the Board membership, administration, faculty, parent body and student body continuously changing, there is an inevitable tendency constantly to redefine the school. Thus the school – in terms of its philosophy, purpose and programme – becomes whatever its constituents say that it is at any given time. School politics abound, and pressure groups of parents and Board members (and parents are in the majority on many international school Boards) seek to influence the programme and staffing of the school in substantive but not always constructive ways. This is not surprising in the absence of a long-term planning horizon. Fortunately the combined forces of accreditations, external programmes such as those under the aegis of the International Baccalaureate Organisation, the small core of 'permanent' faculty found in almost every international school and, occasionally, the expressed interest of host country education authorities, lend the school a certain amount of stability. Without them there would be virtually no assurance of continuity from year to year.

Other reasons for the dearth of long-term (strategic) planning in international schools are that a good deal of time and energy on the part of everyone is required to produce a plan, after which a commitment must be made to use the plan as the guide for all teaching and decision-making in the school. If what is contained in the curriculum and what is taught is not derived from the mission, goals and objectives of the school's plan, the plan is without effect. Implicit in the design of a long-term plan, however, is the awareness that much of what is done in the school – pre-eminently the curriculum – will likely need to undergo comprehensive revision to reflect the values and objectives of the plan. Not only is this time-consuming work, it also requires the acquisition of new knowledge and new skills; it means surrendering the comfortable and familiar to move into new pedagogical terrain. All of this can create a formidable resistance to planning on the part of faculty. Most teachers believe they already have more to do than time permits. When teaching is done conscientiously and well, it is, indeed, a very demanding and time-consuming responsibility. Planning is often regarded by faculty as one more 'add-on'.

Another serious potential fault line in strategic (long-term) planning is the failure on the part of the Board and Head of school to assure that the connection is made between developing the plan and implementing it. This requires diligence and determination as well as the allocation of a substantial portion of the Head's time to the ongoing supervision of the Principals, who are the vital link in the entire process, because it is clear that if the curriculum of the school – what the faculty teach – does not follow the plan, then there is not one curriculum but, rather, as many as there are teachers.

One of the major obstacles to successful strategic planning is the failure to include in the process those who will be most directly affected by it: faculty, staff and students. In spite of the fact that the membership of these constituencies will change fairly rapidly, the insights of current members are essential. If they are ignored in the planning process, the plan that results will have little or no impact. The mere fact that they were involved will give the plan credibility with the new faculty and students who take their places over time.

If a strategic plan is developed with the participation of all the school's constituencies, approved by the Board and implemented by the administration and faculty, if that plan is updated at least annually, if new Board members are oriented to it, and if all key management and instructional decisions are based on it, the school will cease to be a *tabula rasa* for each new wave of Board members, Head, faculty and parents. Instead, long-term directions can be set, respected and followed. The school can maintain its identity, character, purpose, values and curriculum in spite of the ceaseless changing of the cast of characters in the various constituencies. In short, the school will no longer undergo continued reinvention.

Everything in the life and organization of a school ought to be the result of planning: the school's mission, its educational programme and policies, its staffing and staff development, its budgets, its physical plant and educational equipment, its size and organizational structure. It is the responsibility of the governing body (by whatever title it is known: Board of trustees, Board of directors, governing Board, Board of governors, etc) to make certain that this planning takes place, to participate in it at the macro-level and to evaluate periodically its effectiveness as it is implemented.

Leadership and management planning

Planning is the key leadership responsibility and a major function of management. What does this statement mean? At the least it asserts that management and leadership are not synonymous and, implicitly, that they may involve different people. Educational organizations, in spite of their consultative culture and commitment to democratic decision-making, are still largely hierarchical structures in governance and management. Those expected to provide leadership and to manage are a relatively small number of people in the organization, and are typically the governing Boards, and the executive officers who report to them. This model is still a more, rather than less, accurate reflection of K-12 education and small colleges.

Before going further, it is important to note that leadership and management differ from one another in several critical ways. Management is essentially a rational process relying upon certain acquired skills. Managers motivate by assuring promotions, salary increases, bonuses and a wide array of other perquisites, nearly all of which have a monetary value. Leaders, on the other hand, are energized by a vision of what might be, along with a single-minded determination to achieve that vision. The leader influences others by words (inspiration) and example (charisma), winning their commitment to participate in the achievement of the vision. Ideally, leaders are effective managers, and vice versa. However, we have all known people with wonderfully exciting ideas who had no idea how to implement them. Leaders who are not good managers need to find and empower others who are, and work in tandem with them.

It is difficult to imagine how an international school – or any other school – could achieve and maintain a programme of the highest quality without strategic planning. A school must define what high quality means in every aspect of its programme and operations. This, in turn, requires a comprehensive understanding of the school's external environment (in its widest sense) and the demands it makes upon the school and will make in the future, along with a realistic assessment of the school's capability to meet the demands. A standard of the highest quality also means that beyond meeting the demands placed upon it externally, the school has a larger agenda. Particularly in an international school, this larger agenda (which should be consistent with its general founding purpose, its specific mission and its philosophy) is to inspire, educate and train its students to become active, lifelong champions of peaceful resolution of conflict, of sustainable development, of the eradication of poverty and disease, of the democratic political process and of a more equitable distribution of the world's riches.

There is widespread lip service paid to the foregoing criteria, but a rigorous review of a typical international school's curriculum, teaching resources, policies and practices too often does not reflect a pervasive practical commitment to them. Schools cannot develop such a profile without an explicit decision to do so, as well as the resources and ability to implement that decision. At the heart of strategic planning is the realization that the future does not yet exist. Its impact on us can be influenced and shaped by us, first by making decisions about what we want that future to be and then by taking all necessary steps to assure that the curriculum, staffing, educational materials and equipment, facilities and assessment procedures are in place.

Planning as a whole-school commitment

There is nothing mysterious or exotic about strategic planning. It is neither a highly technical nor an arcane process. External expertise, while it may be helpful, is not required, nor are significant additional financial resources. Strategic planning is not difficult to implement if there is a determination to do it on the part of all the school's constituencies, beginning with the governing Board.

Although there is no one 'right' way to plan strategically, a number of characteristics of successful models consistently manifest themselves. Chief among these are the following:

1. The process begins with a documented consensus among the governing Board, administration, faculty, staff, parents and student representatives about the most important knowledge, skills, values and commitments the students should acquire and develop.
2. Consensus is then reached and documented among the same constituencies about what the school needs to become (its vision) at the earliest practical time, in order to enable the attainment of those aspirations.
3. The school's entire programme: curricular, co-curricular and extracurricular, is reviewed for consistency with the school's newly declared aspirations. A work schedule is developed for making whatever revisions and additions to the programme are necessary to ensure consistency.

The above three steps become the framework of a written plan which documents major courses of action to be taken (strategies), the major results expected (goals), a time frame for specific interim results derived from the goals (objectives) and the resources required (fiscal projections and budgets). This written plan also includes a description of the procedures to be used to monitor progress and assess results. A carefully crafted strategic plan is in reality a comprehensive organizational plan in that it includes all aspects of the school – governance and leadership, philosophy, educational programmes, student life and performance, teaching, facilities, and fiscal – for both the near and long term. Finally, characteristic of all effective strategic plans is that they are continuously calibrated and are comprehensively reviewed and revised annually. This is a vital part of assessing quality in the process.

Life is evolution and change. Institutions and organizations also evolve and change. Since the purpose of schooling is to produce young people who can function successfully in a constantly changing world and, in fact, lead that change, all schools, including international schools, must be changing themselves in order to meet that need and that purpose. But the evolution and change in the school should be a planned and guided one – based on a chosen future. Strategic planning enables schools to adjust and adapt to a mutable external environment while remaining true to their essential purpose and aspirations.

References

Hayden, M C and Thompson, J J (1995) International schools and international education: a relationship reviewed, *Oxford Review of Education*, **21** (3), pp 327–45

Hawley, D (1995) How long do international school heads survive? A research analysis (Part II), *International Schools Journal*, **14** (2), pp 23–36

Chapter 14

Strategic planning for international schools: a roadmap to excellence

Niall Nelson

Strategic and long-term planning

Without proper planning – strategic planning – the goal of achieving a high-quality standard of education in international schools is likely to be ephemeral. If somehow achieved, whether through fiat, intuition, an initial burst of energy, or some other combination of circumstances, it is unlikely to be maintained. Building and sustaining excellence takes forethought, hard work and the effective harnessing of all available talent. This is nowhere more evident than in the complex environments within which international schools operate, as captured by Glickman (2000) in pointing out that 'We live and breathe based on the vitality of the economy and the whim of the corporate and diplomatic world. These conditions pose a challenge in planning…' In accepting the challenge, schools will increasingly, as Caldwell and Spinks (1992) note, 'require a high level capacity for strategic planning, that is to see the larger picture and on a continuing basis set and reset priorities.'

Recognition of the importance of strategic planning is increasing, both within international schools and among the organizations that support them, such as accrediting agencies. The European Council of International Schools (1997) includes the following statement among its standards for accreditation: 'There shall be evidence of long-range educational planning with a strategy for accomplishing the school's goals.' Noting that the terms used to describe the planning process may vary, Leggate and Thompson (1997) observe that 'The growth of interest in school improvement and effectiveness over recent years has brought with it an increase in the volume of literature and debate relating to the value of development planning in schools, and its relevance to a wide range of contexts.'

The descriptor 'strategic' planning is often used interchangeably with 'development', 'long term', or 'long range' planning. Hargreaves and Hopkins (1994) comment that 'Development planning is a response to the management of multiple innovations and change, and the perceived need for a systematic and whole-school approach to planning, especially where schools are expected to be more self-managing.' Brown (2000), meanwhile, suggests a distinction between strategic and long-range planning, as follows:

> Strategic planning, involving review of mission and philosophy, long term resource commitments, goals, action plans and stakeholder participation, is the culminate time-consuming activity... Long range planning, a look into a shorter-term future of where current mission, philosophy and programs will take the organization, also demands a great deal of time, albeit less than the process of community organization for strategic planning.

Independent School Management's *Ideas & Perspectives* (1997), a US independent school publication, sees the distinction between the two in a different light, pointing out that 'In our parlance, "long range" indicates comprehensiveness in a planning document, whereas "strategic" refers to a more limited viability-focused (and, thus, finance-oriented) planning document.'

The term 'strategic gap' is referred to by Walker (2000), who finds it helpful in distinguishing between the status quo and a desired future; referring to the draft strategic plan of the International Baccalaureate Organisation (IBO), he writes that: 'A strategic plan starts from where the Organisation is now, today. We must ask first what will happen in, say, five years' time if the IBO goes on much as it is now. We then ask what must be done if we want to end up somewhere different. That difference, between what is *likely* to happen and what we *want* to happen, is sometimes called the "strategic gap". In order to close that strategic gap, something has to change.'

These descriptions and definitions explicitly or implicitly embrace the premise of anticipating and managing change; of proactively committing time, energy and resources to riding the wave of forward momentum, rather than being drowned beneath it. Cook (1988) goes further by introducing the notion of strategic planning as consisting of both a discipline and a process:

the *discipline* being the substantive ingredients or components of the plan itself; the *process* the method or procedure by which the plan is created. To argue the relative value of either is moot; to attempt completely to separate them is foolish. Both are inextricably connected and, if properly interwoven, will provide a superior plan.

The *discipline*, if properly applied, will render the process entirely meaningful because it forces a complete and final resolution of all relevant issues. The *process*, if properly followed, assures substance in the discipline because it provides a controlled concentration of rational effort on the issues involved.

The involvement of key school constituents in this discipline and process is clearly pivotal if lasting quality is to be attained, and this point will be expanded upon later. Certainly, strategic planning is demanding of time, but so too is the alternative – not planning! Being in a constantly reactive mode is time-consuming, wasteful of resources and ultimately debilitating to students, staff and parents alike. A well-crafted, flexible, strategic plan can be a powerful way of saying 'no' to whimsical, ill-conceived, or politically motivated ideas, from whatever quarter they may emanate. The challenge for the proponents of new ideas or proposals is then to get them into the strategic planning cycle, to convince others of their deserved ranking among competing priorities.

The role of school Boards

Where, then, does the responsibility for strategic planning properly belong? Brown (2000) places it firmly in the hands of school Board members and argues that they abrogate this primary duty at great risk to the school:

> No other individual, group or organization is charged with it. Nor can anyone else do it as well as the Board, although many have tried and will continue to try to usurp this prime function reserved to a school's Board. However, and unfortunately, if the Board does not fulfil this obligation, by default it will be pirated by others not entitled to exercise the authority legally given to the Board. Most likely, the results of such usurpation will be undesirable to the Board and to the community who has entrusted its precious children to it. That one prime onus that should command the full and constant attention of all Board members is the determination of the future of their institution.

Brown does not confuse responsibility with execution, or contend that Boards should write or implement the plan; he abhors what he describes as '"micromanagement", the time-consuming assumption by Boards of the decision-making authority and prerogatives of the hired professional administrators of their institution'. He also recognizes that 'Effective Boards unite their communities in involvement in, and commitment to, sound plans developed jointly for the growth of their institutions.'

In addressing Board chairs and Heads of schools, Daignault (1999) stresses their combined responsibility for spelling out how their strategic plans are forwarding the mission of their schools and '(addressing) areas of concern for the foreseeable future'. She continues:

> We all know about the importance of partnership in your school: the chair and the Head. But I contend you need more than that. Just as the Head of school needs an administrative team that is cohesive and forward thinking, the Board chair needs to have the whole Board working together on the strategic issues facing the school. This kind of total teamwork doesn't just happen. You, as Board chair, have to develop your Board into a cohesive unit.'

Board retreats, with administrators and other key stakeholders present, can provide a powerful forum for considering strategic directions. They allow time to focus on the big picture, often difficult during regular Board meetings.

Leggate and Thompson (1997) reinforce the importance of the Board accepting responsibility for planning while ensuring a proper role for other stakeholders, in noting that:

> In many countries both state and independent schools are discovering that the determination of the future of the institution lies within the control of members of their school Boards, composed of elected, or selected, governors working with the Head and teaching staff, each with a responsibility for a particular role in the process. In such a situation the need for an overall school development plan, or the school's equivalent to the corporate strategic plan, becomes even more pressing. For in a negotiated plan there exists a vehicle for the translation of the shared vision of the school community into some form of coherent reality, through prioritized strategies and action plans within an agreed time schedule.

As the school's Chief Executive Officer, and the sole employee appointed by the Board, the Head must play a central part in developing the institutional strategic plan, in ensuring its implementation and in maintaining a process of regular review and revision. The Board must hold the Head accountable for accomplishing these tasks. The wise international school Head will, in turn, draw on the talents of the staff, which will typically represent rich and varied experiences in a range of national and international settings. As Hawkes (1991) observes: 'the Strategic Plan can increase the synergy of a school, particularly if the community has a real sense of ownership of the plan'.

The context of planning in international schools

Before examining an approach to strategic planning used successfully in one international school, it is worth reflecting on a question which represents something of a paradox: if the case for strategic planning is so compelling, why aren't all schools doing it? Survey research by Leggate and Thompson (1997) reaffirms the premise that international school Heads overwhelmingly recognize the importance of planning. Yet up to a quarter of the schools surveyed lacked any plan in which short-, medium- and long-term goals had been identified and prioritized. Free-response comments provided by the Heads offer some explanations for this deficit, summarized by Leggate and Thompson as follows: 'Among the suggestions made for hindrance to the process of long-term planning were the variety of cultural expectations of such an exercise, linguistic and legal complexities, the impact of transiency on financial planning particularly, limited input from alumni and uncertainties generated by external forces, political or climatic.'

Ironically, this list underlines the essential strength of the case for strategic planning. If schools' futures were predictable, secure and absolute, the need to anticipate and manage change would recede, if not disappear altogether. Because they are not, because international schools are complex organizations and experience high levels of student mobility and constant turnover of Board members, administrators and teachers, planning is absolutely essential. Individuals may move on, but as long as the institution remains, the Board retains the ultimate responsibility for planning. The greater the degree of institutional flux, the greater the need for building flexibility and regular review into the strategic-planning mechanism. There is evidence to suggest that the very attempt to impose order on chaos has a salutary effect, in and of itself. Hawley (1994), for instance, found that Heads of international schools that had Board policy manuals remained considerably longer in post than did Heads in schools that had none, while Littleford (1999) found that there is a direct link between length of service of Board chairs and the tenures and successes of Heads. The longer the term of the chair, it is suggested, the longer the tenure of the Head, not least because of the value of historical memory in preventing upheavals.

Independent School Management's *Ideas & Perspectives* (1999) contends that, because of the importance of 'Board memory' to future planning efforts, a Board might usefully create an *ad hoc* committee to develop the school's strategic history:

> Help the Chair keep the goal clearly in mind: a brief strategic history in bul-
> let-point format, summarizing the past in order to highlight the (implied)

constraints and opportunities affecting the organization's strategic future. Make sure the committee Chair is clear that, given the fact that the Board of Trustees must operate fundamentally as a planning entity, a *brief, accurate, user-friendly*, strategic history is by definition a core Board document.

Such an approach would surely help greatly in mitigating the effects of rapid Board member turnover in many international schools.

Other criticisms of strategic planning charge that it is antithetical to firm leadership by the school Head, impedes innovation and creativity, is cumbersome and takes undue time. Broman (1999) encapsulates these views in arguing that:

> inhibiting our schools from a bold advance into the future are the excessive time, resources and total community involvement that are poured into the process of deciding the next vital steps in a school's progress. This process, often called 'strategic planning', can be a costly and lengthy affair... Long complicated planning processes with widespread community involvement seriously undermine both in concept and execution the bold, engaging leadership that is needed to improve our schools. We must put the process and the responsibility back where it belongs – in our trained, professional school leaders.

The unstated, and unproven, assertion here is that, in the absence of strategic planning, schools would advance boldly into the future. Indeed they might, and might even do so successfully for a while, particularly if they have a lucky or charismatic leader. But, as argued earlier, fiat or intuition is not sufficient to sustain institutional excellence over time. Bold leadership and personal conviction do not always deliver the goods. General Custer, for example, might well have benefited from a little strategic planning before his last leadership act; his troops would doubtless have wished he had sought counsel from others not anointed to lead but more knowledgeable about terrain and context.

Ad hoc, non-collaborative leadership is rarely a good fit for those complex microcosms called international schools, with their diverse staffs and inquiring, expectant, migratory parent bodies. The challenge for the leadership is how best to tap into the talents of the school community to inform the planning discipline and process and increase the likelihood of successful implementation of action plans. Strategic planning may indeed be demanding of time and effort, certainly in the early stages, but it need not be onerous or unduly complicated. In helping to prioritize demands it can be reassuring. In providing for the rejection of frivolous or off-agenda requests it can be liberating. It does not necessitate building cumbersome bureaucracies, or abandoning decision-making, but it does require the leadership to be clear, consistent and willing to forego conservation of power for the prospect of receiving creative ideas and innovative insights from unexpected quarters.

A perspective from Jakarta

As a means of illustrating many of the points raised so far, the remainder of the chapter will briefly describe the discipline and process of strategic planning at Jakarta International School (JIS), a large pre-K–12 institution established in 1951 in Indonesia. Since approval by the school Board in its first iteration in 1992, the JIS Strategic Plan (2000) has undergone several substantial revisions. The current version, covering the years 2000 to 2005, represents the seventh update of the original plan. In fact, each successive plan is but a snapshot in time; the planning cycle is ongoing and undergirds the operation of the whole school. A Strategic Planning Committee (SPC) was formed during the first semester of the 1991–1992 academic year and consisted of representatives of the Board, administration, faculty and parent body; about 15 in total. As the newly appointed Headmaster, the development of a strategic plan was a major performance objective during my first year (and has rarely been absent from my annual goals ever since). Members of the SPC added to their residual knowledge of planning by reviewing publications on the subject and by listening to such experienced voices as were available. Undoubtedly the most helpful and informative source was *Bill Cook's Strategic Planning for America's Schools* (Cook, 1988).

It was quickly evident that, while the SPC would provide direction and continuity, elements of the wider school community would need to be consulted and involved on an *ad hoc* basis if the plan was to succeed. The drafting of a school mission statement gave us an early opportunity to test our direction. We invited comment and input on successive drafts from all constituencies, including students, and eventually developed the statement that has stood the test of time until the present, and represents a 'clear and concise statement of the school's purpose and function, which acknowledges reality and aspires to an ideal vision'. At the outset the plan defines terms used; specificity is essential to avoid vagueness and confusion. The school's philosophy statement, which also benefited from community input, is one which 'describes how the school will conduct its day-to-day business with stakeholders. The philosophy's foundation is a shared set of convictions and beliefs, which manifests itself in the school's operating behaviour. It is the standard used to judge the appropriateness of all actions.'

Next came the development of planning assumptions: 'important forecasted planning parameters within which the school will operate over the five year planning horizon'. These assumptions are revisited each year. The same is true of our position audit, or SWOT analysis: 'a tool used to identify the school's Strengths, Weaknesses, Opportunities and Threats in order to gain understanding of potential environmental impacts which may affect the school's ability to accomplish its mission'.

Five main sections follow: curriculum, facilities, finances, human resources and community relations. Each of the five is broken down into objectives, strategies and action plans. Objectives are 'broad, sweeping, realistic aims or goals that are critical in meeting the school's mission'. Strategies are 'broad courses of action which require the manoeuvring of substantially all of the school's resources'. Action plans are 'detailed tactical plans or series of actions established to effect the strategies'. In the curriculum section, for example, a five-year curriculum plan review cycle is shown. In the facilities section an action plan timeline is laid out, also pointing towards a five-year horizon.

Control charts are published annually for each section. A control chart is 'a specific report format used to track the progress of the key implementation elements of an action plan.' For each action plan, a bar chart shows the projected completion date within the July–June time frame, or indicates that the action plan will extend into a subsequent year. The person ultimately responsible for the completion of each action plan is also clearly specified. Since the whole point of strategic planning is to turn ideas into action, the critical importance of effective implementation cannot be over-emphasized.

Successive drafts of our first strategic plan were tested with different constituents as they developed. An open forum was held when the final draft was ready, prior to school Board approval. Our plan is now published annually on JISNet and hard copies are made available to all constituents through our libraries and offices. As the planning discipline and process have become better integrated into the fabric of the school's operation, the work of the SPC has become less onerous. In essence, it provides oversight of the cycle whereby the document is extended a further year into the future, as more information becomes available and fine-tuning is applied to the intervening years.

A word about financial forecasting is apposite here, since facilities, staffing and other plans are unlikely to be translated from intention to implementation without the establishment of fiscal projections. An important two-part budgeting question is 'what do we want our school to look like five years from now, and how will we ensure solvency *en route*?' Five-year enrolment projections follow naturally from answering this question as accurately as possible and, in turn, provide the basis for developing year-by-year cost forecasts.

The JIS Strategic Plan was extensively tested in 1998 as economic uncertainty and political and civil unrest swept Indonesia. Although we could not have foreseen all that happened, we had at least posed some of the right questions and had explored alternative strategies and courses of action. The plan was of great benefit in helping us navigate the difficulties posed by a dramatic drop in enrolment from 3,160 to 2,400, and to locate opportunities for institutional improvement in the midst of threats to the school's future well-being.

Any strategic plan can be improved upon, but it is easier and more fulfilling to seek improvement than to have to start constantly from scratch. Seeking a balance between preservation of mission and strategic change, anticipating bends in the road ahead, and being as flexible and agile as age and size will allow, are all keys to success. Luther put it more elegantly quite some time ago:

> We are not yet what we shall be
> But we are growing toward it,
> The process is not yet finished
> But it is going on,
> This is not the end
> But it is the road.

References

Broman, F (1999) Complicated planning undermines leadership, *The International Educator*, **XIII** (4), p 8

Brown, G C (2000) *Long Range and Strategic Planning*, in *Memo to the Board, A Development Program for American/International Overseas School Board Members*, Association for the Advancement of International Education, New Wilmington, PA

Caldwell, B J and Spinks, J M (1992) *Leading the Self-Managing School*, Falmer Press, London

Cook, W J (1988) *Bill Cook's Strategic Planning for America's Schools*, American Association of School Administrators, Arlington, VA

Daignault, S (1999) NAIS Leadership Through Partnership, *Leadership Forum*, Fall 1999, National Association of Independent Schools, Washington, DC

European Council of International Schools (1997) *The ECIS Guide to School Evaluation and Accreditation*, ECIS, Petersfield

Glickman, J (2000) Changing Enrolments, *American Overseas Schools*, Phi Delta Kappa Educational Foundation, Bloomington, IN

Hargreaves, D H and Hopkins, D (1994) *Development Planning for School Improvement*, Cassell Educational, London

Hawkes, T (1991) *Some Thoughts on Strategic Planning for Schools*, paper delivered to the Association of Independent Schools, Victoria, Australia

Hawley, D B (1994) How long do international school heads survive? (Part I), *International Schools Journal*, **XIV** (1), pp 8–21

Independent School Management (1997) Your strategic financial plan, *Ideas & Perspectives*, **22** (5)

Independent School Management (1999) Strategic continuity: the importance of 'Board memory', *Ideas & Perspectives*, **24** (9)

Jakarta International School (2000) *Strategic Plan 2000–2005*, Jakarta, Indonesia

Leggate, P M C and Thompson, J J (1997) The management of development planning in international schools, *International Journal of Educational Management*, **11** (6), pp 268–73

Littleford, J (1999) Leadership of schools and the longevity of school heads, *International Schools Journal*, **XIX** (1), pp 23–34

Walker, G R (2000) *A Draft Strategic Plan*, International Baccalaureate Organisation, Geneva

Chapter 15

International schools, globalization and the seven cultures of capitalism

James Cambridge

This chapter considers the structure and activities of international schools and schools offering international education in the context of globalization, one definition of which is the spread of capitalist values around the world. International schools are characterized by diversity (Hayden and Thompson, 1995), which in turn implies a range of values applying to every dimension of their practice. The organizational culture of an international school therefore represents the reconciliation of a dilemma between the formation of a monoculture in terms of the educational values espoused by the organization, and the cultural pluralism of its teachers and students. This is a dynamic process and, as the components change over time, so the nature of the reconciliation also changes. Multiculturalism in education can be 'a substantial mono-culturalism as to values, mitigated by tolerance of exotic detail' (Zaw, 1996). It may be argued, however, that parents choose to send their children to international schools because of the values that the institutions embody in terms of curriculum offered, organizational style and human relations practised between teachers and students.

The view of the structure and function of the international school as embodiments of particular values resembles a model of entrepreneurism in business described by Hampden–Turner and Trompenaars (1993), who argue that capitalism provides a cultural framework for economic and ethical values. Institutions, whether they are schools or business organizations, are the products and expressions of cultural values.

Managers of organizations are constantly attempting to reconcile the opposing points of view of competing interest groups. Such challenges are a fact of life, and they are likely to be increased in a multicultural setting in which the participants often start from fundamentally different sets of values.

Capitalist values, however, are by no means monolithic since there are at least 'seven cultures of capitalism' (Hampden-Turner and Trompenaars, 1993). International schools are theatres in which a variety of intercultural encounters are rehearsed between administration, teaching staff, support staff, students, parents and the local community. The form and content of these encounters will have a profound effect on the procedural and transformational quality of the structure and activities of the international school.

Globalization and international schools

International schools, and other schools offering international education, operate in a context of increasing globalization, which has been described as 'the widening, deepening and speeding up of world-wide interconnectedness in all aspects of contemporary social life' (Held *et al*, 1998). Three ways of interpreting globalization have been proposed, and trends in each may be identified in the activities of international schools.

One approach is the hyperglobalist thesis that globalization is 'the denationalization of economies through the establishment of transnational networks of production, trade and finance' (Held *et al*, 1998). This is a trend that results in the application of the same standards everywhere, so that international schools may be identified as being part of a process of cultural homogenization. For many globally mobile expatriates, this would be an attractive proposition because international education may be compared with other globally marketed goods and services such as soft drinks and hamburgers; a reliable product conforming to consistent quality standards throughout the world.

A second approach is sceptical about globalization because it argues that the world economic order is no more globalized now than it was in the past. The tasks of governments are to regulate and facilitate international trade. International, national and regional markets are converging, but there is no evidence to support the view that superstates which transcend national frontiers are emerging. Furthermore, identification with national and regional cultures is becoming more – not less – prominent at the present time. Certain countries appear to tolerate rather than encourage expatriate educational institutions in their territories, and may legislate to prevent the participation of their own citizens in them. International schools therefore offer an opportunity for the provision of an encapsulated education, based on the transplanted educational values of other national systems and insulated from the local cultural environment (Sylvester, 1998).

A third transformationalist approach to globalization brings together the global with the local. In a world where the electronic media facilitate rapid and widespread communication, distribution of cultural difference may depend less on geographical dispersion and more on the distribution of wealth and resources. As John Lowe observes elsewhere in this volume, members of the socio-economic elite in a country may have less in common in some respects with their poorer compatriots than they have with their peers in another country. On the other hand, they will still share certain national cultural values and ways of seeing the world with their compatriots, identifiable with what Hofstede (1991) calls 'software of the mind'. Members of the local socio-economic elite may select an international education for their children because they lack confidence in their home country's educational system and/or because of the opportunities for advancement which are offered, leading to entry into the higher education systems of other countries. International schools may offer scholarships to widen the participation of host country nationals from a range of social classes, alongside their fellow students from the globally mobile expatriate community.

Seven cultures of capitalism

It is my contention that the hyperglobalist view of the spread of one particular set of capitalist values throughout the world is a myth, since there are at least seven cultures of capitalism, exemplified by the contrasting value systems expressed in the national cultures of the United States of America, Great Britain, Japan, Germany, France, Sweden and The Netherlands (Hampden-Turner and Trompenaars, 1993). It is no accident that these nationalities comprise the majority of the consumers – and suppliers – of the services of international schools. They are the most economically developed nations which not only provide the capital to finance multinational businesses, parastatal organizations and development aid agencies, but also supply the globally mobile personnel who staff them.

The framework has become dated since market liberalization, particularly in India and China, has brought the economies of those countries into more prominence globally in the past decade (Fitzgerald, 1997; Kobrin, 1999), but I do not think that this necessarily invalidates it. Its authors recognize this and the values of the South-East Asian economies are addressed in a later publication (Hampden-Turner and Trompenaars, 1997). It will be interesting to see how the global impact of the emerging Indian and Chinese cultures of capitalism unfolds in the twenty-first century, especially in terms of how their values influence the development of international education. The number of institutions offering international education is increasing in both countries.

Valuing processes applied to international schools

Hampden-Turner and Trompenaars (1993) propose that the cultural values of seven major capitalist countries can be described and analysed as dilemmas about how we relate to other people, time and the external environment. They argue that all cultures are confronted with the same basic problems but differ in how they solve them; indeed, this is how we recognize different cultures. Coincidentally, there are not only seven cultures of capitalism but also seven sets of 'values in tension' which describe those dilemmas. They comprise:

- making rules and discovering exceptions, contrasting the need for universally applied rules with the need to recognize particular exceptions to them;
- constructing and deconstructing, which contrasts integrating (building up a world view by looking at whole patterns, relationships and wider contexts) and analysing (breaking down phenomena into their component parts);
- managing communities of individuals, contrasting the needs of the individual with the needs of the community;
- internalizing the outside world, contrasting personal judgements, decisions and commitments (inner direction) with the signals, demands and trends of the outside world (outer direction) as guides to action;
- synchronizing fast processes, contrasting views of time as a sequence and as synchronization;
- choosing among achievers, contrasting attribution of status to individuals by what they have achieved (status by achievement), with some other characteristic important to the institution such as age, seniority or gender (status by ascription); and

- sponsoring equal opportunities to excel, which contrasts treating
  employees with equality with the establishment of authority through
  hierarchy.

How might these valuing processes be applied to the description and
analysis of international schools? The statements that follow are
tentative, and provide a set of hypotheses which may be tested in the
context of the organizational cultures of international schools.

Making rules and discovering exceptions

This valuing process contrasts the tendency to apply general rules to
situations (universalism) with making special exceptions (particu-
larism). For illustration, consider traffic speed limits. Are they absolute
limits to speed to which all drivers must conform, or are they ideal
speeds to which drivers should aspire but which may be broken under
special circumstances? The former is a universalist solution to the regu-
lation of traffic speed (the rules apply to everyone), and the latter is a
particularist solution (the rules apply to everyone – except me when
I'm in a hurry).

   In the context of international schools, to what extent are the rules of
the institution applied to all persons, in the same way and at all times, or
are exceptions made? For example, school admissions criteria may be
stretched to allow a particular student to enrol. Certain countries may
have employment legislation making it difficult to recruit expatriate
teachers but there may be ways of circumventing these laws if the school
has 'friends in high places'. However, 'oiling the wheels of business' in
one culture may be interpreted as corruption of government officials in
another. A maze of legislation may be faced by the international school
manager and a steep part of the learning curve associated with starting a
new job will involve developing an understanding of the ways in which
it is applied. Misunderstandings may abound as individuals from
different cultures interpret situations differently, by placing emphasis on
different things, and failing to recognize the limits of what is permissible.

Constructing and deconstructing

What is the relationship between the whole and its component parts?
This valuing process contrasts how some cultures take an holistic view of
systems in their entirety, whereas others analyse systems by breaking
them down into their component parts. Hampden-Turner and
Trompenaars (1993) propose that the values of Japanese and German

business organizations show a preference for synthesis, in contrast to British and North American companies which prefer analysis.

In the context of international education, to employ the metaphor proposed by Thompson (1998), are we looking at the wall or at its constituent bricks? The curriculum may be seen as either discrete subjects or as a coherent programme embracing not only learning within a balanced selection of academic subjects, but also interstitial learning 'between the subjects', and learning at the level of the whole institution. Consider the timing and purposes of educational assessment. Does assessment take place in isolation from learning, as a terminal examination, or is it integrated into the entire learning programme? Formative assessment can be used for many purposes, including course evaluation by the teacher and to provide valuable feedback about progress to the learner.

Managing communities of individuals

Is it true, as a politician once declared, that 'there is no such thing as society, only individuals and their families'? This valuing process contrasts the view that it is more important to focus on the enhancement of the individual with the view that more attention should be paid to the community.

School policy may indicate a preference for considering the learner as, for instance, part of a group over the learner being recognized as an individual. Educational assessment may be either norm-referenced, where the performance of a learner is compared with others within or beyond the immediate school community, or criterion-referenced, where performance is matched against a set of assessment criteria (Frith and Macintosh, 1984). Norm-referencing may be competitive, especially if the comparison of learners is made public knowledge, whereas criterion-referenced assessment is less competitive to the extent that performance is individualized.

Individualism can take different forms. It is remarkable that the educational system of the most strongly individualist nation – the USA – requires college entry information in terms of norm-referencing. College application forms which solicit a recommendation from teachers frequently ask questions such as 'Where in the class would you place this student?' Interviews conducted by the author with teachers of International Baccalaureate Diploma Programme subjects, however, indicate that they are strongly influenced by the values of criterion-referenced assessment. This appears to exert a backwash effect on the assessment culture of IB schools, which tends to take the form of being strongly individualist, non-competitive and against norm-referencing, manifested as a preference not to rank students according to achievement. Reporting student performance for US college entry can thus become a difficult task, and one for which some respondents have expressed repugnance.

Internalizing the outside world

This valuing process contrasts the way in which our actions are either self-motivated or influenced by those around us. Consider this obser-vation about the contrasting ways in which a familiar consumer product may be used: 'Akio Morita of Sony... conceived the notion of the Walkman while he was searching for a way to enjoy music without disturbing others. This is in sharp contrast to the normal motivation for using a Walkman in north-west Europe and North America, where most users do not want to be disturbed by other people' (Trompenaars and Hampden-Turner, 1997).

The 'Japanese' use of the Walkman exemplifies 'outer-directedness' through concern about disturbing others, whereas the 'European and American' use exemplifies 'inner-directedness'. Hampden-Turner and Trompenaars ascribe the success of North American capitalism to the inner voice of Puritanism, coupled with strong individualism. Japanese companies, however, show strength in terms of quality assurance by attending to the needs expressed by customers.

The autonomous, active student who has learnt how to learn exem-plifies inner-directedness. Some appear to be self-motivated to complete problems and find solutions, but others require external encouragement. Outer-directedness may take the form of rewards or punishments (depending on the culture) and competition. Competitive behaviour between students has been a controversial issue in international education. Peterson (1987) relates how competitive team games were discouraged by Kurt Hahn, who considered that they encouraged 'trib-alism'. On the other hand, Hahn encouraged the types of physical pursuits, such as sailing and climbing, which test the individual personally and which appear to require a large component of inner-directedness. Thus some of the most influential ideas about international education can be identified with the universalist application of values derived from a particular cultural context.

Not everybody feels the same way about competition in education. For some it encourages excellence, whereas for others it discourages the losers. On the other hand, the 'all must have prizes' philosophy of non-competitive education is regarded by some as a recipe for mediocrity.

The challenge to educational institutions is how to reconcile the dilemma between encouraging all students to give their best, and recognizing their achievements without discouraging any of them.

Some may argue that the combination of rugged individualism with inner-directedness is a source of the world's problems, and that schools should intervene to socialize young people by encouraging them to share and cooperate. Teamwork is evidently a work-related skill to be encouraged and it appears among the assessment criteria of International Baccalaureate diploma courses, such as the coursework component of Science subjects (IBO, 1999).

Karacs (1999) discusses a study into the origins of xenophobia which contrasts the values of former West Germany (inner directed) and East Germany (outer directed) in terms of toilet training in early childhood. Systems of rewards and punishments are a frequently debated topic. In international schools there appears to be an overwhelming preference for inner-directedness, to the exclusion of that most clear-cut form of outer direction of behaviour, the physical punishment of children.

Synchronizing fast processes

This valuing process contrasts the ways in which we conceive of time as either a sequence of discrete events or the synchronization of many events together. Cultural stereotypes abound concerning contrasting attitudes to time. Expatriates frequently admit exasperation, for example, with what they perceive to be the 'mañana' culture of some parts of Latin America. Rhythms of daily life vary according to geography. Business practices that operate in temperate latitudes cannot always be transplanted to the tropics.

Different cultures embody different concepts of time. O'Connor and Seymour (1990) cite work which proposes that time can be conceived either as 'through-time' or as 'in-time'. Through-time is 'the Anglo-European type of time where the timeline goes from side to side. The past is on one side, the future on another and both are visible in front of the person.' In-time is 'Arabic time, where the timeline stretches from front to back so that one part (usually the past) is behind you, and invisible. You have to turn your head to see it.' Trompenaars and Hampden-Turner (1997) describe a circle test to measure contrasting approaches to time. The relative diameters of the circles and the intersections between them, it is claimed, describe the perceived relationship between past, present and future.

Punctuality is generally encouraged by schools. They have timetables, and students and teachers are expected to be in the right place at the proper time. Schools impose time deadlines; homework must be handed in at this lesson, examination entries must be complete by that date. Time management in a culturally diverse organization may be difficult because of contrasting concepts of time. Some people have a preference for completing one job before starting the next, whereas others can manage many different tasks simultaneously. The establishment of an effective organizational culture requires acknowledgement of such differing perceptions.

Choosing among achievers

This valuing process addresses the ways in which people from different cultures attribute status. Status may be given according to what a person has achieved, for example in terms of academic qualifications or relevant professional experience, or according to what qualities are ascribed to that person. Would it be acceptable to take gender or age into account when considering a person for promotion? To what extent should a school manager from one culture defer to the values of the host country culture? For example, certain colleagues might find it unacceptable to work with a female Head of Department if in their culture that role would always be taken by a male member of staff. Status may increase or diminish with age. Would it be unacceptable for colleagues to work with a Head of Department who is younger than themselves? High status is ascribed to the elders of certain cultures, such as those of Asia, but in Western cultures emphasis often appears to be on the dynamism of youth. Family affiliations may also contribute to the ascription of status. How should these be taken into account? Should the fact that a candidate for a job is related to a powerful person in the local community influence the decision about whether or not to employ that person?

Another topic that highlights issues about the attribution of status involves how we name people. Should a school have a policy concerning how students address teachers? Are students encouraged to use a familiar form of address, such as a teacher's first name, or is more social distance between teachers and learners encouraged by the use of titles such as Mr, Miss and Sir? How do students interpret the apparent familiarity (or lack of it) between themselves and their teachers? Students and teachers from some cultures may experience embarrassment at being on familiar terms and might prefer to use a more formal style of address. Such a reaction might be expected to be particularly common among individuals from cultures that prefer recognition of status by ascription over achievement.

It could be argued that ascription-based cultures encourage continuity. If seniority in a culture is ascribed as a result of long service, then the longer a person is in a job the higher his or her status will become. However, employment patterns of staff in many international schools appear to be short term and with high rates of turnover. There is a tendency towards the implementation of short-term solutions, with pressure on incoming employees to institute change early in their tenure. As noted elsewhere in this volume, Hawley (1995) has indicated that Heads of international schools have a high rate of turnover, with many staying in post for only two years or less, and cultural misunderstandings with governing Boards being cited as a contributory factor. It would be useful to enquire whether the countries with the most rapid turnover are those whose cultures attribute status by achievement or ascription.

Sponsoring equal opportunities to excel

This valuing process highlights the dilemma between preferences for hierarchy and equality in the organization. We have already considered conventions for naming people in the context of the attribution of status, and such conventions also reflect perceived social distance between teacher and learner. Does the guru or master figure dominate the relationship with the learner, or are teachers and learners equal citizens in a republic of ideas? Do the names they attach to each other reinforce a sense of hierarchy, or is the relationship on more of an equal footing?

Organizations may take the form of flattened or steeply tiered hierarchies (Handy, 1993). Does the Head of a school direct the teachers or serve them? Who are the most important people in the school staff; are they the Head and administration, the teachers, or the support staff including cleaners, cooks and gardeners? In schools with a strongly hierarchical culture the Head takes on the role of the Chief Executive Officer of the organization, but in a more egalitarian culture the Head is 'first among equals' as a team member.

Another aspect of hierarchy within the school relates to who makes the decisions about policy and appointments. It may be the Head alone, or the governing Board of the school. In more egalitarian organizational cultures, the teaching staff may be involved in making staff appointments. To what extent are the students involved in the running of the institution? Some schools solicit evaluation reports on the work of teaching staff from the student body.

Quality and the international school

The dilemmas discussed above make clear how the values of the teachers and students may vary in a multicultural international school. Proponents of total quality management such as Sallis (1996) argue that 'the customer is king' and that the organization should always be structured to serve the needs of the client. This means, when translated into the context of education, not only that the school exists to serve its students and their parents, but also that the administration exists to serve, amongst others, the needs of the teaching staff. Organizational management is the act of creation of organizational culture and, with such diverse multicultural inputs as are found in an international school, it is important that educational managers consider the cultural preferences of their colleagues. By acting in a culturally sensitive manner, school managers should be able to build an effective organizational culture that treats people of all cultural viewpoints with equity.

References

Fitzgerald, N (1997) Harnessing the potential of globalization for consumer and citizen, *International Affairs*, **73** (4), pp 739–46

Frith, D and Macintosh, H (1984) *A Teacher's Guide to Assessment*, Stanley Thornes, Cheltenham

Hampden-Turner, C and Trompenaars, F (1993) *The Seven Cultures of Capitalism*, Piatkus, London

Hampden-Turner, C and Trompenaars, F (1997) *Mastering the Infinite Game: How East Asian values are transforming business practices*, Capstone, Oxford

Handy, C (1993) *Understanding Organizations*, Penguin, London

Hawley, D (1995) How long do international school heads survive? A research analysis (part II), *International Schools Journal*, **14** (2), pp 23–36

Hayden, M C and Thompson, J J (1995) International schools and international education: a relationship reviewed, *Oxford Review of Education*, **21** (3), pp 327–45

Held, D, McGrew, A. Goldblatt, D and Perraton, J (1998) *Global Transformations*, Polity Press, Cambridge

Hofstede, G (1991) *Cultures and Organizations*, Harper Collins, London

IBO (1999) *Teacher Support Material: Experimental sciences internal assessment*, International Baccalaureate Organisation, Geneva

Karacs, I (1999) If only Adolf had worn Pampers, *Independent on Sunday*, 25 July

Kobrin, S (1999) Development after industrialization: poor countries in an electronically integrated global economy, in *The Globalization of Multinational Enterprise Activity and Economic Development*, eds N Hood and S Young, Macmillan, Basingstoke

O'Connor, J and Seymour, J (1990) *Introducing Neurolinguistic Programming: The new psychology of personal excellence*, Mandala/HarperCollins, London

Peterson, A D C (1987) *Schools Across Frontiers*, Open Court, La Salle, IL

Sallis, E (1996) *Total Quality Management in Education*, Kogan Page, London

Sylvester, B (1998) Through the lens of diversity: inclusive and encapsulated school missions, in *International Education: Principles and practice*, eds M C Hayden and J J Thompson, Kogan Page, London

Thompson, J J (1998) Towards a model for international education, in *International Education: Principles and practice*, eds M C Hayden and J J Thompson, Kogan Page, London

Trompenaars, F and Hampden-Turner, C (1997) *Riding the Waves of Culture*, 2nd edn, Nicholas Brealey, London

Zaw, S K (1996) Locke and multiculturalism: toleration, relativism and reason, in *Public Education in a Multicultural Society*, ed R K Fullinwider, Cambridge University Press, Cambridge

Part D

CONCLUSION

Chapter 16

International education: connecting the national to the global

George Walker

The original philosophy for international education

There is, I believe, a misconception that international education was created for the internationally mobile student, the so-called 'global nomad'. To explain why I do not believe this to be true I need to go back briefly to 1924, to the origins of international education and thus, indirectly, to the origins of the International Baccalaureate Organisation (IBO) (Knight, 1999). In 1924 the International School of Geneva was founded for the children of the new breed of international civil servant working at the League of Nations and at the International Labour Office. This was not a vote of no confidence in the local school system; on the contrary, a Swiss group of educators was closely involved in the project and the school's first working language was French. Rather it was a combination of pragmatism (these children would return one day to their own countries) and vision (an education based on the values of the League itself). Even today, 'Ecolint', as it is known around the world, has a charter which commits it to preparing young people for re-entry into their own, as well as entry into different, cultures.

A generation after its foundation, the school was almost bankrupt. It had survived the Second World War, but most of its students were now refugees who were unable to pay their fees, and in 1947 the school was forced to sell its land back to the state of Geneva. From the receipts of this sale 10,000 Swiss francs were sent to New York to help to found a sister school, the United Nations International School (UNIS). Today, UNIS not only serves the United Nations, but is also widely respected as a significant player in Manhattan's education provision.

A good idea needs three supports to keep it upright, and in 1962 a new kind of school opened its doors in Wales, in the United Kingdom: Atlantic College, the first of the United World Colleges. Based on the philosophy of Kurt Hahn, Atlantic College welcomed students who were funded by scholarships awarded by national committees to young people selected as outstanding ambassadors of their countries. And the rest, as they say, is history. In the late 1960s these three schools, Ecolint, UNIS and Atlantic College, supported by several others around the world, pioneered the IB Diploma Programme. And the point I wish to stress is that none of them was able, or would have wished, to detach this international education from the national education systems from which all of their students had come and to which most would return. This point is made clear by Alec Peterson in his book *Schools Across Frontiers* (1987), where he explores in the final chapter the relationship between international education and what he called 'patriotic education'.

Since the award of the first IB Diplomas in 1970 there has been a dramatic growth in the number of international schools and, although opinions and definitions vary, the total today must be at least a thousand. This growth has been largely driven by the expansion of international trade, which has created that unattractively labelled group, the 'third culture kids', young people who have neither the culture of their passport nor that of their temporary host country. Many recent developments in international education, such as attempts to rationalize syllabuses, conditions of service and standards of accreditation, and indeed the rapid growth of IB schools and the welcome given especially to the IB Primary and Middle Years Programmes, have been part of an uncoordinated movement to create a global education for the expanding population of mobile families whose children will spend much of their school lives in some kind of international orbit.

Global mobility was certainly one of the driving forces behind the creation of the IB Diploma Programme. It was not, however, the only such force, a point which brings me back to the earlier and more challenging issue: the relationship between international education and national education systems. Why more challenging? First, because the simple logic of numbers tells us that if we want to change the world it will have to be done through state education. Second because, before we get very far, we have to ask ourselves whether the very concept of a global education does not contain a contradiction in terms. And third, because there is clearly a growing interest amongst governments in the possibility of building bridges between their national education systems and the IBO.

Education begins at home

Education has always been the peaceful weapon in the nation state's struggle to create and maintain its identity (Green, 1997). It has been used differently by different nations during different periods of their history, depending upon the need for national myths and heroes, an articulate electorate, a patriotic army of conscripts, an administrative elite, a contented group of tax-paying citizens or (most recently) a competitive economic workforce. Let no one imagine that when in 1998 the British Prime Minister, Tony Blair, listed the first three priorities of his government as 'education, education and education', he had in mind the future welfare of the European Community, the Commonwealth or the United Nations. No: like charity, education still begins at home.

Nonetheless, there have been some important shifts in the focus of state education, especially in the developed world. Generally, it has become less concerned with national identity and more concerned with economic performance in an internationally competitive market. A generation ago there was a trend in the developed world towards education for greater individual autonomy, but since then concern about increasing social alienation has brought a new emphasis on education for responsible citizenship, including parenthood. Today, governments still view education as the essential vehicle of economic and social development, one of the few remaining instruments of national policy.

However, it is not surprising that many countries are less confident about education for building national identity. What national identity? Today 188 different countries belong to the United Nations but, of those, only about 20 have any claim to be 'nation states' by containing within their boundaries people of common descent, language and history. By contrast, it is estimated that there are about 2,000 different 'nations' making some kind of territorial claim to various parts of the planet. It is against this background that I will examine first some aspects of the relationship between education and globalization. Since this is my first use of the term, let me say, for the moment, that 'globalization' (Ossipow, 1998)

nous rend voisins et contemporains de tous sur n'importe quel point du globe, et permet de vivre cette proximité en temps réel: les échanges de marchandises, mais aussi les échanges de signes ne connaissent plus d'obstacles, d'autant moins que les transferts sont de moins en moins de marchandises physiques et de plus en plus d'informations et de symboles qui circulent à la vitesse de l'électricité (makes of us all, in whatever part of the world, neighbours and peers and allows this close relationship to be conducted in real time: exchanges of goods, as well as exchanges of symbols, no longer encounter obstacles, not least because such transfers are less and less of physical goods and increasingly of information and symbols which circulate at the speed of electricity).

International cooperation

It is astonishing to discover how little has been written about the likely impact of globalization on systems of education. One widely welcomed outcome, however, has been the opportunity to share successful national practice (see, for example, Barber writing in Mortimore and Little, 1997). I will call this 'international cooperation' in order to distinguish it from international education. One can sense renewed confidence amongst the developed nations (confidence, incidentally, which the developing and underdeveloped nations never lost) that education really can make a difference, and research on school effectiveness and reform is now being shared, with measurable benefits, across the world. Such optimism is not new; perhaps what is new is the conviction that it might after all be justified.

> The ancients who wished to illustrate illustrious virtues throughout the kingdom first ordered well their own states. Wishing to order well their states, they first regulated their families. Wishing to regulate their families, they first cultivated their persons. Wishing to cultivate their persons, they first rectified their hearts. Wishing to rectify their hearts, they first sought to be sincere in their thoughts. Wishing to be sincere in their thoughts, they first extended to the utmost their knowledge. Such extension of knowledge lay in the investigation of things.

That expression of faith was written two-and-a-half millennia ago by Confucius.

It seems to me that the process of international cooperation is no different in kind to the exchange of ideas between continental Europe, Britain and then America that goes back to Rousseau and includes Matthew Arnold, Montessori and Dewey. The scale is certainly different, facilitated by greater mobility of teachers, researchers and students, and, with global communication and the high quality of modern research, there is less excuse for ignorance of its implications.

However, I have something rather different in mind. Our knowledge of international education, developed over the past 75 years and first put into a global framework by the IBO, can surely make a distinctive contribution to the nations of the world. Now that 'globalization' has arrived on every doorstep, is it not the moment for those who have studied its impact on education for more than three generations to explain what they have learnt and how it might connect to other systems? But first, we need to look in more depth at the concept of globalization. Not surprisingly, we shall find there is rather more to it than CNN, cheeseburgers and the World Cup.

Popular globalization

At some point in our daily lives, globalization touches us all. In 1999, for example, travel and tourism accounted for nearly 12 per cent of the world GDP, and no one was asked for a smallpox vaccination certificate. Personal communication, particularly in developing countries, has improved dramatically with the use of mobile telephones, and international sport, which created unparallelled excitement once every four years when I was a boy, has been turned into a boring daily ritual. Visually dramatic images from space remind us of both the beauty and the fragility of our planet. In schools, we try to support the United Nations year of the culture of peace, we try to relate our study of economics to the needs of the global village and we try to encourage a policy of environmentally sustainable development for our 'spaceship earth'. Intellectually, though, we mistrust these popular metaphors which hide our ignorance of a complex reality and encourage our fear that, whatever that reality is, it is already beyond our control. We no longer fully understand.

To the annual toll of oil-tanker disasters, we have recently added the case of the Australian gold-mining company operating in Romania that poisoned huge stretches of the River Danube, creating a major environmental disaster in several countries downstream. Or did it? As with most of these dramatic stories, after the initial blast of outrage, our global media networks move on without ever leaving behind a wholly satisfactory answer. We no longer fully understand.

There is concern, too, that the major problems caused by globalization can only be solved by putting together even bigger globalized solutions in an increasing spiral of global resources that lie beyond conventional political control. For example, more than 22 million of the 34 million people in the world infected with HIV/AIDS are Africans. In Botswana, Namibia, Zambia and Zimbabwe about 25 per cent of people aged 15 to 49, in the prime of their lives, are infected. The major effort to deal with this epidemic is being led by UNAIDS and the World Bank. How many of us could explain to someone else the functions of the World Bank, and its political relationship with the United Nations? We no longer fully understand.

Three theories of globalization

It is perhaps not surprising that we do not fully understand, since those who spend their lives studying the phenomenon of globalization do not agree amongst themselves. There are currently at least three different, if overlapping, theories of globalization (Held *et al*, 1999), as referred to by Jim Cambridge earlier in this volume.

The most extreme is *hyperglobalization*. The hyperglobalists (including Reich, 1991 and Ohmae, 1990) believe that the global marketplace has become so advanced that the nation state has become obsolete. They would argue that this is a good thing, because the market is more rational than governments can ever be. Politicians are becoming irrelevant and they could quote the example of Hong Kong, which, they would argue, will play a role in the global economy that is largely unrelated to its political environment, which just happens to be in China. All that will remain within the borders of a nation will be its people with their knowledge and skills.

Challenging the hyperglobalists are the *global sceptics* (such as Hirst and Thompson, 1996). They question the whole concept of a single global market and instead point to the increasing internationalism of trade, which is in some ways a reversion to the nineteenth century, when borders were open and few people bothered with passports. Only the other day I read this reference to Ghana: 'The English, Dutch, French, Danes and other nations have factories upon this coast', and it is only when we read on 'and purchase slaves and their commodities, for the benefit of their employers' that we realize it was written in the eighteenth century. It is interesting to reflect that the gazetteer in which I found that description contains, in one modest volume, descriptions of every place in the world known to Europeans in 1782 and the focus of every description is economic: fairs, markets, commodities, natural resources and fertility of land. What we see today, argue the global sceptics, is not a single market but the development of regional economic *blocs*. The huge increase in trade between certain countries has left others marginalized. Globalization is an ideology of the political right rather than a reality, and this is clearly a view shared by the increasingly violent anti-WTO protestors in Seattle and Geneva.

It is hard to deny that huge economic differences have arisen, with very clear global winners and global losers and no evidence that the rich becoming richer is likely to improve the prospects of the poor. For example, 1 in 40 of the world's population are now enjoying the economic and social benefits of the Internet. In South-East Asia, however, the figure is one in two hundred and in Africa it is one in a thousand. This means that 95 per cent of Internet activity (and in 1999 that meant linkage with about 56 million computers) is located in the developed world.

'Globalization looks very different when it is seen, not from the capitals of the West, but from the cities and villages of the South, where most of humanity lives', writes the director of the Agenda Peru programme on development strategy and democratic governance. He might have quoted the recent UNICEF report (UNICEF, 2000) which estimates that 5,000 children die every day from water-borne diseases. The author of the report asked what the developed nations' response might be if 12 jumbo jets full of children crashed every single day of the year. Would we be better able to grasp the extent of the problem and thus feel compelled to do something?

A third view of globalization (which is sometimes linked to the political programme known as 'the third way'; see, for example, Anthony Giddens, 1990) looks more closely at the relationship between the large-scale global and the small-scale local. It is also known as the *transformationalist* view because it is not a question of the global market removing the powers of the nation state but rather of the global market transforming these powers, by challenging existing institutions and encouraging greater local autonomy. Paradoxically, the new global movements have both stimulated and facilitated interest and participation in the national, the local and even the parochial. Increasingly, we shall see the familiar north/south and developed/undeveloped paradigms illustrated within cities rather than dividing the world. Indeed, large Mercedes cars are already as numerous in the streets of Mumbai as the beggars on London's underground system.

If I were knocked down in the street, what would passers-by find on me to establish where I belong? First of all my maroon passport identifies me as a member of the European Community and, although I was sad to surrender my trusty blue British passport, I am very pleased to enjoy the additional benefits of EU membership. They would find my security pass to the United Nations headquarters in Geneva, the Palais des Nations, where important decisions are taken on global issues such as human rights and nuclear disarmament. But they would also find my membership card of the National Trust, an organization which is quintessentially English. Although I have not used the card for years, I pay the annual subscription to support an organization that defends an important part of my national heritage. Clearly, I am happily operating at the global, the transnational and the national levels, without even mentioning my credit cards!

International education and hyperglobalization

If we were to accept the imminent arrival of hyperglobalization and the demise of the nation state, then as international educators we would be challenged to create a unitary system of education that would be valid not merely throughout the world, but for the world. In a very modest way, the IBO has already picked up this challenge through the Diploma Programme. The Middle Years and Primary Years Programmes are, however, likely to be more regionally influenced in their development and, in any case, does a total of just over a thousand schools, spread thinly over one hundred countries, entitle us to use the description 'global'?

Let us take note of the bolder project proposed by Joseph Blaney (1991), then Director of UNIS, and launched by the International Schools Association five years later (ISA, 1996). Blaney wrote: 'Education systems rooted mainly in national concerns and constrained by national ideologies cannot educate young people to live meaningfully in a world society which is global'.

More than 20 schools, a mixture of private and public, located in every continent, were invited to test the feasibility of an international schools system. As with most ambitious projects, this one was seriously underfunded and, as a feasibility study, it remains inconclusive. Two major lessons emerged, however: the ability of schools across the world to cooperate electronically, and the eagerness of national schools to expand their horizons through interaction with international schools. As for the 'system of international education', it was never really put to the acid test of requiring project schools to surrender significant areas of their own autonomy in the interest of the greater good of the system. In fact, the project went little further than the IBO had already gone; schools all around the world (including 400 state schools) have already signed up to the 'system' of the International Baccalaureate. If one believes, as I do, that education will remain a basic national priority, then that is probably as far as we can go to satisfy the hyperglobalists. The IBO offers an education system throughout the world, but not for the world.

International education and the global sceptics

The global sceptics force the international educator onto the defensive.

From this perspective, instead of saving the world, international education will seek to protect the interests of those who are distant from their national system and especially those who are in isolated expatriate enclaves in countries that cannot afford high-quality education. International education now becomes the safety net for the children of international executives, who, in the interests of international trade, are here today but somewhere else tomorrow. It also becomes an option for the nationals of the host country who are dissatisfied with their own system and are in a position to afford, or in some cases even to build, an international alternative.

A third strand of international education is opened up by the global sceptics. If the wide discrepancies caused by unequal access to a globalized economy are to be addressed, then perhaps we need a special kind of education for those destined to be the world's future leaders. Education for leadership has never been far from the agenda of the international schools movement, and I sometimes wonder if the criteria used by international schools that offer scholarships today are so very different from those laid down by Cecil Rhodes a century ago. As with Rhodes, the leadership issue is given moral overtones as in this recent quote from an experienced international school principal: 'It's a mission to graduate students who are aware that they are truly privileged and are aware of the world's inequities.' This message is clear: international education is different, is separate and has a mission to make other systems work better.

International education and the transformationalists

For reasons explained earlier, I believe that national education systems are here to stay. But today, when the face of Nelson Mandela is more familiar to many of us than that of our next-door neighbour, it would be absurd to imagine that state education can remain untouched by globalization. Let us suppose we reflect a national system in the mirror of a global economy sustained by global communication; surely its image will come back transformed. I believe that international education can play a supportive role in that transformation because we have been there before; we know what it is like. So what special contribution can international education, and the IBO in particular, offer to the national system of education?

For me, one word encapsulates that contribution: diversity. Globalization is changing the cultural mix of nations, and the numbing spread of the culture of Nike, Coca Cola and McDonald's is being fiercely resisted by the strengthening of local cultures reflected in the celebration of linguistic differences, the sharpening of ethnic awareness and the protection of minority rights. As the world shrinks, we are having to learn to live with our differences. I like my dictionary's definition of diversity as 'unlikeness' because there is a toughness about the word; it is something we are going to have to work at; it does not come naturally.

Valuing diversity

The international educator believes in pluralism (Orellana Benado, 1995). All human beings share the same human condition, but it is displayed in many different cultural variants. International education celebrates that diversity and ensures that every act, every symbol, every exchange involving teachers, administrators, students and parents reinforces the belief that, in the end, human diversity is an enrichment and a source of strength. Such a belief was made uncompromisingly clear by a former directrice of Ecolint, the remarkable Madame Maurette, when she told her students: *'aussi furieux que vous soyez, vous ne devez jamais vous servir de la nationalité ou de la race comme terme d'insulte. C'est dans cette école, le crime des crimes'* ('however angry you may be, you must never use nationality or race as a term of abuse. In this school, that is the worst of all crimes').

In the same year, 1948, the United Nations ratified the Universal Declaration of Human Rights, with its famous first article: *'Tous les êtres humains naissent libres et égaux en dignité et en droits. Ils sont doués de raison et de conscience et doivent agir les un envers les autres dans un esprit de fraternité'* ('All human beings are born free and equal in dignity and rights. They are endowed with reason and conscience and should act towards one another in a spirit of brotherhood').

The same sentiment can be expressed in fewer words, and I noticed only recently on the letterhead of an IB school in France a lovely quotation from Paul Valéry: *'Enrichissons-nous de nos différences'* (Let us be enriched by our differences).

The IBO's mission statement makes it clear where we stand when it speaks of: 'respecting the variety of cultures and attitudes that makes for the richness of life', but however it is expressed, such a philosophy needs working at, reinforcing, explaining and justifying.

Personally, I believe that the IBO has a great deal to offer in addressing such a range of tasks. The combination of the IB's language policy, its breadth of curricular studies and its students' engagement with a variety of modes of learning, does, indeed, give those of us committed to the IB the right to say to national educators 'we believe we have something well worth sharing with you'. It is important to note here that I refer to all three of the IBO's programmes when I make that offer. It is also worth noting that, already, 40 per cent of IB schools are state schools.

The relevance of international education to national education systems is not a new concept. Since 1974, UNESCO has officially supported a definition of international education and in 1995 its General Council encouraged member states to integrate it into their own systems. I believe the IBO is in a strong position to support that process, and I would like to conclude this chapter with a statement made in 1997 by the previous Director General of the IBO, Roger Peel, which sums up in a modest way what the IBO would like to achieve. He wrote: 'Ideally, at the end of the IB experience, students should know themselves better than when they started, while acknowledging that others can be right in being different.' If we could begin to spread that message across both international and national schools then, in a modest way, I think we should have left the world a better place than we found it.

References

Barber, M (1997) Education, leadership and the global paradox, in *Living Education: Essays in honour of John Tomlinson*, eds P Mortimore and V Little, Paul Chapman, London

Blaney, J J (1991) The international school system, in *International Schools and International Education*, eds P L Jonietz and D Harris, Kogan Page, London

Giddens, A (1990) *The Consequences of Modernity*, Polity Press, Cambridge

Green, A (1997) *Education, Globalization and the Nation State*, Macmillan, Basingstoke

Held, D, McGrew, A, Goldblatt, D and Perraton, J (1999) *Global Transformations: Politics, economics and culture*, Polity Press, Cambridge

Hirst, P and Thompson, G (1996) *Globalization in Question: The international economy and possibilities of governance*, Polity Press, Cambridge

International Schools Association (1996) *The International Education System Pilot Project*, ISA, Geneva

Knight, M (1999) *Ecolint: A portrait of the International School of Geneva 1924–1999*, International School of Geneva, Geneva

Ohmae, K (1990) *The Borderless World*, Collins, London

Orellana Benado, M E (1995) Pluralism and the ethics of internationalism, *IB World*, **8**, pp 29–30

Ossipow, W (1998) *De La Globalization et des Societes*, Academie Suisse des Sciences Humaines et Sociales, Berne

Peel, R M (1997) *Education for Life*, International Baccalaureate Organisation, Geneva

Peterson, A D C (1987) *Schools Across Frontiers*, Open Court, La Salle, IL

Reich, R (1991) *The Work of Nations: A blueprint for the future*, Vintage Press, New York

UNICEF (2000) *Paper presented to Second World Water Forum and Ministerial Conference*, The Hague

Index

Visit Kogan Page on-line

Comprehensive information on
Kogan Page titles

Features include

- complete catalogue listings,
  including book reviews and
  descriptions

- on-line discounts on a variety
  of titles

- special monthly promotions

- information and discounts on
  NEW titles and BESTSELLING titles

- a secure shopping basket facility
  for on-line ordering

- infoZones, with links and
  information on specific areas of
  interest

PLUS everything you need to know
about KOGAN PAGE

http://www.kogan-page.co.uk